PREFACE

The trademark of American public education has been to expand the curriculum to meet the individual needs and differences of children. Unfortunately, curriculum change has been confined largely to differences in children's abilities for academic achievement. Little attention has been given to the learning styles, ethnic and cultural backgrounds, and other characteristics of the individual. As a result, the system of public education has been very selective in terms of those who have received the full benefits of "schooling." The academic high achiever receives the rewards, while the so-called "non-achiever" is systematically excluded from participation in many school activities and, eventually, from continued schooling. Those who are in the mainstream of middle-class culture receive the rewards; those who are not are excluded. Those whose belief system is congruent with that of the school staff receive the rewards; others do not . . . and thus it goes for those who are different.

This book describes the efforts of an urban school system, working in partnership with three universities and community personnel, to create a different kind of school environment— a school environment in which people recognize, accept, and seek to develop the uniqueness of each individual. Each school's program focused on the implementation by teachers and students of experiences designed to develop pride in one's ethnic and cultural heritage, to expose students to alternative lifestyles and cultural options, to develop understanding and appreciation for the validity of others' ethnicity, and to fill the education voids that most students have concerning cultural and ethnic diversity. Some people call this "Multi-Cultural Education." But, in reality, learning experiences focused on the culture of the school and society should be a priority objective within all education.

The process and activities described in this book were created by a diverse group of dedicated people. College professors, graduate students, community personnel, school principals, and, most significantly, classroom teachers assumed new and unfamiliar roles to develop a completely new program, often working in risk-taking situations.

George Peabody College for Teachers, Middle Tennessee State University, Tennessee State University, and the Metropolitan Public Schools of Nashville-Davidson County must be recognized

iii

for making administrative arrangements and policy changes that encouraged the development of the multi-cultural program in Nashville.

Three public schools—Wharton, Ford Greene, and Washington, all located in North Nashville within the portion once known as the Model Cities area—constituted the training complex. Because of a unitary school plan, the three schools are integrated by race and socio-economic levels. Approximately 120 teachers at these schools participated in the development and implementation of the multi-cultural program.

Dr. Michael Pasternak, Associate Professor of Education, George Peabody College for Teachers, provided the leadership for the development of the multi-cultural program. Dr. Pasternak was a staff member for the Corps Member Training Institute, 1975; a consultant to the Multi-Cultural Task Force, Mid-South Teacher Corps Network, 1976-77; and a trainer in multi-cultural education for two Network workshops. He has been a member of the Nashville Teacher Corps's instructional management team and has made significant contributions to other components of the Nashville program, including leadership training and the development of a middle school workshop for inservice personnel. Beginning with multi-cultural needs assessment and culminating with the conception and development of this book, Michael Pasternak has made a noteworthy contribution to public education's helping people appreciate their uniqueness and the uniqueness of other people.

James M. Yonts, Jr.
Executive Director
Teacher Education Alliance for Metro
July 1977

ACKNOWLEDGMENTS

Creating this publication involved many individuals. First off, I wish to acknowledge with gratitude the contribution made by the efforts of the teachers and administrators in the Nashville Teacher Corps schools who created multi-cultural opportunities for their students and contributed their ideas to this book. Likewise, none of the work could have been accomplished without James M. Yonts, Jr. who, as the Nashville Teacher Corps Project Director, provided the spirit, leadership, and commitment necessary to assemble this successful multi-cultural team effort.

The roles of others were also indispensable. Robert Dellanoce, Jane Smith, Kate Williams, Martis Okpalobi, Betty Jane Martin, and Vicki L. Sullivan carried out discussions and research activities with teachers, administrators, and community participants to identify clearly the multi-cultural opportunities in the Nashville Teacher Corps program. Jane Smith and Robert Dellanoce also assisted me in adapting the teacher activities for the book. Vicki L. Sullivan worked far beyond *reasonable* hours typing and retyping the manuscript. Appreciable improvements in the presentation of this work were contributed by the editing of Norman R. Moore. Generous editing assistance was also given by Katharine Martin.

Sherrilyn Pasternak assisted with several phases of the book's development. She adapted activities, completed the initial editing, and provided the encouragement and support for me to complete this project in the extraordinarily short period of five months. I am especially indebted to Jack Miller for the initial idea that our project accomplishments were significant and should be shared with others through publication.

The many contributing authors in this undertaking deserve special mention. Those associated with George Peabody College for Teachers are: Jerold P. Bauch, Judy Davis, Robert Dellanoce, Algund Hermann, Edward V. Johnson, Charles B. Myers, Martis M. Okpalobi, Jane Bandy Smith, and Kate Williams. Others are Robert Eaker and James Huffman of Middle Tennessee State University; Carol Stice of Tennessee State University; Ella Lett Gandy, John Lifsey, and Aldorothy Wright of Nashville's Metropolitan Public Schools; and James M. Yonts, Jr., Joan Johnson and Elizabeth Thompson of the Teacher Education Alliance for Metro. The opinions expressed herein by these contributors,

v

however, should not be construed as necessarily representing the opinions of the institutions with which they are affiliated.

Special recognition and gratitude are also due to the following:

Teacher Corps and its leadership in promoting American education.

Teachers, parents, students, and administrators of three Metropolitan Public Schools of Nashville-Davidson County, Tennessee: Ford Greene Elementary, Wharton Elementary, Wharton Junior High, and Washington Junior High.

Teacher Education Alliance for Metro supported by George Peabody College for Teachers, Tennessee State University, Middle Tennessee State University, and Nashville's Metropolitan Public Schools.

Arthur Justice, Executive Secretary, and the Board of Directors of Mid-South Teacher Corps Network for encouragement and support.

The Office of Educational Services at George Peabody College for Teachers for facilitating publication.

Additional manuscript assistance: Katharine Martin and Ruby Fisher, Advanced Programs for Curriculum Leadership Personnel, George Peabody College for Teachers.

Photographs: Jacob Eleasari, producer and director of the Ami Ron film, "What's the Difference Being Different: The Nashville Teacher Corps Multi-Cultural Program."

Cover Design: Linda Hazen, McQuiddy Printing Company, Nashville, Tennessee.

Our efforts have reached culmination in this publication. Hopefully, its usefulness will justify the efforts of all those preceding which made it possible.

M. G. P.

TABLE OF CONTENTS

Introduction

Helping Kids Learn Multi-Cultural Concepts is designed to develop among future and practicing educators an increased awareness of multi-cultural education. It provides a wide selection of activities that teachers can use in their classrooms. It also delineates the leadership roles teacher educators can assume in a multi-cultural education training program. The book is intended to influence people to become involved in creating processes to help children, educators, and other community members enhance and support cultural literacy and pluralism in our schools.

The present book arises from an educational need of our times. Teacher Corps attempted to respond to the national need to develop schools that support multi-cultural concepts. The materials in this book began when the Nashville (Tennessee) Consortium Teacher Corps decided to include an innovative multi-cultural education program in its training opportunities. So often new areas of study are initiated by scholars on the college campus and brought to and applied to the teachers on the firing line. Such was not the case with this multi-cultural program. At the invitation of James M. Yonts, Jr., project director of Nashville Teacher Corps, and Haroldine Miller, the project's program development specialist, I planned the multi-cultural foundations program with George Cox, assistant dean of the graduate school at Tennessee State University, and Martis M. Okpalobi at George Peabody College for Teachers, *and* 84 teachers, interns, administrators, and community members. As a result of our initial training successes I designed, along with Yonts and the project's management team, a means for implementing multi-cultural education in the curriculum of schools and in all of the training opportunities for teachers. From the beginning, the program was a joint venture between teacher educators (myself included), teachers, and community members. We have learned from one another and the kids are richer for it.

Following the positive responses to our multi-cultural program at a Teacher Corps network presentation we were awarded a developmental grant to share our accomplishments. Along with this book, a 16mm color film entitled *What's the Difference Being Different* has been created to explain the Nashville program.

1

A major portion of this book consists of activities that focus on helping students develop increased multi-cultural and multi-ethnic understandings while building healthy human relationships and enhancing the learners' self-concepts. These activities were adapted from strategies used by teachers in the Nashville multi-cultural program who were committed to improving the multi-cultural climate of their schools. Although created and developed for students aged 10-13, the activities can easily be adapted for use with any age level. They offer a broad range of examples of what could be integrated into any school program.

The examples provided should influence you to create your own strategies to reflect the uniqueness of your school or class-room. You will notice that while some of our activities are beyond identifiable disciplines, others are obviously interdisciplinary. A uniqueness of our work with teachers in developing strategies was our willingness to support and encourage any viable process to accomplish multi-cultural purposes. The result was that teachers, regardless of teaching level or subject orientation, found ways of supporting cultural and ethnic diversity in their classrooms.

Another portion of the book provides a description of how to develop a multi-cultural resource center. You will find there a valuable, extensive listing of resource materials for supporting teachers' and trainers' efforts. A final portion outlines the organization, management, and implementation of the multi-cultural program as it was integrated across all of the inservice efforts in the local Teacher Corps complex. It also includes a series of brief selections written by teacher trainers describing some of the leadership roles and training processes in the program. Some of the motivators for the participants are also included.

It is difficult to capture in print the enthusiasm and success the teachers in this training program expressed as they created and implemented multi-cultural strategies. The real value of these learning experiences will be seen in the kids in the years to come. As one teacher related, after completing a multi-cultural activity: "Wow, the feelings generated by what we've done. The students profited from a feeling of self-worth and each came away with the benefit of a sharing experience." That's what this book is about.

Michael G. Pasternak
July 1977

Part 1

Strategies and Activities
For New Understandings

A Word To The Teacher

The activities for multi-cultural learning described in this book, and their underlying strategies, focus on three interrelated areas. These areas are the important objectives of:

1. Enhancing multi-ethnic and multi-cultural understandings.
2. Building healthy human relationships and self-concepts.
3. Improving the multi-cultural climate factors of a school.

If you emphasize only one or two of these areas rather than all three, you will seriously limit the success you will experience in your classroom, school, or inservice training program. Some of the activities described in Part I include all three areas; others, one or two. Some activities take nine months to complete; others, less than thirty minutes. Many build on one another, support one another, and/or can be used simultaneously by one or more teachers in team teaching situations. For these reasons, you should read through as many as possible before you begin to use them.

While each of these strategies and activities might add to the multi-cultural nature of your classroom, it will take far more than a few of them to accomplish the whole task. The development of a multi-cultural spirit or attitude within a faculty, school, and community requires the long-term commitment of individual teachers, administrators, supporters, and teacher trainers. It must include the opportunity to make mistakes—to try it and "blow it" and try it again. Creators of the following activities had the opportunity to "try it." Hopefully, you also will be supported by others as you use, modify, and improve upon these activities and strategies.

Always be mindful, finally, that regardless of your grade level

3

or subject orientation, something can be initiated in your classroom almost every day to enhance multi-cultural understandings.

A. Activities Generated In The Classroom

DO-IT-YOURSELF LEARNING CENTERS

One way to establish multi-cultural education as an ongoing
part of the curriculum is to create individual learning centers that
generate continued interest in and sensitivity to uniqueness between individuals and various ethnic groups. A learning center
is an area set up in such a way that students who participate in it
are able to do so independently. Any directions, requirements,
regulations for using materials and equipment, sequential steps,
or other pertinent information is provided for the students prior to
opening up the center for use. After that the students are able to
use the center whenever possible with a minimum amount of in-
tervention from the teacher. Anything goes as long as it supports and fosters an appreciation of uniqueness and differences!
Most of these centers are not only multi-cultural but also multi-
disciplinary and can be integrated into almost any academic
area with great success.

Presented in this first selection are several ideas for multi-
cultural learning centers. But the beauty of the learning center
concept is that you can create your own, or have your students
create theirs, tailored to fit the specific needs and interests of
your class.

GETTING TO KNOW YOU

Everyone gets to help in this activity. Each individual (including the teacher) will collect autobiographical data. The data
could include appropriately mounted and labeled photographs of
parents, sisters, brothers, aunts, uncles, cousins, family homes,
vacations, previous residences, pets, friends, baby picture of self
and so on, illustrations, essays, souvenirs, personal "treasures,"
anecdotes, self-portraits, family trees, pictorial and/or written autobiographical story, or anything else that would help people who
will look at it to know and understand that individual better.
Although you would want everyone's "autobiography" available
to look at and share at all times, you might want to pick one or

4

two individuals a day and let each share his/her collection with the entire class. This could continue until everyone had a chance to have the "spotlight." The particular center might be useful early in the school year to help everyone get acquainted more quickly.

SEE THE U.S.A.

Gather materials about the fifty states of the U.S.A. Ask the students to help by bringing anything they might have, e.g., postcards, travel posters, artifacts, photos, etc. Be certain that the multi-cultural nature of our country is reflected as the students learn about Indian Reservations in New Mexico, Chinatown in San Francisco, the various ethnic communities in our larger eastern cities, the expansive farms of the Middle West, the Eskimos of Alaska, or the sunny beaches of Hawaii. Highlight birthplaces of famous men and women of all races. In other words, let the diversity of this country speak for itself as students see that as part of the strength and beauty of the U.S.A.

FOLKTALES

Include folktales from around the world, drawing from Chinese, Arabian, German, English, Scottish, African (various tribes), and American (East, West, North, South) sources. You might eventually let those who are interested write their own folktale and add it to the learning center.

MULTI-CULTURAL CRAFTS

Fill the center with reference materials on arts and crafts and the legend and tradition behind them (include domestic as well as foreign crafts), and the necessary materials for making the crafts.

The students should be instructed that before they can use the materials to make a craft they must do some research and understand, well enough to explain to the rest of the class, the origin and significance of the crafts. Provide an exhibit area in the center so that the finished crafts can be left for the others to see.

Following are a few ideas for possible inclusion in the center:

—Chinese writing —Japanese fish kite
—African masks (or make-up) —Indian totem poles
—Spanish castanets —Tiki masks
—Mexican sundial —Mexican yarn art

5

"I took the song, 'The Black Man', from Stevie Wonder's new album, 'Songs In the Key of Life', and dittoed the words. This song portrays the contributions of Black people. As a follow-up, each student went to the library and looked up the biography of one person named in the song . . . and told someone else about that person's life."

—Aztec calendar
—Wood carving
  (Appalachian Mountain crafts)
—Basket weaving
  (American Indian)

—Japanese paper folding
  art (origami)
—Piñata (Mexico)
—Soapstone carving
  (Alaska)

MULTI-CULTURAL MUSIC

Beg, borrow, and tape friends' records, and check out library records, tapes, and cassettes in order to assemble a collection of music that reflects as much artistic and cultural diversity as possible. Provide an information file on the origin and development of each category, including specific artists, songs, composers, and techniques. Have earphones attached to the record and tape players so that several students can listen to different selections without disturbing others. Tell the students that before listening they must read the available information on that type of music. Encourage them to spend time listening to music that is new and different for them. This center can be therapeutic, also! It's a great place for kids who need some alone or cooling-off time. Some suggested musical categories are:

—Rock
—Jazz
—Soul
—Marching Bands
—Classical
—Folk
—Country Western

—Show tunes
—Pop
—Opera
—Music from other countries
  (Mexican Mariachi Bands,
  Polkas, Irish Ballads, Russian
  Folk Songs, etc.)

MULTI-CULTURAL READING CENTER

Fill the bookshelves and tables in this center with books (fiction and non-fiction) about different cultures—the people, the places, the problems, the joys, and the accomplishments. Let the students browse and look at pictures and enjoy the books. Ask each student to find eventually at least one that looks particularly interesting to him and read it. But require that the book chosen be about someone from a different culture or about a place other than his home environment. Ask each student to

6

plan on sharing his book with the rest of the class. How he does that is up to him—it can be a writing, a picture, a diorama, a dramatization—so long as he shares what significance the book had for him and what he learned from it.

CREATIVE WRITING CENTER

Ask the students to help you get this one ready. Have them bring in magazines, brochures, postcards, or anything having pictures. You supply a box which can be used as a "file," have the students decorate it, and begin to fill it with pictures they have cut out and mounted on construction paper or oak tag. (If you have the resources, have the pictures laminated. They will last longer.) When you have at least twice as many pictures as students (twenty-five students = fifty pictures), you're ready to open the center for all the authors in the class.

Ask the students to choose a picture and write something about it. It may be a story, poem, newspaper article, parable, lyrics to a song (sung to the tune of . . .), or limerick; just about anything is OK. After they finish, they can put their work back in the file behind the picture that was their inspiration. There will eventually accumulate, behind each picture, different writings that the children can read and enjoy. Advise your students not to read what others have written about a certain picture until *after* they've written their own (so they won't be influenced by someone else's work.) Also suggest to students that they be on the lookout for new pictures which can be added to the file.

You will find that students are amazed and delighted at the very different results derived from the same stimulus. It is a great way to help students look at differences, appreciate uniqueness, and try out their own creative genius.

CURRENT EVENTS

Keep a current collection of newspapers and news magazines. Encourage students to cut out and bring in articles from home that they find particularly interesting or pertinent. The objective of this center is to have students read about and become aware of what's happening outside their own immediate world. Within a one-week period, each student will be asked to use the center and read at least one article from each of the following categories:

An event occurring in another country
An event occurring in a different state

A local event involving a cultural or ethnic group different from the student's

An article of their choice

Prepare a record sheet on which the students will write brief responses and turn in to you. Among the kinds of questions on the sheet might be: What is the source? Author? (if any). Give a *brief synopsis* of the content. Why was it interesting to you? What were your feelings and impressions after reading it?

The key to keeping this center alive and interesting to students is to keep the reading material current and varied. Have a bulletin board for key articles or extremely relevant information. You might want to have some stationery and envelopes in the center so that students can write letters to people in the news (mayors, presidents, celebrities, premiers, etc.). They might want to write for additional information to gain expanded perceptions or viewpoints from potential newsmakers.

LANGUAGES

Want a fun way to let students explore languages? Your curriculum lab or public library will probably have beginning language lessons complete with records or tapes to go along. Get as great a variety as possible. The French, Spanish, German, and Italian lessons might be good starters. Supplement these with foreign language dictionaries, pronounciation guides, and commonly used phrases (those books travel agencies provide for tourists to other countries contain simple conversational phrases).

Have assignment sheets available in the center. Some suggested activities are these:

—Translate ten words you use daily into another language.

—Find five words that we use as slang that are real words in another language (amigo, for example).

—Tape a brief conversation between yourself and a friend in another language.

—Translate your ten favorite foods into another language. Why do you think you might not be able to find certain foods?

If you have any students in your class who speak a second language, appoint them aides in the language center to assist the others in any way they can.

This center continues throughout the year but is changed each month when a different country is featured. If you have children that come from another country or whose parents are first or second generation Americans, be sure theirs are the first countries highlighted. Have the center full of information on the country. Include pictures, costumes, examples of housing and/or communities, political organizations, natural resources, foods, geographical differences and so on. Have a place for students to sign up if any of their ancestors came from that country, explaining who they were/are and when and why they left. Provide another place for students to sign up if they've ever visited the country themselves. You might want the children responding to questions such as:

How is this country different from where you live?
What do you like about it?
What do you not like about it?
How is it the same as where you live?
What else would you like to know about it?

Adapted from exercises by: Nancy Edwards, Linda Therber, and Paul Cotton, Teachers, Ford Greene Elementary

---

THE BOOKIES

Children are often asked to write book reports. This activity takes them several steps further into learning how to write and make books for your classroom multi-cultural library.

A critical point in the process is that the children must select a country, geographical area, or ethnic group that they are *really* interested in. Asking children to express "why" will help in determining if they are motivated to focus on their topic. This is a long, involved activity and requires a high level of student motivation. Be most concerned that the students understand that they may choose from the list of choices you provide for them or from alternatives not on the list, and that it's *their* own selection. You may wish to encourage some students who select the same topic to form a group to work cooperatively on one book.

Explain to your students that they will be making books on different domestic or foreign cultures. Also explain the book-building process and possible secondary activities such as: that they will be provided with an outline that will be a useful guide, that they must make use of outside-the-school resources in addition to library materials, that they must explore the reasons for making their topical selections, that they will make display items to go along with the textbooks they make (for example, a scroll with Japanese writing), that they will introduce their books in a variety of ways to the class, that they will have opportunities to watch filmstrips and order films related to people they write about, and that they will learn how to write letters to the United Nations and other organizations for information. Here is a sample outline that you might improve upon and give to your students:

MAKING YOUR MULTI-CULTURAL BOOK

1. What will you learn?

   Do people have the same *basic* needs such as food, shelter, clothing, and safety? Why are cultures always changing? Why must people who live with others who are different learn how to interact successfully with those cultural differences?

2. What will you do to complete your book successfully?
   Write at least five questions that you would like to answer. Put these in your folder so you can answer them later.

   Watch filmstrips about people/cultures in the listening center. Read at least six books and/or articles. List the titles of your books and the number of pages read.

   Write the U.N., an embassy, or cultural organizations for more information.

3. Read at least six of the booklets listed below and list ideas about what you want to compare in your topic with those of other students. (This list is an example received from the U.N. and travel agencies.)

London	Dar Es Salaam	Helsinki, Finland
Valparaiso	Kuwait	Tikai
Bangkok	Mohenjo-daro	Bern, Switzerland
Zanbabrue	Moshi	Nakluya Eurasia

4. Choose a book from the selected list below (or identify another, with your teacher's approval) and complete your project at school and at home by (*date*). Try to depict the features of the people you choose to write about. *Remember, you may choose one not on this list.*

"As an all-school project we went on a city tour. It was conducted by the Historical Commission and we explored the historic downtown and government in Nashville, including churches. Next we will see all of the city and study the ethnic groups that live here."

Books about peoples in or from:

Greece	India	Africa (many nations)
Holland	Spain	Germany
Russia	England	Korea
Israel	Denmark	Vietnam
Mexico	Japan	Poland
Iran	Egypt	Brazil
Argentina	China	Ecuador
Ireland		Italy

or, the many American cultural, geographic, and ethnic groups:

Jewish Americans	Afro-Americans
American Indians	Japanese Americans
Hawaiians	Puerto Ricans
Chicanos	Chinese Americans
Philippinos	Appalachian—
Eskimos	Mountain cultures

5. After choosing your book topic, here are some areas of information you are expected to discover and write about:

Peoples' lifestyles	Art/music
Family—male/female roles	Religion
Language/language patterns	Government
Dress—male/female, young/old	Weather
Customs—important traditions	History
Education/schools	

Also—

List the resources you have used including films, film-strips, tapes, persons interviewed, etc.

Design a super book cover. (Teacher, don't forget to find someone to help laminate the students' book covers.)

Some suggested ways for sharing during and after the book-making process are plays, drawings, pantomime, dramatizations, and films. Be certain that your new library is available to other classrooms in the school and to your parent group.

Adopted from an exercise by: Gebee Hodges and Ann Clay-brook, Teachers, Ford Greene Elementary

11

T.V. CULTURE

Regular T.V. watching activities tend to be favorites with the kids because it's something they do "anyway" for hours a day. Select several shows a week to identify similarities and differences between the lifestyles, beliefs, values, and language patterns portrayed. Chico and the Man, Sanford and Son, Six Million Dollar Man, Good Times, and Charlie's Angels are just examples of clearly identifiable differences in culture.

Several different approaches can be used in T.V. watching. Here are just a few. One, ask the students to write and act out commercials that reflect the culture of the T.V. show they watched—e.g., dress, language patterns, styles, and products associated with the culture of that show.

Two, ask the students to work in groups and create a T.V. show that reflects their own neighborhood lifestyles based upon their own friends and family . . . comedy, tragedy, science fiction, thriller, detective story, sports show, etc.

Three, ask the kids to turn off the T.V. program (an assigned show they all will be watching on the same evening) ten minutes before its ending. Don't let anyone see what *really* happened at the end. In a super creative writing activity, each student will write his or her own ending . . . and compare it to what really happened when the teacher tells them in class.

Each of these T.V. activities provides the opportunity for students to discuss differences in their own perceptions of cultural characteristics, their communication patterns and stereotypes, and their multiple approaches to what they would do if they were creators of T.V. shows for others. They represent a successful way to use the students' T.V. reality world to learn communication skills and multi-cultural concepts.

Adapted from an exercise by: Tom Sloan, Teacher, Wharton Elementary

---

UP WITH WOMEN

As students become more aware of human rights (President Carter, the news media, classroom activities, it won't be long before they will want a cause to champion. One of the more timely issues is that of women's rights.

"I made a bulletin board in the main hallway of outstanding women that identified women of all races and ethnic groups . . . interesting how many teachers told me which groups I had forgotten and suggested representative additions . . . the board continued growing for a long time." (Examples: Mary McLeod Bethune, Louisa May Alcott, Amelia Earhart, Georgia O'Keefe, Elizabeth Blackwell, "Babe" Didrikson Zaharias, Marian Anderson, Susan B. Anthony, Helen Keller, Anne Sullivan, Eleanor Roosevelt.)

Provide some time for looking at women's roles from an historical perspective. Some of the areas you might explore are : 1) significant contributions made by women (scientists, stateswomen, humanitarians, etc.); 2) old and current text books, magazines, ads, etc. and how they depict a woman's role; 3) laws, past and present, that reflect inequities for women; 4) "double standards" that exist for men and women in social behavior; 5) statistics on women in certain traditionally male professions, i.e., engineers, doctors, lawyers, business, etc. (it would be helpful if current statistics as well as some from about 10 to 15 years ago were available in order to detect any trend of women entering these fields); and 6) the "equal pay for equal work" issue; providing specific instances, if possible, where women receive less for the same job done by a man.

Now that you've had a chance to look at the "facts," give the students a chance to digest all that information and explore their own beliefs and how those beliefs support or come into conflict with women's rights. You may expect some real differences in perceptions from students representing different minority groups. Black students may have a very different idea of women and their role than Chicanos, whose culture tends to put a woman on a pedestal and keep her in the kitchen. One way of helping students look at these issues would be to pose the question, "Do you think a person should not be allowed to do a certain job just because he's Black (Chicano, American Indian, etc.)?" Then turn it around and say: "Should a person's rights be any less because that person is a woman?"

It's now time for an action plan! Suggest to those who are interested (especially the more "militant" girls) that they make and carry signs, suffragette style, protesting the denial of their rights. Let them choose their own slogans, depending on what they feel is important.

Ask others to decide what they can do to help out mothers

13

who work. Maybe some of the boys would like to exercise their rights and learn to cook. Ask others to write letters to authors, employers, editors, senators, or even the President, protesting the denial of women's rights through prejudicial laws, books, and hiring practices. Ask the students to come up with their own ideas for registering a protest—articles in the school paper, bulletin boards, leaflets, a special school assembly. Ask them to practice their civil right to protest in a reasonable and effective manner.

Adapted from an exercise by: Tom Sloan, Teacher, Wharton Elementary

---

FRONT PAGE ANCHORPERSON

Request your students to become involved, on a regular basis, in newspaper activities. These will lead to many other multi-cultural activities including discussions of cultural groups, minority problems, and the value of cultural pluralism. Put together a regular radio or T.V. show where students become reporters by presenting brief news summaries covering activities of the world. You may select, along with the students, the articles that best reflect the variety of news items. Ask them to write in a few sentences the major ideas of the story. Taking turns as anchorperson is fun for the kids as they direct others in presenting news items. Each student reads his/her news to the class or puts it on a tape recording. The exploration and discussion of the Indian caste system, African separation, the Middle East conflicts, white minority rule, school integration, Black athletes, earthquakes in Turkey, and the weather are just a few examples of what may be stimulated by this activity as it relates to multi-cultural understandings.

No doubt, this is also designed to turn kids on to the newspaper and a variety of communication skills.

Related discussion questions:

Which is the most distressing story in the news?

What's happening in this world where people are really "together"?

If you were _____, what would you do to bring those people "together"?

14

SLAVIN' AWAY

After gaining the cooperation of other teachers and obtaining parental permission, designate some of your students as "slaves." Have them wear slave tags around their necks. The other students are considered "free" for a day (within reason and school rules). The slaves must sit in one section of the room, drink from one water fountain only, stand in the rear of the line, etc. Some students may rebel during the day, indicating they don't like what's happening. At mid-day request that the children switch free/slave roles.

At the end of the day ask the students to identify some of the feelings, values, and attitudes they have experienced. Some discussion sentence stems to stimulate sharing are:

I felt worst when . . .

I missed being able to . . .

I liked being free because . . .

I still feel bad about . . .

This reminded me of . . .

Many of these kinds of feelings, values, and attitudes that are explored will relate to freedom and intolerance. Explore what happens when "differences" are not valued.

Applications of this activity may be developed to relate to any cultural, ethnic, and other groups which have experienced prejudice and discrimination, such as:

> Females
> Students (adolescents)
> Amish
> Southerners
> Appalachian Whites
> Polish Americans
> Afro-Americans
> Mexican Americans
> Asian Americans

Adapted from an exercise by: Tom Sloan, Teacher, Wharton Elementary

CRAFTS AROUND THE WORLD

Here is an introduction to the history and customs of other cultures.

By participating in crafts activities, the student may learn:

—About a variety of cultures and the authentic products of the cultures.

—How different cultures developed utilitarian items prior to industrialization.

—About superstitions and/or traditional customs observed by other cultures.

—How symbols are used by other cultures for the purpose of written communication.

—How other cultures use natural materials to produce items for aesthetic and decorative purposes.

—About musical diversity among other peoples and how to make musical instruments representative of various cultures.

—About toys used by children from other cultures.

—About units of exchange in other cultures.

The effectiveness of this activity lies in the actual production

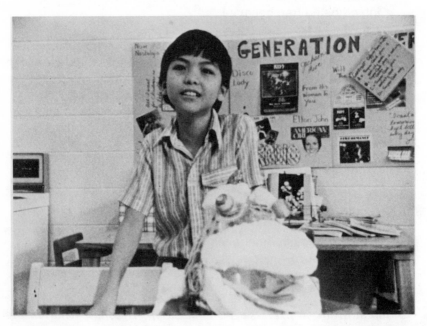

A VIETNAMESE STUDENT ASSISTS CLASSMATES IN LEARNING NEW CRAFTS SKILLS.

of the crafts which reflect the cultures from which they come. The students can fly the Japanese fish kite, hang the Philippine wind chimes in a breeze, click out a rhythm on the Spanish castanets, write messages in Chinese, wear Tiki masks, and display other works for all to view.

The students will be more responsive to exploring the history and customs of other cultures as they relate "their" products and their uses in the cultural contexts from which they originated.

The materials used for this activity are available through S & S Arts and Crafts, Colchester, Connecticut. Although you could research and develop your own projects, the materials are easily and effectively used and the prices for them are reasonable. Here is the list of materials and their cost per package at this writing. (Each package contains enough material for 25 projects.)

World Explorer Learning Guides	$1.95
Philippine Wind Chimes	3.75
Japanese Fish Kites	2.95
Chinese Calligraphy	2.95
African "Saying Goodbye" Cloth	8.75
Mexican Sundials	3.75
Spanish Castanets	2.95
Foreign Coin Key Holder	4.50
Tiki Masks	7.95
Indian Totem Plaque	10.50
Mexican Yarn Painting	6.95
African Masks	9.95

Adapted from an exercise by: Linda Therber, Teacher, Ford Greene Elementary

---

KEEP A JOURNAL

If creating an environment of trust, respect for cultural differences and support of uniqueness in your class is a high priority for you . . . and you are looking for ways to help kids better understand "what's happening" as they move through new experiences . . . then a journal might be just what you're looking for!

Explain to your students that a journal is a record of a journey and they will record their journey through the nine months you spend together. The journals (spiral notebook, notebook paper stapled together, or whatever is available) should be kept at school at all times. Make it clear that although there will be specific time allotted daily for journal entries, individuals may make an entry any time they want to. Confidentiality should be guaranteed—no entry shall be shared with the class without the individual's permission; even then, they may choose to have the teacher share it and have authorship remain anonymous.

Your guidance (at least until the students get the idea) is critical. Allow follow-up time for journal entries any time the class explores relationships, group process, acceptance of differences, conflict because of differences, other cultures and/or cultural patterns, or anything demonstrating the need for a better understanding of each person's uniqueness and how that can be an asset to the group as they learn from one another. To help them get started, you might suggest they consider answers to such questions as these:

—How did they feel during the experience?

—How and why did they respond to certain individuals after the experience?

—How and why did they perceive others' responses to them?

—How may what they learned from their experiences be related to other situations?

You can use the journal entries as a springboard for other discussions and/or activities. As you periodically spot-check the journals, choose entries which reflect differences in perception and outlook or those which record significant insight and share those (with the author's permission) with the class. This gives them another experience in how unique we all are—to the point that each of us may perceive a single event in a different way.

Periodically, and at the end of the year, ask the students to reread their journals and look for specific instances of their own growth and change, especially as it relates to an understanding of the need to support and nurture uniqueness. Ask them to share with others some of their personal feelings as a result of this growth.

Although not required, it would be beneficial if you also kept a similar journal and occasionally shared some of your entries with the class. In this way the students can appreciate your becoming a learner with them—as everyone explores how best to meet the needs of the complex and multi-cultural group that lives in your class and your world.

Adapted from an exercise by: The Teaching Team, Wharton Elementary

COOKING, TASTING, EXPLORING

An adventure in taste is a great way for everyone to experience different cultures. This activity can be extended for an indefinite period of time and take on such multi-disciplinary aspects as math (measuring, equal portions, etc.), language arts (describing what they ate and how it tasted), science (nutrition and how our body functions), social studies (the origins of certain foods and the reasons for their popularity), and community resources (as people from the community assist in identifying and preparing culturally unique foods).

Begin with a discussion of the students' favorite foods. Look at the similarities—ice cream, cake, or other foods universally

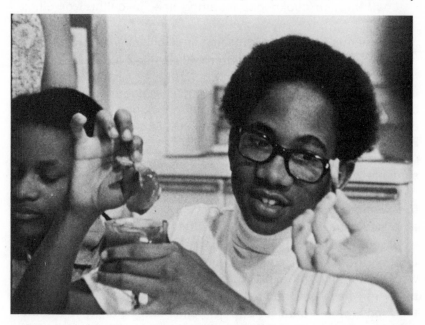

WHAT'S THAT? LEARNING ABOUT CULTURES THROUGH NEW FOODS LOOKS "RISKY AND FUN."

popular with kids. Then take a look at some of the differences. If you have a classroom with different cultural and ethnic groups represented, begin to probe for food preferences that seem to be unique to those cultures. Suggest to the students that it might be interesting to learn more about foods that are different from those in their own diets.

Start with the cultures represented in your class. The obvious cultural groups will include Black, Chicano, Oriental, and Middle-Eastern, but don't overlook those children who come from families with a German, Irish, or other heritage whose daily diet might reflect uniqueness. Another consideration would be regional differences, i.e., the foods families eat along the coast of Maine or in the bayou country of Louisiana.

Make a list of the different cultures you are going to explore through food. Taking one at a time, find out all you can about the typical dishes of that culture. You may, for instance:

Ask children to describe and/or bring recipes of favorite dishes.

Ask parents to contribute recipes and talk to the class about them.

Look through cookbooks featuring special cultural or ethnic foods.

Get menus from restaurants that specialize in ethnic dishes.

After looking at many different possibilities, ask the students to select five or six foods they would like to sample. Select by food categories and get a sample for each category. For example, choose one fruit or vegetable, one main dish, one bread or pastry, one dessert, one appetizer (soup, cheese, snack foods) and so on. Enlist the help of parents in preparing foods and do as much as possible in the class with the students participating. If you have students who are suspicious of certain new foods, you may indicate that if a student wants to taste any *one* food he *must* try all five or six. In that way all students will taste all foods and be able to decide for themselves how they feel about each.

If interest is still high after the students have sampled foods from all the different cultures represented in the class, they may want to continue by exploring foods from countries and/or cultures they have not tried yet. When it's time to move away from the foods-related studies, a great culminating activity is a multicultural smorgasbord. Have each child bring a dish representative of a particular culture, invite the parents, and have a feast! (Oops, don't forget to invite the principal *and* the custodian.)

Adapted from an exercise by: Diane Kern and Catherine Greene, Teachers, Wharton Jr. High

---

REACHING OUT

In this activity kids learn about human diversity and how it affects the behavior of others.

Divide the class into groups of 6 to 8 students. Have each group sit in a circle. Ask all students to remove any rings or bracelets they are wearing. Have one student in each group wear a blindfold and have another come forward and allow the blindfolded student to explore his or her hands. Instruct the students to note texture, size, nails, fingers, and similar features. Then, with blindfold removed, ask the student to go around the circle touching and exploring the hands of those in the group until

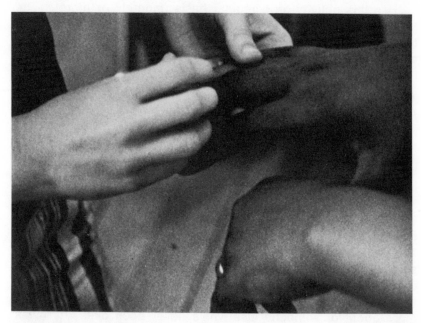

"FEELS WEIRD!" LEARNING ABOUT DIFFERENCES IN PEOPLE BY TOUCHING OTHERS BRINGS US CLOSER TOGETHER.

he/she identifies the hands explored while blindfolded. Repeat the activity until all students have had a chance to participate.

Now call the class back together and have them consider the following questions:

Were there obvious differences among hands? Discuss some of them.

Were you ever surprised to find out which hands belonged to who? Why? (Look for reasons that involve a stereotype, i.e., a girl's hands should be soft, black skin should feel different than white skin, etc.)

How did you feel about touching or being touched?

How did others react to you when you touched them?

Why do we react in the different ways we do? (Explore reasons that stem from racial, cultural, social, familial, and sexual taboos or mores.)

Can the diversity of responses to touching result in misunderstandings between people? Give examples.

Do you feel any different about touching others than you did prior to the activity? Does touching influence how you feel about others? How?

Use this activity on a regular basis (monthly or more). The kids like to do it and it can be the stimulus for pulling the class together to begin a related activity. Remember, the more the students interact in these ways the better will be their cooperation in other class activities and relationships outside of school.

Adapted from an exercise by: Dixie Vogel, Teacher, Ford Greene Elementary

---

GUESS WHO?

Let's help kids get to know one another, discover shared interests, and develop relationships based on trust and respect! They will discover that kids they thought very different from themselves share a favorite sport, or that kids they thought dumb have a skill or talent that few others possess; or they'll find someone who has visited a far-off place they've always wanted to know more about or someone else who's never been over fifty miles away from home. They might even find a girl who loves baseball and a boy who cooks. At any rate, there will be a few happy surprises when they discover that some talents and interests take on the flavor of a particular culture while others span cultures and provide for some common interests in the most unlikely places.

Here's what you do . . . have the students complete sentence stems such as:

My favorite place to be is. . . .

The thing I do best is. . . .

School is. . . .

The three most interesting places I've been to out of town are. . . .

My favorite animal is. . . .

I am different from others because. . . .

Add as many as you need until you feel that the answers will *really* give each student a chance to tell something interesting or significant about himself/herself. Tell the students *not* to put their names on the papers when they hand them in. You, in turn, will distribute the papers randomly among the class, making sure that no one has his or her own paper. After all students have read the answers, announce that they must find the person who wrote the paper they hold. Rules for finding the correct person are:

1. Students must move around the classroom, asking questions, until they find the person who wrote the paper they hold.
2. Before asking questions, they must join hands with the person they want to question.
3. Students may *not* simply ask a person whether they are holding his/her paper.
4. They *may* ask three questions based on information given in the paper they hold. For example, they may ask: "Is a tree house your favorite place to be?"
5. If the response is no, the person questioned must say where his or her favorite place really is.
6. After one person asks three questions, the other may also ask three questions to determine if the first questioner is

the owner of the paper he or she is holding. This is true even if one of the pair already knows whose paper he/she holds. In this way, everyone continues to participate and interact even after they know who their mystery person is.

Follow up by asking the students if they would like to know more about someone. This could involve such things as a student giving a demonstration, several students getting together and discussing a common hobby, or someone bringing in slides of a foreign country, a geographical area, or a special place they have visited or are from. Be certain to discuss with the kids the significance of the interests and talents which crossed cultures, sexes, and backgrounds, and their new learnings about others in the class—both the surprises and the "I knew that all the time" reactions.

Adapted from an exercise by: Dixie Vogel, Teacher, Ford Greene Elementary

---

MOVABLE TYPE EXPLORATION

A printing frame, ink, tools, and two point sizes of movable type are relatively inexpensive to buy (about $75.00). This equipment will provide an opportunity for many experiences for your students which support cultural pluralism. This activity suggests a few ways, but the possibilities are limited only by your imagination!

One, ask the children to think of some way they believe their family is unique from others and write a poem about it. Print each poem on a single page and then let the students do a collage representing what they have written. Put them on display in the room. Read and discuss them. Talk about how the values of our families affect us. Look at the differences and similarities. Are some things seemingly unique to a specific culture while others cross cultural boundaries? Can anyone think of a stereotype that someone's poem proved to be wrong?

Two, a *Community News-Poster* is especially beneficial if you have students attending school from different communities. Assign a different student group each week (making certain that the group reflects all communities) to research newspapers, interview other students, talk to parents, and explore any other source which might provide information for them to include on a news-poster. The poster might include such things as want ads, items (or pets) for sale, current and coming events, and news items featuring community residents (e.g., births, illnesses, deaths). The news-poster can be printed and put up within the school on a weekly basis. The advantage of this activity is that as each child takes his turn on the reporting team he becomes actively involved in what people from other cultural or neighborhood groups are doing. Some moments of discovery will occur as many realize that long-held stereotypes do not apply, and new interest will be generated as students become acquainted with communities and people with whom they were unfamiliar.

Three, present a list of topics for essays that are likely to reflect differences of opinions. Some possibilities are:

—What's the perfect age for getting married?
—How do you feel about being bused to school?
—Should children go to church?
—Is it "OK" to date someone of a different ethnic background?

Pick those responses that best represent different opinions, have them printed, distribute them to the class, and discuss them. The students may want to start printing a weekly editorial page to be circulated schoolwide. But if this is to be meaningful, you must take the time to discuss with your class the differences reflected in what is to be printed and the impact these differences have on people as they interact with one another.

Four, a "How-To Book" can give each child the chance to share with other students something he or she is good at. Ask students to submit directions for doing, making, or participating in something. Have each entry printed with bylines. Illustrations or diagrams can be added later. Assemble entries in book form and distribute to class members. They may find something they'd like to do together, e.g., if someone is good at making kites, maybe he/she might show the whole class how to do it and then everyone can go to the park (or school yard) and fly them. This is great for enhancing everyone's self-concept as well as providing the opportunity to find out more about the skills and abilities of individuals.

Adapted from an exercise by: John Roeder, Teacher, Washington Jr. High

"I have a Vietnamese child in my class who could write English before he spoke it. The class enjoyed looking at his writing because it had such a lovely form. I would pass it around and display it in the room. I did it to improve the child's self-concept and support peer acceptance."

ETHNICALLY SPEAKING

If you would like an activity that promotes an understanding and appreciation of cultural diversity that can be extended over a period of time and that is rich in multi-disciplinary possibilities—read on. The core thrust is foreign language, but the spin-off is exploring a culture other than one's own through another language. The possibilities for the extension of this activity are limited only by the interest of the students and the energy you are willing to put into it. Although some knowledge of another language would be helpful to your implementing this activity, it is not essential. You can rely on records or tapes, pronunciation guides, and/or friends, relatives, or colleagues who have some background in another language and are willing to help.

The first thing you need to do is decide on which language you will be exploring. The choice may be obvious if there is one you have had more experience in than others. Other considerations that might influence your decision would be the availability of materials and resources (both human and others), interest of the class, or how it fits into your other curricular areas. You may find that after going through the activities using French the class might want to do similar studies using Spanish or German.

After selecting a language explain to your students that, although they will be learning some words and phrases, the primary goal is to learn more about an unfamiliar culture. We have included a suggested sequence of activities—but remember there is nothing sacred about these. Add, subtract, and improve upon them based upon your classroom needs. The very essence of multi-cultural education is that the concept be customized to reflect the class—for its journey through other cultures.

WHERE AND HOW THEY LIVE

Bring out the maps, globes, encyclopedias, films, books, etc., and find out where the people live who speak the language you have selected. Do people in more than one country speak the language? Can you explain this? Take a look at their housing, their families, their dress, their customs. What do their towns look like? What kinds of schools do the children attend? This can be done as a total class, or the students can divide into groups, choose a topic, and report back to the class. Whatever the process, when all the data is in take time to explore such concerns as:

How are our lives similar to those of people in (country)?

What problems would a student from (country) have if he came to our town and our school?

What problems would we experience if we were to move to (country)?

Name some ways you would help someone different from you feel more comfortable.

NAMES

Look at common names in the language. Where applicable, talk about name equivalents (i.e., Joe—José). Make a list of boys' and girls' names and ask each student to choose a new name. Tell them that any assignments turned in about the language study can have their new name on it. Encourage your students to refer to one another using their new names. After a day or so ask them to discuss several questions related to these:

—Were you embarrassed when others outside the class heard your new name?

—Did anyone make fun of you?

—Have you ever heard someone made fun of because of his/her name? How do you feel about that?

—How do we help people to respect and value different names?

WORDS, WORDS, AND MORE WORDS

Time to have some fun with the language itself. Transform your room into a foreign language dictionary. Make color and number charts in the language you're studying. Label everything in the room (chairs, desks, tables, record player, floor, lights, etc.) with foreign names. Ask the kids what new language words they would like to know. Make charts with the English (or a pictorial representation) and the foreign language word. Make other charts dealing with common phrases such as "how are you," "where is," "goodbye." Don't stress memorization. Leave the charts up so, as the students experiment with using the language, they can easily find the words they want. Play tapes and records of the language so they can get a better idea of pronunciation and accent. Be certain to note similarities in words to English (i.e., blue—bleu). Discuss slang usage and how what we say might often be confusing for someone who had learned "dictionary English." Encourage the students to play with the language and use it whenever they can instead of English. Their self-esteem is going to soar as other members of the school hear them saying words in a different language.

CAN YOU TASTE A CULTURE?

Have your students participate in a little research into what kind of food is typically eaten by the peoples speaking the language you're studying. Is our food influenced at all by their culture? Have we (America) had any influence on what they eat? Ask those who have experienced some of the food to try to describe how it tasted. Ask your students if they can figure out why a particular food is more popular in that country than it is here. After exploring different foods, select a recipe to prepare in class. Unless you have access to a stove, it would probably be more feasible to choose something that can be prepared in the classroom with a hotplate or electric skillet or some other easily transportable appliance. It might be worthwhile to prepare the recipe in the other language and have the students translate. Keep the recipe simple and encourage students to try it out at home.

A DIFFERENT KIND OF "BREAD"

If you don't have access to coins from other countries, have the students make some "play money" from poster board. Look at the different units of exchange and the value of the American dollar. Try to present some price of food, clothing, and housing in that country. Compare that to average income. Have the students make budgets and decide where it is cheaper to live. What things might be cheaper there than here in America? Then turn it around and look at what might be cheaper in the U.S.A. than in other countries. Look at and compare taxes, government support of education, medical care, child care, welfare benefits, etc. Have the students list the pros and cons of the monetary aspects of both countries.

HEROES AND HEROINES

Choose popular heroes, heroines and/or patriots from the cultures you are exploring. Learn about their contributions to their countries. Find out something about their personal lives. How do the countries commemorate them (holidays, monuments, memorials, etc.)? Ask your students if these persons would have been heroes or heroines in our country. Look at some of the people we honor for their contributions to our country. Do we place emphasis on or value different attributes than other countries? Discuss those differences and similarities. Is it necessary for us to better understand values before we can appreciate other cultures? What implications does this hold for world peace? Do the same concepts apply in order to assure a sense of brotherhood among Americans who differ from one another?

Where you go from here is up to you and your class. Ask them what else they would like to know about other cultures and countries. Would they like to pick another language and launch another voyage? Be daring and have some fun while you look at the languages and cultures that make up this big wide world of ours.

Adapted from an exercise by: Ella Lett Gandy, Teacher, Ford Greene Elementary, and Edward V. Johnson, George Peabody College

---

I AM

This activity is most effective if done early in the school year and then repeated later towards the end of the year. It provides an opportunity for you and the students to look at your own growth and how your perceptions of yourselves and others change.

Ask the students to draw a picture of themselves including any physical (or other) characteristics that they feel make them different from others. Give them an outline of a person on a blank sheet of paper. Then ask them to finish the sentence "I am . . ." at least five times at the bottom of their picture. Encourage them to include the things they feel contribute to making them unique. Provide some time during which students can volunteer to share their pictures and tell something about themselves. Be certain to highlight, in a supportive fashion, any differences based on culture or ethnicity. This is often useful in the beginning of the year to help students get to know one another

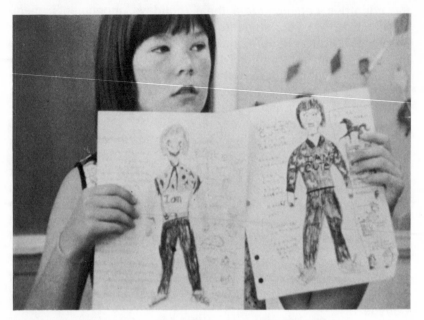

UNDERSTANDING HOW WE CHANGE AND HOW WE DIFFER IS LEARNED IN "I AM."

better. Display the pictures for at least several weeks and give everyone a chance to look them over before you take them down and put them in safekeeping for later in the year.

Repeat the activity towards the end of the year. Pull out the same activity done seven to eight months earlier and let the students compare their two pictures. If you and your class have spent time during the interval exploring differences and learning more about your own uniqueness, you will probably notice some obvious changes in the students' responses. They should reflect a greater awareness of self as well as an extended awareness of their fellow students.

Be sure to ask the students how they perceive the differences in their responses. Can they explain why or how they've changed? Do they notice any change in their friends? Do they remember where they were when they did the first one? How do they feel about the change?

Adapted from an exercise by: Loretta Green, Teacher, Wharton Elementary

30

GENERATION GAP

Because teachers represent one generation but teach a classroom of young people, they are perhaps in a unique situation to examine and understand differences in generations. As a class activity, have students conduct a survey of family members and close neighbors to determine their favorite television shows, magazines, foods, or activities. Let your class compile their lists and compare the likes and dislikes of the older generation with their own. Why do we like certain things and dislike others? How do we demonstrate our likes and dislikes? Does one generation absorb likes and dislikes from another? Can your class give examples of one generation borrowing from another? What about dances—where do they originate? do they go in and out of vogue?

The following *Generation Super Cards* represent an instructional process designed to help your students understand differences in generations. Find out your students' interests in: music, T.V. shows, fashion, cars, food, and sports. Keep a careful record of individual responses and then list your own favorites in the same categories. Are any of these areas able to cross the generation gap? Ask your kids to do at least one of these cards a week and to have someone else of a different generation do it also. Then compare the answers and report to the class. Periodically update the cards so they maintain their contemporary flavor.

Activity Card I: Write a record review about any of the works by the following recording artists: The Jackson Five, Lynyrd Skynyrd, Parliament Psychedelics, Elton John, Kiss, Led Zeppelin. (Other artists may be approved by the teacher.)

Activity Card II: Listen to the records "Roll Gypsy Roll" and "Double Trouble" by Lynyrd Skynyrd. Interpret the record's meaning for the older ears of your teacher.

Activity Card III: Listen to the record "Welcome Back" by John Sebastian. Watch and review the T.V. show "Welcome Back Kotter."

Activity Card IV: Listen to a sportscast on T.V. or radio. Keep a record of slang used to describe the specific sports event. Go to a school basketball game and record crowd phrases and slang in the cheers.

31

Activity Card V: Watch the T.V. shows "Good Times" and "Happy Days." Contrast and compare the two shows as to fashion, slang, and content.

Activity Card VI: Several magazines are displayed for your enjoyment. Please browse through them. Report to the class on the contents of a particular magazine and tell why you chose that selection.

Activity Card VII: Write a biographical sketch about your favorite sports hero or heroine.

Activity Card VIII: Talk with a classmate of the opposite sex and a different race. Discover the person's likes in terms of music, clothes, food, and favorite recreation. Report your findings. Be sure to include interests you both share.

Activity Card IX: Make a dictionary of slang words from the T.V. shows "Happy Days" and "Good Times." Just for fun, try some illustrations.

Activity Card X: Organize a fashion show or fashion review. Include dress and sports wear. Write a narrative that will be given orally to the class. You may persuade classmates to be models, or use pictures as you wish.

Activity Card XI: Pretend that you are a disc jockey. Use a

IN "THE GENERATION GAP" STUDENTS LEARN ABOUT SOMEONE OF A DIFFERENT AGE/RACE/SEX.

blank tape to record your own radio show. Include some of your favorite songs, an advertisement, tell someone happy birthday, and pretend to do at least one request.

Have a "Generation Day" where students come dressed to represent a certain period of American history. They could also be prepared to provide the rest of the class with historical incidents of that period, what music was popular, and the like. It would be fun to have students talk with older family members who might have had personal experiences during that time period; these stories could be shared as "Timely Reminders." Your class might even want to collect these stories to make a book. Be certain to include a discussion of why we don't understand, differences between age groups or how it feels to be old. Do we talk differently to old people than we do to each other? Why, if we do? Do all of you have the same kind of relationship with your grandparents? Let the students discuss how they feel about their grandparents. What activities have they had in common with older family members? American Indian and Oriental cultures have traditionally had different ways of reacting to and treating elderly people than the traditional American culture. What are these differences?

Adapted from an exercise by: Catherine Greene, Teacher, Wharton Jr. High

------

THE COVER-UP GAME

We all react to situations in a manner that is determined by previous experiences. Scenes that appear real to one student, will not to another. A human figure that one student sees as helpful may intimidate another student. Remember, it helps students clarify their feelings when they can analyze them in a relaxed, accepting environment. This activity provides a vehicle for students to explore diversity and their many responses to differences.

Collect an assortment of realistic pictures from news or picture magazines and mount them on construction paper. Cover one part of the picture with a small square of paper. Ask the class some questions about the covered part. If it is a person you could cover the face and ask what type of person is pictured,

STEREOTYPICAL EVALUATIONS ARE MADE AS STUDENTS LEARN FROM "THE COVER-UP GAME."

or why he or she is in the picture. A good example for this activity is a picture that shows the consequential action but the "cause" is covered.

It will be possible to hear stereotypical evaluations emerge as the class analyzes the pictures. Figures engaged in certain activities will be prejudged to be either male or female, or associated with one ethnic group rather than another . . . or old rather than young. After the class has a chance to guess what's under the covered part of the picture, show it to them. Then help them identify why they responded as they did and how their assumptions affect behavior.

As a follow-up activity, you can encourage your students to locate pictures to be used. For variety, you could project a frame from a filmstrip or a 2″ x 2″ slide with the lens out of focus. Slowly adjust the picture to be in focus while the students are trying to determine the content of the picture. Discuss how difficult it is to adjust your thinking once you believe you know what the picture is. Compare this characteristic with the manner in which prejudices keep our minds from making accurate assessments by blocking or keeping information out-of-focus. Exploring further what's happening in the pictures (or comparing pictures) is a grand way to focus on cultural lifestyles.

Adapted from an exercise by: Jacob Eleasari, Producer and Director of the multi-cultural film, "What's the Difference Being Different"; and Kathy Bryant, Teacher Corps Intern, Washington Jr. High

---

PORTRAIT PLURALISM

Appreciation of uniquenesses within individuals goes further than simply recognizing differences. It must include a true valuing of those differences as good and desirable. This activity provides an experience for students to give a positive value to differences while getting a real boost for their self-concept at the same time.

Either have students draw self-portraits, help each other make silhouettes, or if time and money permits, photograph each child in 5" x 7" or 8" x 10" size . . . or use the yearly school pictures (wallet size) taken in most schools. Mount each picture on a three foot sheet of butcher paper and hang up around the room. Explain to the students that at any time they may write something *true* and good about someone in the class on that person's picture paper. They may or may not choose to sign their names. Stress the point that everyone has good qualities and they are to discover as many of those qualities about their classmates as possible. To avoid a newcomer to the class or a less popular student getting little written under his picture, tell students that before they write a comment about a friend they must write at least one positive comment about someone they do not know as well. The teacher should also feel free to add comments. Encourage students to read the comments written on the sheets of other classmates.

At the end of the week, ask the class to discuss the comments written about them. Discuss the following points:

Did you begin to feel any differently towards your classmates when you were really concentrating on their good qualities?

Were you surprised by the good qualities you discovered in students you had not known well?

Why do you think you never noticed their good qualities?

35

(Stress reasons that reflect stereotypes of how certain people are "supposed" to be.)

Do you feel a closer bond to your classmates now than before? Why do you think that is?

Allow each student to take his sheet home. Parents are generally pleased to see their children are supported and appreciated for their good points. You may repeat this activity whenever you feel that the class needs a boost in appreciating the differences among themselves.

Adapted from an exercise by: Loretta Green, Teacher, Wharton Elementary

"I paired a White boy (with a twelfth grade reading level) with a Black child that was performing poorly in academics. The purpose was that the White boy was too "bookish" and needed to learn some street knowledge and the Black child needed some help with scholastics. The two boys have become close friends and often chide each other. The White boy is more accepted by the group and the Black child is doing much better classwork. When the White child had his Bar Mitzvah he invited the entire class, and most of them attended, including this Black teacher."

ETHNIC IN THE NEWS

This activity is exciting. It provides the next best thing to a first-hand visit to various ethnic communities. The students may wish to delve even deeper into some of the topics suggested in order to better understand cultures. Your responsibility is to keep all discussion non-judgmental and to stress the great contribution ethnic differences make to our society.

Many ethnic groups publish periodicals dealing with their particular community and interests. You can find a listing of such publications in *Urich's International Periodicals Dictionary* (R.R. Bowker Co., New York), under the heading "Ethnic Interest." Some examples:

Chinatown News, Chinese Publicity Bureau Ltd., 459 E. Hastings St., Vancouver, B. C. V6A 1P5, Canada.

Parola del Popolo, Parola del Popolo Publishing Assn., 6740 W. Diversey, Chicago, Ill. 60635 *(In Italian and English)*.

Yughtruf, Bainbridge Ave., New York, N. Y. 10467 *(Student's quarterly in Yiddish and English)*.

Send for some of these periodicals and ask each student to look through them to initiate some of the following activities.

—Find out what the locally published "ethnic" newspapers are in your community.

—Look for differences and similarities between these papers and those sent to you.

—Look at and compare sections of the papers. What traditional parts have been included (editorial page, vital statistics, classified ads, comics, etc.)? What has been excluded or added? Can you think of *why* the paper follows the format it does?

—Check out how the different publications treat such issues as children speaking both English and the ethnic language and prejudices about their community supporting and preserving their ethnic culture (foods, social organizations, churches, dancing, music, arts, talent, etc.)

—Look at the advertisements. Do the businesses that have ads reflect the culture? Do the grocery store ads specialize in ethnic foods? Do you see anything you *didn't* expect to find in an ethnic newspaper?

—Do political concerns take a different slant from paper to paper? What are some of the differences? Do you understand why there are these differences?

Adapted from an exercise by: Karen Safley, Teacher, Ford Greene Elementary

---

WHY ARE WE WHAT WE ARE?

Why are we what we are? All of us, including the students in your class, are interested in why and how we are what we are. This activity is a genetic experiment that shows how traits are inherited from parents.

Order some Albino Corn Seed from the Carolina Biological Supply Company, Burlington, North Carolina 27215. The parent plants have a recessive trait for albinism that will reveal itself in subsequent plant generations. This activity can be year-long and have students involved in charting the characteristics of each generation. As a parallel, students could explore one of these physical characteristics and see what family members have the same trait . . . a map of family similarities and differences.

An interesting variation for genetic discovery is the breeding of fruit flies. This activity is suitable for responsible students in grades seven through ten. A Breeder Kit can be ordered from Carolina Biological Supply (#67-4050) for $14.00 that includes everything but the Drosophilae culture. *Drosophila? . . .* that's a fruit fly's proper name!

Several characteristics can be used in comparing the fruit fly offspring, but the easiest to use is whether they are winged or wingless. From the same source, you can order the cultures for $6.50—all the fruit fly culture you'll need. The kit will have full instructions, but it is not too complicated. The culture is placed in plastic tubes with the "food" and soon the larvae appear. It takes ten days for each generation. Students will be able to tell whether the flies are winged or wingless by visual examination.

To determine sex count, it is necessary to use ether to put the flies to sleep. This is not dangerous for your students, but it does call for responsible action. The male fruit fly has a black tip on the abdomen and can be distinguished in this manner. Your students will discover that the count is roughly 50-50 for each generation—just as for them.

An effective filmstrip to use before this experiment is "The Fruit Fly," Filmstrip of the Month Club, 355 Lexington Avenue, New York, N. Y. 10017.

Adapted from an exercise by: Ann Von Cannon, Teacher, Wharton Jr. High

---

UNDERSTANDING HOW WE DIFFER

We are all combinations of many characteristics and features and these combinations make us unique. Understanding and acceptance of our differences, as well as those of others, forms the basis for multi-cultural education.

Because we are all fascinated and interested in the human body, this interest can develop into activities that explore our differences. These differences are not related to sex or race, but fall across those categories. For example: obtain some P.T.C. Taste Papers from a science supply company. When students put these small slips of paper in their mouths, some will taste a very bitter taste, others will taste nothing. Approximately 65 percent of all people who do this experiment taste the bitter taste. Why? Because there is a difference in our taste buds.

Likewise, some people have attached earlobes and some people have unattached lobes. Some people can roll their tongue up toward the roof of the mouth so that it forms a cylinder; other people can do this only slightly, or not at all! There are differences in the way we clasp our hands together. Which thumb do you place on top? This characteristic is generally constant so that you will repeatedly place the same thumb on top unless you really think about it.

Let your students test themselves for these human characteristics and then group off. This activity is kind of a human body "Four Squares" because it will form groups that have no relationship to sex or race. It will be interesting for students to find out who is "like" them and "different" from them on each of these characteristics. Discuss with your class how they would feel if one way was right . . . tongue rollers were not as acceptable as non-tongue rollers. What determines whether we can roll our tongues or not? You can change how you clasp your hands, but how would you feel if someone in authority told you that you had to do it a certain way? How would it feel to deny your own way?

Adapted from an exercise by: Ann Von Cannon, Teacher, Wharton Jr. High

---

I LIKE YOUR TYPE!

This activity was originated for a unit on genetics and inheritance aimed at middle school and junior high students. It dramatically points up the basic sameness in man's development while highlighting the differences in characteristics—it will give your students some bloodcurdling insights! It's best to obtain parental permission for this one.

Blood typing is a process that will teach students about the four types of human blood and that these types are inherited. It is very interesting to find out what type of blood you have. The

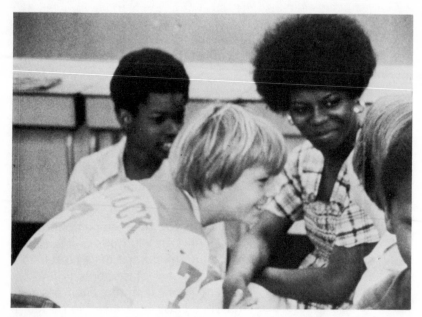

ROLE PLAYING IS A SUCCESSFUL INSTRUCTIONAL TECHNIQUE IN A MULTI-CULTURAL EDU-CATION PROGRAM.

teacher that used this activity related that students wanted to "be different" . . . to have one of the rare blood types. However, during a discussion of which blood type was "best" there was agreement that all blood types do the same job for the body; no matter what type blood, it would carry oxygen to body parts, aid nutrition, and fight disease. Their discussion concluded that blood is different, but the same! This can be correlated with people, since they too are different but the same.

You are probably intrigued but apprehensive about this activity. It really is not as complicated as you probably think it is. For supplies, you will need: sterile disposable lancets that are individually prepackaged, typing serum, alcohol, toothpicks, glass slides, and cotton balls. You can get adequate supplies for an entire class for around $6.00. Directions for this activity are as follows:

1. Draw two circles on a microscope slide with the felt tip pen. Label one A, the other B.
2. Clean the tip of one of your fingers with cotton that has been soaked in alcohol.

3. Either you, your lab partner, or teacher will prick your finger with a sterile lancet.
4. Squeeze two drops of blood from your finger into each circle on the slide. Work rapidly. Do not let the blood harden on the slide.
5. Place one drop of anti-A typing serum into circle A. Do not touch the dropper to the blood.
6. Place one drop of anti-B typing serum into circle B. Do not touch the dropper to the blood.
7. Gently mix the blood and typing serum with a toothpick. *Use different toothpicks for each circle.* Take no more than 10 to 20 seconds to mix the blood and serum.
8. Immediately match your slide with the proper combination in the blood typing chart (below) to determine your blood type.

BLOOD TYPING CHART

Type	*Results*
AB	Slide will have clumping on label A and label B
A	Slide will have clumping on label A only
B	Slide will have clumping on label B only
O	Slide will *not* have clumping on label A or B

A book that is good to use for the study of blood is *Laboratory Biology: Investigating Living Systems,* Charles Merrill Publishers, Columbus, Ohio 43216. On page 128 of this book is a table that shows a break-down of blood types by ethnic groups. It is interesting to note that Eskimos have only two of four possible blood types, Type O and Type A. Also, 76 percent of American Indians have Type A blood.

If you are interested in trying the blood typing activity in your classroom, you may want to contact your local Blood Bank or American Red Cross Chapter to see if they have any services connected with the study of blood. For supplies, contact a science supply house or surgical supply company.

Adapted from an exercise by: Ann Von Cannon, Teacher, Wharton Jr. High

FOREIGN NEWSPAPERS ARRIVE

Kids are fascinated by foreign newspapers. Giving children access to them can heighten their awareness of other countries and cultures as real places in which real people live. You could incorporate this in several areas of study, for instance:

In Social Studies—What kind of government does (country) have and what are some of the problems arising from this form of government? What is the economic level of the (country)? What do the people do for work? For entertainment? What are their lifestyles? The characteristics of culture go on and on! Food, art, play, music . . . look for them all in the news!

In Math—A study of metrics. If the grocery ads are given in metric units, convert the foreign currency into dollar equivalents and compare the prices.

In Science—Climatic conditions, ecological and conservation concerns. How advanced is their technology? What are their natural resources? And so on.

In Language Arts—Compare the styles of writing. Look at differences in paper format. Write imaginary (or real!) letters to the editor or rewrite articles so that they more closely reflect the student's own culture.

A good source for English-language periodicals is the *1977 Ayer Directory of Publications,* Ayer Press, Philadelphia. The following are some newspapers you might use (also see page 163 in the resource section).

> *Star,* Jim Beebe, Editor, 2149 2nd Avenue, Whitehorse, Yukon Territory, Canada.
>
> *Bermuda Sun,* John Ellington, Editor, Hamilton, Bermuda.
>
> *Guardian,* Leon Turnquest, Editor, P. O. Box N. 3011, Nassau, Bahamas.
>
> *Star and Herald,* Luis C. Noli, Editor, Box 159, Panama City, Panama.
>
> *Times,* Pedro Calomarde, Editor, Cor. D. Jakosalem, Gullas Street, Cebu, Republic of the Philippines.

Adapted from an exercise by: Karen Safley, Teacher, Ford Greene Elementary

MOVEMENT FOR EDUCATION

A great way to learn more about different cultures is to dance through them. Dance has always reflected the spirit and the music of a culture and most students enjoy learning more about how to do different dances.

The best place to begin is right at home. Find out how many students have had some experience in (or at least exposure to) dances representative of a different culture. Don't exclude the "youth culture" with the latest dance crazes, square dancing, or any other dances which your students might have experienced.

As you begin to look at dances less familiar to your students, be sure to explore such questions as the social religious origin of the dance, the music (tempo, instruments, etc.), and the current status of the dance in its culture. Check out any other area of interest that might arise from exploring a culture through the medium of dance. Actually learn and participate in as many of the different dances as possible. Exceptions, of course, are those dances in which the level of skill and expertise needed make them unfeasible. Some possible places to begin looking for resources for this activity are your school media center, public libraries, ethnic restaurants (which often feature ethnic dancers), Y.M.(W.)C.A. (which sometimes offer classes in ethnic dancing), your P.E. teacher, and any community members who might have expertise in a particular dance. Some rich initial possibilities to explore are Mexican, American Indian, Greek, Polish, Russian, Latin, Japanese, Puerto Rican, and Jewish dances. Of course, any dances that intrigue you and the kids should be included.

Adapted from an exercise by: Sherrilyn D. Pasternak, Instructor, Middle Tennessee State University

---

GAMES IN MANY CULTURES

Games are universally popular. As long as man has existed, there have been games for relaxation, for ceremony, to prepare for war, or to ward off demons. There is a commonality in games, and it is often possible to see variations of the same game in many cultures. For instance, Blindman's Buff, popular with

> *"Thomas is our new student from Hawaii. He told the class all the things he could remember about his early childhood there—the straw house he lived in, where he played, how his parents spent the evening dancing. He also brought a necklace of shells that his grandmother made. We talked about the location and climate of Hawaii and how it has changed. The kids want to know more."*

boys and girls in the United States, was played by children in Rome. This game is also played in many European countries and is known as Blind Cow or Blind Hen.

See how much your students can discover about other cultures by exploring games. If your school library does not have the materials you need, bring in resources from a local public or university library. Another good source would be people from the community who have some expertise in the games played in many cultures. Tell your students to be alert to ancient games that might have influenced games or sports in the U.S.A. and those in other countries that may have originated in America.

Many times games will reflect the culture in terms of values (strength vs. skill), natural resources available (game equipment made of stones, sticks, leather), social order (Who is allowed to play? Is the winner awarded a particular prize?), technological advancement (Is any of the equipment used mechanized?), and many other interesting facts about the culture.

Described below are games from two cultures as examples of the activities that can be developed from this interest area.

NATIVE AMERICAN GAMES

Native Americans especially enjoy playing games. They would often gather together for competition between tribes. Foot races and horse races were popular. Some tribes in the northwestern portion of the continent even competed with song contests. Accompaniment was with native instruments: drums, rattles, whistles, flutes, and notched sticks rasped together. These instruments are easily made from items found in the home like oatmeal boxes, gourds, etc. Why not let your class plan a song competition with accompaniment?

Indians also like games of chance. One particular favorite is the hand game where a player holds two wooden pieces in his hand. One piece is marked and the other is plain. The opponent tries to guess which hand has the marked piece.

The bowl game played by Native Americans is similar to a

dice game in that seeds, marked with different designs representing different amounts, were tossed into a bowl. The amount won depended upon the designs that were showing.

Indian boys enjoy ring and pole games, such as seeing how many rings one can catch on a stick when they are thrown by another player. It is possible to construct this game very cheaply, using jar rings and any kind of stick or dowel. Also, Indian children like throwing a pointed stick to see who could throw it the farthest. Sometimes the stick was painted like a snake. Today, boys in the United States compete in the punt, pass, and kick contest . . . same thing.

GAMES FROM THE FAR EAST

Kite flying is very popular in China. Let your class make miniature kites of colored paper with straws as a frame. Since the kites in China are usually made in the shapes of fish, dragons, butterflies, birds, and bumblebees—let your students be creative. The finished products can be assembled into a mobile for an attractive room decoration.

A variation of kite-making from tissue paper is to make a Japanese Carp Kite. Draw a large fish on tissue paper and cut out two sheets at the same time. Draw scales, eyes, and decoration on the fish. Glue the fish together at the edges, except for the mouth. Then stuff the scrap tissue paper gently into the fish's mouth. Tape a string to the mouth for displaying. Or don't stuff the fish and let the students see if they can fill the fish with air by running with it (outside, of course).

As in other countries, Chinese boys and girls like to play games of chase. One game, called Peacock Feather, has everyone but two children in a circle. The remaining two are inside the circle blindfolded and try to catch each other. The students in the outside circle walk around reciting: "Peacock feather on a plum limb, you catch me and I'll catch him." After one child inside the circle is caught, another student is selected to enter the circle and be blindfolded. The game is repeated.

Adapted from an exercise by: Jane Bandy Smith, Multi-Cultural Instructor

45

"In Smash Ball children get into a circle and throw the ball as hard and fast as they can. The object is to make the other person miss. Everyone but one person has to lose. The purpose of the game is to help children to learn that it's O.K. to lose sometimes; it's not always the 'jock' that wins . . . sometimes the very best people make mistakes, are beaten, but never give up."

OLYMPIC TRIALS

The Olympic Games represent a multi-cultural event that is enjoyed by millions of people. These games, begun in Greece in ancient times, and later revived by a Frenchman, combine the efforts and interests of most of the world's nations. In the ancient Olympic Games, the outstanding event was the Pentathlon. Five events comprised the Pentathlon: the discus throw, the long jump, the javelin throw, the stade race (a sprint the length of the stadium), and upright wrestling.

Why not have a class activity built around these events of the Pentathlon? Ask the class to divide into groups representing countries other than the United States.

They can even make a paper flag to represent their country and find out about the people, language, landscape, etc., of that country. Next, have the groups decide on one member to enter each event of the five Pentathlon events—only change from athletic tasks to information-finding tasks. For instance, have the Discus Throw be a search for information on the sixteen major sports of the Olympics—where they originated, star performers, equipment needed, and so on. Put the country's name on a construction paper discus and advance the paper discus as each report comes in. Instead of measuring the feet the discus is thrown, measure the different facts that are presented in the research report. Carry out a similar change with each of the other four events, substituting tasks like: finding out the record holders in other sports; having a group quiz on who's who in sports; giving points for group members that locate and teach the class a game or dance from another country; or researching the biography of an outstanding sports figure from a minority group.

Some possible biographies are: Henry Aaron, Wilma Rudolph, Allie Reynolds, Lee Trevino, Jack Johnson, Olga Korbut, John O. Crow, Joe Louis, Jackie Robinson, Isaac Murphy, Archie Moore, Billie Jean King, Robert Hayes, Jim Thorpe, Hosia Richardson,

Charles Albert "Chief" Bender, Arthur Ashe, Jesse Owens, Floyd Patterson, and Althea Darben.

A good resource for this activity is the *Guiness Book of World Records.*

Adapted from an exercise by: Carolyn Gunter, Teacher, Washington Jr. High

---

FEASTING—A FESTIVAL OF ACTIVITIES

Using cultural feasts as the focal points of many multi-cultural activities on a monthly or bi-monthly basis provides the opportunity for indepth ethnic study experiences. The new learnings necessary for students to hold a cultural feast are enormous—lifestyles, language, history, beliefs, values, customs. Pulling all of this together into a feast-festival provides the impetus for a variety of guests, films, readings, and visits. Most ethnic groups, cultures, and subcultures lend themselves to the festival approach.

Such activities could be continuous throughout the school year. For example, your class could make a ceremonial igloo from sheets and each child contribute something to the cereony in traditional Eskimo style. Students might write songs about another student who assumes the role of a hunter in the wilderness. As Eskimos they could vent some frustrations by singing songs they compose about their lives. Some could read poems they have written (as Eskimos) and others could do string art (Jacob's Ladder, etc.). Eskimo games could be played. Foods, including raw fish, can be eaten Eskimo style. If several classrooms wish to do so, "all-school" multi-cultural festivals could be developed on a regular basis with parents and friends invited.

Adapted from an exercise by: Mary Parker, Teacher, Head Elementary

"I identify all of the cultural oriented restaurants in the yellow pages and have the kids and parents go and do reports . . . sometimes we earn the money and the whole class goes . . . I love Chinese, Kosher, country. . . ." (Social Studies Teacher)

LABELING IS FOR JELLY JARS

This activity may be used with small groups or with the entire class. Choose a concept, such as the opposites short and tall. Then label appropriate students as "good" or "bad." For example, label certain students (who share tallness) as good, then label other students (who share shortness) as bad. The others in the group try to guess the criterion on which the students were labeled. Variations of this activity might include specific rules on what those who are labeled are allowed to do. For instance, those labeled "bad" cannot participate in the group discussion, while those labeled "good" automatically assume leadership roles in the group.

After discovering the criterion used, the students could explore concepts such as value judgments, stereotyping, and prejudicial treatment. Input from those who were labeled as to how they felt when the others responded to them in a negative (or positive) way is valuable. Did they feel as though they could "control" the circumstances? What were their feelings toward those placing value judgments on them? Contrast the feelings of the "good" and the "bad" students.

Repeating this activity with student-chosen criteria and labeling enables more students to experience being labeled and to discover how they might respond. Discuss the different reactions of the students. For instance, did those labeled "good" feel powerful, guilty, a sense of well-being, lucky, etc.? Or did those labeled "bad" feel angry, frustrated, ashamed, shy . . . and so on?

Adapted from an exercise by: Johnny Thompson, Teacher Corps Intern, Washington Jr. High

---

WHEN I GROW UP . . .

In this activity, which may be used as an exercise for career development, students are encouraged to think about occupations they might like to enter. After selecting a career (but not sharing it with the others), a student volunteers to field questions from the class as it tries to guess what career he is considering.

As the students explore a variety of careers they will also be encouraged to look at such questions as . . .

Does everyone choose the same career for the same reason?
Does self-concept have an impact on one's career choice?
Do we stereotype certain careers using race, sex, or socio-economics as criteria?
Do we place value judgments on certain careers? What criteria are used . . . money, prestige, visibility, education, skill, morality?
Are some careers more prestigious in one culture than another? Why?
Do some careers require different lifestyles than others?
Discussion along these lines should support and highlight the value of differences as the class probes the diverse needs and opportunities generated by a diverse society.

Adapted from an exercise by: Johnny Thompson, Teacher Corps Intern, Washington Jr. High

---

WHO'S THAT?

A necessary step in helping students develop healthy relationships with other members of their class is to design activities in which they look at why they seek out certain individuals as friends and tend to shy away from other individuals, or perhaps groups of individuals. This activity should lay some groundwork for exploring what is involved before one person feels he can trust another and some of the ways a trusting relationship can be developed.

Ask for several volunteers. Explain that they will be blindfolded and led by another student on a walk and ask them to choose the individual they would like to serve as their guide. When they have decided, tell them that the guide's job is to be sure the partner is safe at all times—i.e., doesn't bump into anything or fall down stairs. The guide should also give the partner as interesting a walk as possible. They might go up and down stairs, or to places with different noises, try walking backwards, and so on. After the walk, ask the partner to remain blindfolded and select different guides, keeping the identity of the new guides from the blindfolded partner. When selecting a guide, choose someone with whom the other doesn't usually associate.

After everyone has returned from their walks remove the blindfolds and let them see who their anonymous guide was.

Then ask both the participants and observers of the experiment to discuss what they felt happened. Some ideas for generating a discussion are:

1. Why did you choose certain people to guide you and not others?
2. Did you feel there were certain individuals or "groups" you could not trust to guide you safely?
3. If so, what were your reasons for feeling this way? Would they feel the same about you? Are these judgments based on cultural, racial, economic, or other stereotypes?
4. Did you feel or act different when you did not know who was guiding you? (Ask observers if they noticed any different behavior.)
5. Did you feel differently toward your anonymous guide at the end of your walk? Were you surprised to find out who it was?
6. Do you feel as though you could now trust that person? How could you demonstrate that you could be trusted?
7. List some ways that individuals in the class can develop relationships based on acceptance and trust with someone who "looks" very different from themselves.

Adapted from an exercise by: Dixie Vogel, Teacher, Ford Greene Elementary, and Robert Dellanoce, Multi-Cultural Instructor

---

CULTURAL ART

Choose an abstract concept such as love, peace, anger, honesty or fear. Have the class break into small groups of three to five students and give each group a large piece of paper and something to draw with—paints, markers, colored chalk, crayons. Ask each group to draw a picture representing the concept in question. Put the finished products on the wall and have a representative from each group explain their drawings.

Discuss the drawings with the class. Capitalize on the differences in representations of the same concept. Talk about uniqueness, showing that it is valuable and valid. If love is one thing to one person and something else to another, does that mean one is "right" and the other "wrong"? Explain the consequences of such feelings. Are any of them tied to cultural, racial

50

or economic stereotypes? How did they feel when someone put a negative value on their conceptual drawing? How did they feel when others seemed to understand and accept it? End the activity by assigning all drawings a grade of A+, showing that you value the uniqueness of each representation.

Adapted from an exercise by: Dixie Vogel, Teacher, Ford Greene Elementary, and Robert Dellanoce, Multi-Cultural Instructor

CULTURAL COMPLIMENTS

Much of how we respond to people and situations is a result of our "culture." Helping students understand this is an integral part of multi-cultural education. This activity can help students become aware of how their own culture influences them as well as help them relate to each other by discovering and appreciating each individual's uniqueness.

Arrange chairs in a circle and ask each individual to think of a compliment to give someone else in the class. Volunteers are then called on to express their compliments. Observe which students are uncomfortable with paying someone a compliment. Is there a pattern of giving compliments to those that most closely reflect their own culture? Are different values reflected in the nature of the compliment, i.e., dress, skin color, hair color or texture, voice quality or accent, and the like? Discuss with the students how culture influences their values and how they feel about complimenting others. Look at the differences in value systems: some students hold certain attributes in esteem while others value some entirely different ones. Talk about how being aware of those differences helps us to be more sensitive to how people feel and more appreciative of their uniqueness.

Students may be shy about complimenting at first. But given the chance to "practice" and realize the good feelings that come from saying something good about someone as well as having someone say something nice about you, most students become enthusiastic participants. It certainly enhances everyone's self-concept and helps develop better group cohesiveness.

Adapted from an exercise by: Dixie Vogel, Teacher, Ford Greene Elementary, and Robert Dellanoce, Multi-Cultural Instructor

CULTURAL ROLES

Role playing is a vehicle for getting students immediately and personally involved in the problem solving process. Utilizing the role playing technique to help students explore cultural differences requires an effort on your part to provide realistic and provocative situations to which the students will respond.

This activity suggests a few situations around which role playing skits may be developed using counter-culture groups as the central theme. In all of these experiences the students should be encouraged to look at issues from several points of view. Whenever possible, stress how considering only one viewpoint can lead to a breakdown in cultural understanding and communication. Ask for specific instances from *their* real life experiences that might parallel the points being made in the role plays. Above all, place emphasis on trying to understand values, beliefs, and lifestyles that differ from the student's own cultural experiences.

Try developing further some of the following role play suggestions or create your own.

MALE/FEMALE COUNTER CULTURES

—a dating situation as seen from the boy's point of view (must do the asking, get a car, decide where to go, assume the expenses) and from the girl's point of view (has to wait for the boy to ask her, often in the dark as to what's planned, feels she has to go along with the boy's suggestion).

—a single woman (who has a college degree qualifying her for the job) is getting paid less for the same job done by a married man (without the degree but with more experience).

—the girls' basketball team is getting little or no support while the boys' team is given a spirited backing by the athletic department, the student body, and the community.

—a woman has a good job and loves her career; her husband would rather not work but stay home and expand some of his hobbies, but he feels "pressured" into taking a job.

BLACK/WHITE COUNTER CULTURES

—a great friendship develops between two students, one Black and one White, and they cut school one day; teachers and the parents of the White child place the blame on the Black child.

—a Black girl and a White boy like each other and want to date but neither family will permit it.

—a Black person gets a certain job instead of a White person in order to fulfill a federally mandated employment code.

—the police continually patrol the Black neighborhood, occasionally harassing the residents; but the same police seldom patrol the White neighborhood and usually refer to the residents with politeness and respect.

AFFLUENT/POOR COUNTER CULTURES

—a young man from an affluent family and one from a poor family are both "busted" for smoking marijuana; the affluent youngster is released with a warning—the other is given a six-month jail term and a fine.

—a woman who does housework for a rich family was caught stealing food. She was dismissed and given a poor recommendation so she would not get another job.

—a poor widow is offered a free Thanksgiving Day's dinner by an affluent church group—she refuses.

—a child enters school in worn out clothes and with a dirty face; in his presence, the teacher says he is another one of those "dumb poor kids."

LEARNING HOW WE DIFFER FROM AND RESEMBLE ONE ANOTHER BIOLOGICALLY IS PART OF MULTI-CULTURAL EDUCATION.

—a Puerto Rican boy is put into a class for educationally handicapped children because he doesn't speak English well.

—a worker tells a "Polack" joke at work only to discover later that one of the group was Polish.

—children from a predominantly Spanish-speaking community are told if they speak one word of Spanish they will be punished.

—an ethnic group is ridiculed by their "American" neighbors for their dress, customs, and foods which remind them of the "old country."

Adapted from an exercise by: Dixie Vogel, Teacher, Ford Greene Elementary

---

BLAST OFF

Everyone loves a trip to the moon, but this one takes on new challenges. Each individual must choose a traveling companion and five things to take with him/her. The companion doesn't have to be someone from the class; in fact, it can be anyone, even someone they've never met. First, discuss as a group some of the things they think might happen on such an adventure. Decide if they will have a specific responsibility or if it will be a "pleasure" trip. What are some of the difficulties they might encounter? Next, allow some time for the students to make their lists and decide on their traveling companions.

Now comes the fun! Take a look at some of the lists and chosen companions. Talk about why these decisions were made. Do they reflect the values of the individuals? Are the decisions "right" in view of the reasons behind making them? Is it possible for two people making very different (even opposite) decisions about the same thing to *both* be right? Extend the discussion by looking more closely at the reasons people find different solutions to the same problem.

We are all "culture-bound" to the extent that we use as reference points those practices which are acceptable and standard for the peer (or culture) group we identify with most closely. Many of the decisions on who and what to take to the moon will reflect this. Suggested questions for further discussion are:

1. Can you think of ways your "culture" is different from others? Language? Dress? Attitude towards others?
2. What happens when you bring these differences together without taking the time to understand one another?
3. What would have happened if the class as a whole had been asked to decide on who and what to take to the moon?
4. Is it difficult for some people to accept others who are different from themselves?
5. What are some things we, as a class, can do to help us be more understanding and accepting of differences?

Adapted from an exercise by: Linda Dunlap, Teacher, Ford Greene Elementary

---

SCHOOLUTIONS

This is a super activity for exploring problems that result from schools not being "multi-cultural" and for helping students develop a valuing of the concept of multi-cultural.

Your class is to "become" the local school board. Explain to them the role of the board. Ask the students to research the duties, members, meeting times, etc., of your school board. A visit from one of your board members might be helpful. Ask your class as a whole to take on the role of the school board. You will provide the "board" with problems and the "members" will come up with solutions. Writing out individual solutions to each problem and sharing them usually works well in this activity.

Some suggested problems to be put before the board are as follows:

—The history books in the classrooms portray Native Americans and other minority groups in unfair and negative situations (present examples). What alternatives exist or should be created?

—Girls and boys are discriminated against in the schools because of their sex. Boys must take industrial arts and girls must take home economics. Books in classes always have men and women in stereotyped roles. Boys have a bigger selection of after-school sports than girls (provide examples). What kind of school program would alleviate these problems?

—All of the students from a minority group in a school have petitioned the board to have separate classes only for themselves. How does the board reply?

—A group of students do not want to go to school any more because they think their teachers do not like or care about them. They also think school is boring. What does the board do?

—There are two groups of boys from different ethnic backgrounds always fighting with each other. A teacher tried to stop them recently and was hurt. What action does the board take?

—Some of the children in one school do not speak English and seem to be left out of everything. Teachers do not seem to know what to do about it. The kids look unhappier every day.

—The students in one school are always walking by the special education room and calling the kids names . . . no one seems to be doing anything about stopping it.

These are just some samples for you to use with your kids. Try to create others that reflect the cultural diversity (or the absence of such) of your classroom, school, and community. Your class will probably want to examine the merits of the different solutions offered and select those that seem most feasible.

Adapted from an exercise by: John Culley, Parent, Washington Jr. High, and Clare Carter Baker, Teacher, Ford Greene Elementary

---

PICTURE ME . . . BUT THE WAY I AM

This activity's purpose is to investigate the sex and ethnic stereotyping that can be found in pictures and advertisements.

Ask students to bring in magazine or newspaper pictures that portray femininity, masculinity, or sex or ethnic discrimination. Let each student share one picture with the class and analyze why the picture suggests masculinity, femininity, or some ethnic stereotype. List on the board the characteristics of the pictures upon which they were judged. Next, ask the class to consider those lists and examine them for consistency. For example, if a student identifies a bubble bath as feminine, ask if any of the boys have taken bubble baths. An alternative would be to have

DO MEN REALLY TAKE BUBBLE BATHS??? WHAT IS FEMININITY? STEREOTYPES? THESE ARE PART OF NEW MULTI-CULTURAL LEARNINGS.

the class search for pictures that show women doing jobs characterized as feminine, or people eating foods generally associated with an ethnic group.

Encourage students to examine their textbooks for examples of sex and ethnic stereotypes. In what dress are people pictured? What roles are they filling? Is there an ethnic mixture in the pictures?

Be certain to be supportive as well as analytical as you help your students understand that many of the ways people are pictured are limited stereotypes—many cultures are ignored and neglected and this limits *all* of our opportunities.

Adapted from an exercise by: Jacob Eleasari, Producer and Director of the multi-cultural film, "What's the Difference Being Different?"

WHAT'S IN A NAME ANYWAY?

Ask the students to find out from their family as much about their name as they can. Is their surname reflective of a certain nationality, has it been changed or abbreviated in any way, does it denote a trade or craft, etc.? Ask them also to find out who decided on their first name and why. Was it a family name? Was it a current "popular" name and/or reflective of a specific time or event? Get a globe or a world map and pinpoint probable origins of individuals based upon this information. Discuss how many Blacks have the name of their ancestor's slave masters. Talk about how some Blacks are now taking African names. Does anyone know of someone who has done this? How do the students feel about it? What name would they each like to have if they could change? Provide the opportunity for each child to recognize his own very special uniqueness as reflected in his name. Some follow-up activities are:

—Let each child design a family "crest" reflecting what he discovered about his name.

—Have students give themselves new names they think more closely resemble their current lifestyles and interests.

—Have children draw "mirror" names to display in the room, following these steps: (1) Fold a piece of construction paper; (2) Take a dark (purple or black) crayon and write (must be cursive) along the crease; (3) Fold paper over again on crease; (4) Rub hard behind writing, using scissors to make dark crayon come off on opposite side of crease; (5) Trace over new impression of name; (6) Cut out design made by the original name and mirrored name and mount on a contrasting sheet of paper.

—Have students draw each other's names, then give a new name they think "fitting" for the person whose name was drawn. Tell other students the new name and see if they can guess who it represents. This works better if done in small groups of 8 to 10.

Adapted from an exercise by: Mary Buerger, Teacher, Ford Greene Elementary

---

LEISURE TIME CLUES DIVERSITY

Exploring leisure time choices is often an interestng way of looking at cultural diversity. We'll take a closer look at various leisure activities later; but for now remember that whichever activ-

58

"I get each of the kids involved in something in which they can excell. On an individual basis, I help them explore options and choose something that offers the best chance for success . . . especially our MR students. This does away with many stereotypes and creates new understandings of self and others."

ity you use, be certain the students discuss many of the following questions:

Do you notice any pattern developing in terms of the choices made by individuals from different cultural groups in the classroom?

Do boys make different leisure time choices than girls?

Do you think peer and societal expectations play a role in our choices?

Do we hold certain stereotypes about what certain people do (or should do) with their time?

Do we place value judgments on certain kinds of activities? Why?

Are our personal choices limited by what we have had experience with or exposure to? Did we find out about something we would be interested in trying from someone else?

A few options for looking at specific leisure activities are given below. You may choose any or all, depending on your interest and that of your class.

Entertainment—Ask your children to list their three top choices for entertainment *away* from their homes. After discussing the choices (see preceding questions), ask the students to make an "entertainment directory." They should collect a listing of the entertainment facilities in their community (using personal observation as well as T.V., radio, and newspaper research). Include such places as bowling alleys, parks, eating places, theaters, shopping centers, skating rinks, churches, amusement parks, lakes, or any other recreational facility in their community. The directory could then be duplicated and distributed to the class members.

Hobbies—Since not all students may have a hobby as such, first find out who does and what it is. Explain to the class that they are going to have a hobby appreciation week, month, or semester. Allow each child to explain his particular hobby, how he/she got it started, and how it is maintained. Set up a demonstration table where, if possible, the hobbies can be demonstrated and/or displayed. A possible follow-up would be for students with hobbies to work with small special interest groups in developing their skills in those particular hobbies.

Travel—Tell the students they are going to plan a dream vacation, but first they must look at where they might go. Ask them to bring travel brochures or postcards from home, information from travel agencies and airlines, etc. If certain children have been to places of interest, ask them to tell the class why they did or did not like it. After each one finally makes his/her choice, have him/her share what the decision was based on, travel plans, and what he/she plans to do upon arrival.

Clubs—Have the class do research on the clubs available to them in the school and in their neighborhoods. Find out what the requirements for joining are (prerequisites, fees, age, sex, etc.). Ask the children in the class who belong to clubs to tell something about what they do in the clubs. Find ways to facilitate joining by others who are interested.

Adapted from an exercise by: Johnny Thompson, Teacher Corps Intern, Washington Jr. High

---

CANDIDATE WHO?

As students become aware of the diversity within their school and sensitive about responding to that diversity in an informed and responsible way, it may be time to move them one step further. Although their school may reflect a multi-cultural mixture, it will not fully reflect the complex needs of our country as a whole. This activity is designed to help students apply beliefs supporting cultural pluralism and humans rights to a much broader—much more confusing—world.

Take a look with your students at different political systems around the world. Although you need not go into great depth, it would be useful to cover such points as:

How do the political leaders get into office?
How are major decisions made in the government?
What rights and freedoms do the people have?
What is the general economic level of the country?

Look at our democratic government last and study the same kinds of questions as you did with the others. After the students have a theoretical understanding of the responsibility of a democratic government to reflect the needs of the people, announce that they will now have some fun and creative learning through a simulated election.

Arbitrarily divide your class in half. Explain that each group will form their own political party. From these two parties they will select a candidate who will be their spokesperson and will designate responsibilities to others within their groups. The parties and their candidates must then research the issues until they come up with a "platform" for their candidate that serves the best interest of every "cultural" group in the U.S.A. Your role as the teacher is to function as a resource guide and facilitator. Have available to the students all materials you can find on demographic data, economic issues, conservation needs, etc. Remind the "political parties" that they have to come up with a platform that they feel best represents the needs and wishes of the American people. Be certain they examine the issues that are pertinent to such groups as farmers, urban dwellers, Chicanos, Blacks, Native Americans, other ethnic groups, migrant workers, the labor force, white collar workers, children, the elderly, rich, poor, immigrants, or any other faction that constitutes our diverse society. They should plan and initiate campaign speeches, debates, T.V. and radio "spots," flyers, and pamphlets or any other means to get their message to the different "groups" representing their needs and points of view.

Toward election time pull the class back together and talk about their experiences. Ask how they arrived at their stand on the issues. Did they find certain human rights in conflict with one another? How did they resolve those conflicts? Do they feel *all* the people can be served? Do different "groups" in our society have a right to be different? Is it "OK" to be different? Do they think our government is responding to the diverse needs of the people the way it should? Are they more aware of the complex nature of our society? What do they feel is their personal responsibility to support human rights and the diverse needs of our world?

You may or may not choose to hold the election, depending on the interest of the students. If you do, tell the students to vote for the candidate that most closely reflects their own feelings on the issues and *not* necessarily the one that represents the political party of which they are a member. Although the election itself is interesting, it is secondary to helping students give some serious thought to the diversity of our people and the need for acceptance and understanding of these differences before we can function without conflict and turmoil.

Adapted from an exercise by: Liz Bivens, Teacher, and Johnny Thompson, Teacher Corps Intern, Washington Jr. High

---

BIBLIOTHERAPY

The following activity uses literature for problem solving, multi-cultural understandings, and self-awareness in the classroom. This concept or approach is termed bibliotherapy. Some areas to which bibliotherapy may be applied are: 1) student self-concept development, 2) enhancing student relationships, 3) enhancing student-teacher relationships, 4) learning about other peoples and how to interact with and value their differences, 5) values and value differences, and 6) personal problems and concerns.

Here's how you do it. Identify a specific problem or concern area. For example, the kids in your class make fun of a group of people different from themselves, or you wish to break a stereotype prevalent in your classroom. Next, select a story in literature that focuses on a related problem (as the book *Love Story* focuses on death). Take your time and be selective. Be certain the relationship between your purposes and the story will be clear. Your students may read the story individually or you may read the story to them. Once the story is known, or while it is in process, ask the students questions that will take them close to the emotional content of the literature. For example:

—How do you think the main character of this story must feel?

—How do you think the people who are trying to hurt this main character must feel?

—How can they "get through"' this problem successfully?

—What would you do if you were in this situation?

—What would you do to help someone experiencing this problem?

—What are your feelings and/or your friends' feelings about this?

Be concerned, of course, about the comprehension of the story, but your major emphasis should be placed on the individual's personal interaction with the story and his/her identification with the problem. Put emphasis on the discussion process and helping the students understand the problem.

Form classroom activity groups in order to have small informal "reaction discussions" of the literature. So that you might be able to identify the total group's collective feelings and reactions ask each small group to do some recording. When the group lists are complete, share these reactions and personal feelings any way you wish to direct it.

You might want to take this activity further by asking the kids to write an essay, composition, or book that extends the story's plot and further develops its outcome. Personal values will likely color various unique outcomes. Capitalize on these to help the kids search for new learnings about people—especially if it's a multi-cultural story. Ask the kids to share their unique story outcomes . . . or they, too, might be read, shared, or discussed on a voluntary basis.

Adapted from an exercise by: Robert Dellanoce, Multi-Cultural Instructor

---

DIALECTABLE!!

Things people say and the way they say them are good means of focusing on our differences and similarities. A dialect is the way a language is spoken in a certain part of a country or region. Dialects are found in nearly all the countries of the world. As a matter of fact, dialects can become different languages when people are physically separated for a long period of time. Many years ago, four dialects of the Latin language became French, Spanish, Italian, and Rumanian. Get a foreign language dictionary of those languages and track down some of their similarities. Examine a map of Europe and ask your students to figure out what land features or other characteristics separated these peoples. Let the class divide into four groups representing each of the four Romance language countries and find out as much as they can about "their" country. Encourage the students to learn greetings and common expressions in the language of their assigned country. Follow this activity with a "Full of Gaul Day" where everyone dresses, speaks, sings, and plays the part of people from "their" country.

Dialects enrich the language of the United States. For an activity, let every student record the same statement on a cassette recorder. Then play these recordings and have the class listen for speech differences. Locate students in your school that have lived in different parts of the world and the United States. Ask them to visit your class and talk with your students about their former homes.

Consider with your class the effect that prejudice plays in what we hear when people talk. For instance, a student from Boston might say: "IE drive mye cah ta school." And a student from Birmingham says: "Ah waallk ta scho-ul." Which one is "right"? Who decides what is right in language? Which student would you think was smarter? Why?

Adapted from an exercise by: Carol Stice, Assistant Professor, Tennessee State University

---

EVEN MORE DIALECTABLE!!

On a group of islands off the coasts of South Carolina and Georgia is a subculture referred to as the Gullahs. These black people live mostly in isolation. Dr. Lorenzo Dow Turner was able to study these people and their language in depth. He discovered that over four thousand African words remain in their language today. Some words that the American language has absorbed from Africa are: zombi, voodoo or hoo doo, and banjo. Can your class find out about other African-contributed words?

We also connect dialects with our habits and sentiments. There are characteristic words and phrases that people use in different parts of the country. Let your students interview their grandparents, neighbors, and friends to record the expressions that are part of their culture. Here are some examples to give to your class: "how come?" is a Southernism for "How did it

64

occur?"; "how?" is a New England expression for "What did you say?" When a Californian talks about a bonanza, he means a stroke of good luck. People in the far north know what an air-hole is—an opening in the ice. In Virginia they say "trig" to mean something is trim, neat, or smart.

Make a puzzle sheet for students; ask them what "druthers," "all-fired," "dry crik, "silk-stockings," "make tracks," "get off the track," and other similar words and phrases mean. Compare modern sayings to older ones like, "knock the tar out of," "spic and span," "wolf in sheep's clothing," and "pass the buck." One source for these words and phrases is the book by Clapin, *A New Dictionary of Americanisms* (Detroit: Gale, 1968).

Encourage students to read some literature segments that are written in dialects. George Bernard Shaw, Robert Burns, Bret Harte, Joel Chandler Harris, Mark Twain, and Richard Chase's *Jack Tales* are some possibilities. Examine these selections for expressions. What do sayings reveal about people? How can you figure out a lot about a person's life by hearing words they use in their expressions? Can you tell if people live on a farm? Or if they watch a lot of television?

Adapted from an exercise by: Jane Bandy Smith, Multi-Cultural Instructor

---

IT'S NEWS TO ME

Two of the favorite activities supported by the multi-cultural program were the school newspapers. Such printing endeavors were originated by teachers in two different schools. Though the two newspapers were developed along similar lines, they were different because they reflected the interests and ideas of the students in each of the two schools. That individuality was a multi-cultural attribute in itself!

All schools represent many lifestyles. Our students were encouraged to write articles or stories describing their homes and customs. They also wrote advertisements of their favorite activities, and featured the birthdays of the month as well as honor roll students. One goal was to include as many students' names as possible—not just those that were always getting strokes!

Some other multi-cultural ideas that were included in these papers were: a survey to determine what qualities they looked for in a friend; a survey to find out what students would like to do in a self-improvement effort and why they'd like to change; and re-portings on how students felt about certain issues. These gave students an opportunity for self-exploration and self-expression.

One of the newspapers spotlighted the janitorial staff of the school so that the students and faculty got to know the "real side" of these workers. Both newspapers stressed parent in-volvement in articles written about parents as well as by parents.

Social studies projects and programs make interesting arti-cles to be included in this kind of publication. This is a great way to introduce a new student . . . or to initiate discussion and consideration of a school problem.

A school newspaper is a meaningful source of language arts methods, both in writing articles and examining them after they are printed. Let students look for all the descriptive words used in an issue. Ask them to use a thesaurus to discover other words that could be used in place of those words. Let them see if they can rewrite sentences into questions, or if they can make a poem or adventure story out of an article. How many words have double consonants? There are almost unlimited ways to use newspaper material written by other students.

Newspapers can be related to many subjects. The econom-ics of purchasing supplies and merchandising the newspaper can provide valuable first-hand mathematics instruction. Charts and graphs can be constructed that compare sales from one edition to another or from one class to another.

Organization for your newspaper project can be divided up into departments just like commercial newspapers: news desk, sports, entertainment, social, want ads, cartoons, editorials, human interest, weather, puzzles, and other fillers. Or you can establish an editorial review board to examine work submitted by any student for any category and to decide what will be printed. You would want to rotate the board's membership or establish criteria for membership so that students have an equal chance of being on the board.

For supplies, you will need some mimeograph or ditto sten-cils, several reams of paper, and access to a mimeograph or ditto machine.

This activity stimulates students to look for interesting and different information about the students and faculty in the school.

66

It can provide a vehicle for strengthening the self-concept of students, for focusing praise and attention on little-recognized students, and for promoting school spirit and enthusiasm.

Adapted from an exercise by: Diane Kern, Teacher, Wharton Jr. High; Robert Rice, Teacher, Wayne Betts and Kathy Bryant, Teacher Corps Interns, Washington Jr. High

---

ADVERTISING

Advertising permeates our world—newspapers, T.V., radio, magazines, billboards, signs and so on. This activity should help students not only become more aware of which audience the advertisers are speaking to but also become more sensitive to the many cultural differences that exist in our country.

Ask each student to record the following information about fifteen advertisements:

What ethnic group(s) is the ad addressing?

What members of the group(s) are most likely to be influenced by the ad (men, women, teen-agers, children, elderly)?

To what economic level is the ad addressed (rich, middle class, poor)?

Was it a successful ad in your opinion? Will people buy the product(s) as a result of the ad? Why or why not?

After everyone has their information collected, pull it together and share the results with the whole class. What ethnic groups seem to be addressed most by the ads? What's the general economic level being addressed? Who do advertisers think have more purchasing power—men or women? How do you explain why you found what you did?

Now that the class has taken a look at the nature of advertising, challenge your students to create ads that reflect the diversity of our society. Here are some suggestions:

—Enact a T.V. commercial for a product that would appeal to only *one* ethnic group. Recreate the same commercial so that it would appeal to a diverse audience.

—Do a magazine lay-out that portrays women in a stereotyped role. Do another that reflects the wide range of lifestyles adopted by today's women.

—Ads often portray families in a very stereotyped way. See if

you can do an ad that reflects different family situations, i.e., the single parent, several generations living together, more than one family living together, etc.
—Collect ads from magazines that reflect cultural diversity and make a collage on a large bulletin board. The result should look very much like the world of people with which we live.

Adapted from an exercise by: Catherine Greene, Teacher, Wharton Jr. High

---

"ONCE IN A LIFETIME"

Let's explore the different ways in which people spend their leisure time and the possible priorities they may have concerning leisure time. In order to get your students into this activity, explain that each may go on a fabulous vacation for one week with all expenses paid. The only requirement is that they must write out their travel plans. Allow them five to ten minutes for writing.

After plans are written, a general class discussion is held. Ask for volunteers to share their destinations and general vacation highlights. Then raise discussion questions such as:

Where did you choose to go on your vacation?
How will you travel there?
Where will you stay?
What is this place like? Describe it.
Why do you value this place? Is it something special to you? Why?
Who will accompany you? Why?
What are some things you will experience on this trip?

The activity and discussion will support cultural diversity and individual uniqueness in the classroom by illustrating different choices and priorities in regard to leisure time. Values, attitudes, and differences may be noted and explored.

Adapted from an exercise by: Johnny Thompson, Teacher Corps Intern, Washington Jr. High

RIGHTS AND/OR WRONGS

Label each of the four corners of your classroom with a sign identifying a place where students will move to show their answers to a series of statements you will read to them. One corner should be labeled *Certainly Right,* another *Certainly Wrong,* another *Probably Right,* and the last *Probably Wrong.* Instruct your students to think to themselves about the strength of the feelings they hold about each statement you read to them and then go to the corner which best reflects their opinion about how right or wrong the statement is. Tell them not to depend on how others respond or what others might think about their responses. Read a statement and ask the students to move to the corner of the room which will show their answers. Do not debate which answers are most correct; rather, ask the students to discuss why they moved to the corners they did. Some examples of statements that might be used are:

—A man is right to steal food to feed his starving family.

—All people are basically good.

—If the United States doesn't get its way in getting all the oil it needs at a fair price from other countries it would be right to go to war for it.

—It's all right to tell lies to people you don't like.

—Columbus was the first person to discover America.

Your students should interpret these statements as they wish. Be certain that there is no "right" way to interpret them. Use them as discussion starters to focus on the differences in beliefs and values which individuals share, and the concept of cultural pluralism. Different backgrounds often produce both similar and different responses to value questions.

Have your class make up additional statements from their classwork, current issues, television programs, school policy, musical preferences, and the like. This is an excellent activity to generate discussion about classroom responsibilities children *believe* are important as well as parent-student, teacher-student, and student-student similarities and differences.

Adapted from an exercise by: Tom Sloan, Teacher, Wharton Elementary

SWITCH

Take your students through the exploration of switching roles that follow the theme of a story line. Using a method similar to that of the *Prince and the Pauper,* have the children "rewrite" T.V. shows, current events, and history.

— How would the latest presidential day at the White House go if Jimmy Carter was replaced by a look-alike lion tamer who dressed as such?

— What if a famous basketball player switched roles with your teacher?

— What if your parents were Sonny and Cher?

— What if you and the Mayor traded roles?

Writing and sharing stories and plays about "switches" helps your students to identify what it's like to exhibit lifestyles, beliefs, behaviors, language, and values other than those expected in relationship to a person's "normal" role. It helps them to recognize cultural pluralism, subcultures, and role groups.

The stories can take on an additional multi-cultural switch if the students are asked to add a new geographic location to the role identification switches.

The students can share their switches with one another, put themselves in role plays, and discuss their behavior as representatives of other people, places, and times. Important discussion questions would be: "With whom would you like to switch?" "How would you like to switch with *(fill in the blank)*?" "How would you feel if that switch happened to you?"

Adapted from an exercise by: Tom Sloan, Teacher, Wharton Elementary

---

HONESTLY!

Here is an activity designed to generate class consideration and discussion of honesty. It can also stimulate an evaluation of student-held values.

Ask students to list ten things that are most valuable to them. Next, have the students rank their list of valuables from the most valuable (1) to the least valuable (10).

Share and discuss the students' lists. Ask for their reactions to examining their lists. How much of their list was people-oriented? How much was thing-oriented? Ask them to select item number one on their list and explain how they would feel and what they would do if it was stolen. Then select another numbered item and repeat the process.

Lead the class in a discussion of honesty: What happens to people when someone takes things that are valuable to others? Why do people steal? Do we feel differently about people who steal from businesses or organizations than we do about people who steal from friends and neighbors? Why?

This activity provides a good time to bring in newspaper articles that provide examples of theft. It is important to provide real-world experiences for students to consider *without* utilizing examples of student behavior.

An alternative or expanded activity would be to bring in pictures of many different people from magazines. Mount the pictures on construction paper and use them as a "line-up" like the police stories feature. You could also use an opaque projector for this activity. The purpose is to look at the pictures and act as a judge of the persons' honesty. Have the students select from the pictures someone they would accuse of stealing their valuables. Ask each student individually to examine why they made their choice. Repeat this process with several groups of line-ups. Does a pattern emerge in student selection? In reality, who were the people in the pictures and what did they do to get into the magazines? This activity can be very self-revealing; student-initiated discussion should be welcomed but forced discussion should be avoided.

This activity can easily lead into use of story starters for role playing. For instance, have a student play the part of Robin Hood—rationalizing stealing from the rich to give to the poor. Let the class play the part of the judge and critique Robin's testimony. Or in a more realistic setting, have students act out situations where a man steals food because his family is hungry. Armstrong's *Sounder* provides a well-written example of this behavior and you might choose to use it as an example for class consideration.

It is most important that you arrange for the class to examine their values without evidence of teacher attitudinal interference.

Adapted from a suggested lesson by: Glenda McCaleb, Teacher, Wharton Jr. High

THE ME TREE

One way of helping children become genuinely proud of their own uniqueness is to provide experiences for them to look at uniqueness in the rest of their world. If there isn't a place with trees and bushes within walking distance of the school, arrange for a trip to a nearby park. Ask the children to be particularly alert to the many different trees, leaves, bushes, flowers, grasses, etc., and how they all grow together to make a place beautiful. Ask them if they think it would look as nice or be as interesting if every tree were the same size, shape, and color or every flower was exactly like every other flower. Find out what each individual child likes the best—a majestic tree, a tiny purple wildflower, a blossom-covered bush, and so on. Again, the main emphasis is on appreciating uniqueness.

Once back in the classroom, give each child a loose piece of paper and ask them to draw a picture of something they saw on the trip that they would like to represent them, and to label it with words which they feel describe themselves. For instance, if a child chose to draw a tree he could label the branches with such descriptive words as friendly, tall, quick, black, and so on.

After everyone is through, each child (or selected children) can show his/her picture and read their labels. Talk about how different each of them is from others. Ask if they feel different about their own uniqueness. Allow them to look at things that keep us from appreciating uniqueness, i.e., racial and cultural stereotypes, attitudes of conformity in our culture, lack of understanding, and even fear of people who do not "look like us."

Leave this experience as open-ended as possible, asking the students to make a commitment to understanding and accepting differences between individuals as something desirable. Ask them for suggestions on how their class can best reflect the uniqueness of its members. What activities can they suggest that might help them learn more about each other? The possibilities are as infinite as are the differences that exist in that classroom.

Adapted from an exercise by: Edwina Epps, Teacher, Ford Greene Elementary

GOING PLACES

Group class members into groups of four or five so that each group represents, as nearly as possible, a cross-section of the class as a whole in terms of sex, race, religion, or socio-economic considerations. This will probably mean you will have students working together who do not usually choose to work with each other. Each group will be given a different folder containing several pictures of a geographic area plus some additional information about the habits of people and climatic conditions there. An example would be a picture of Pacific islands with information regarding average temperatures and the fishing and farming habits of the people. None of the pictures should portray a dwelling or the people.

Next tell the groups that they will have to solve the following three problems: What kind of clothes would the inhabitants wear (keeping in mind weather conditions and occupations)? What would they have to be good at? What sort of house would they need? Each group must work together and be in agreement as

KIDS SHOWING OFF THE HOUSE THEY BUILT WHILE STUDYING DWELLINGS OF MANY CULTURES.

73

to its judgments on these questions. Ask the groups to draw pictures depicting their decisions.

When everyone is finished, have each group discuss with the others the results of their work. Have information available on the clothing, skills, and dwellings of the people in question. Some good discussion points are:

—Did what you did not know about the culture get in the way of the problem solving process?

—Did stereotypes about certain cultures influence your group (e.g., all island natives live in grass huts)?

—Weather and natural resources cause people to adopt certain customs and habits. If we hadn't had to consider those factors, would these people's habits look "strange" to us?

—How do you feel after you have really tried to understand the problems of someone whose experiences are different than your own?

—Do you sometimes make generalizations about someone because of the color of his skin or the way he dresses before trying to understand his own "culture"?

—Did you find certain members of your group, because of their different experiences or culture, had a different perspective to offer?

—Do you think you learn more when you work with people who are different from you in some ways or when you work with people who "look like you"?

Adapted from an exercise by: Edwina Epps, Teacher, Ford Greene Elementary

---

MY BEST SELF

Part of creating an atmosphere that encourages an appreciation of uniqueness is providing experiences for each child to have a chance to feel really good about who he or she is. A healthy self-concept is a necessary stepping stone towards positive understanding and acceptance of others who are different from ourselves. This activity is designed to give everyone's self-concept a chance to soar!

Ask the students to form groups of no more than four or five. Each student will have one blank self-sticking tag for each member of his group and a writing implement. Taking turns, each student will complete orally the following types of sentence stems (the teacher may add, delete, or change these as desired):

—I am sad when . . .

—I am happy when . . .

—Things I do best are . . .

—The best thing that ever happened to me . . .

—When I grow up . . .

—If I had three wishes they would be . . .

—My idea of a perfect Saturday is . . .

—I wish I were better at . . .

—My favorite T.V. shows are . . .

—If I had $1,000 I would . . .

While one group member responds to these sentence stems the others in the group write on one of the tags a minimum of three one- or two-word positive comments they think describe that individual. The comments *must* be positive; no negative statements will be accepted. When the one student finishes, the others in the group read what they have written about him/her and then place the tags on the person. After everyone has had a turn, each person should be wearing three or four tags with at least three positive comments written on each one. Allow some time for everyone in the class to mingle and talk and show off their "best self." Don't be surprised if some decide to wear their tags the rest of the day!

Adapted from an exercise by: Edwina Epps, Teacher, Ford Greene Elementary

---

SHOPPING SURVEY

Initiate this activity by asking students to survey the people living in their home to find out where they shop and what products they buy for a one-week period. Have each class member draw a map showing the stores and the distances traveled from the home for shopping purposes. Each student should put his/her map on the walls around the room with a list of the things purchased that week by family members. Give them each a minute or two to clarify their lists and maps for the class. Check out the variations in lifestyles evident in the items bought. What were the most commonly purchased items? What are the items that everyone needs?

Take your class to visit a supermarket and pretend to shop for groceries for their family for one week. Have students write down the items they would buy and their cost. Limit each student's expenditure to $15.00 for the week. Focus on the following:

—When they return to school, ask all students to share their lists. Explore the characteristics of the foods they selected.

—What nutritional outcomes result from eating certain types of foods?

—Was the food purchased for $15.00 the food advertised in the local newspaper's weekly sale items section?

—Would you subscribe to the local newspaper if you were on a limited income and wanted to save money, or would you continue to eat your favorite foods even if more expensive?

This activity has been designed for you to involve the kids in math survey activities with calculation and comparisons, and at the same time to explore their own lifestyles for increased understandings. Remember to support and build on the diversity in what you find rather than to identify "middle-class" standards. Understanding and supporting diversity, developing new relationships, and good nutrition are the important factors . . . but which is most important?

Adapted from an exercise by: Johnny Thompson, Teacher Corps Intern, and Liz Bivens, Teacher, Washington Jr. High.

WHO AM I? . . . WHO ARE YOU?

This multi-purpose, multi-cultural activity helps students be able to provide positive feedback and develop personal regard for others. It also gives them the opportunity to create a book.

Pair off the students in your classroom into pairs of opposites. Use every criterion you can think of to make the opposite distinctions . . . height, weight, number of brothers and sisters, genetic characteristics, etc. Tell each student that they are going to

> *"Two Vietnamese visitors carried on a conversation in their native tongue according to directions given to them by the students in class. Afterwards—a group sharing of experiences and values . . . the activity supplemented a vocabulary unit."*

make a book about the person they have been paired with. Each week have the pairs meet for at least twenty minutes to discuss "what's happening" in the lives of their partners. Some typical questions you might provide for student guidance in the rap sessions are:

What was the best thing that happened to you this week? To your family?

What was your favorite thing to do after school this week?

What did you do out of the ordinary this past weekend?

Each week have the students write a story based on these rap sessions about their partner's "life and times." Pictures (drawings) of fun activities can be added. Information about new weight, height, new favorites can be added over the months of school. At the end of the school year each student will have a biography to present to their partner. What better way to develop new multi-cultural understandings and close relationships?

Adapted from an exercise by: Tom Sloan, Teacher, Wharton Jr. High

---

THE DIVERSITY COLLECTION AGENCY

Encourage your children to be collectors and you will generate long-term opportunities to help them learn more about the values and lifestyles of others. Ask your children to become collectors . . . collecting anything that has "many of a kind," such as: magazines, bottle caps, cans, bird pictures, new words, insects, license plates, bottles, records, travel brochures, cereal boxes, stamps, seeds, and toys. It's the sharing and progress reporting processes that provide the multi-cultural opportunities.

Some questions for you to ask your students on a regular basis to write and/or explain to the other class members are: Which is your favorite? Why? How is it different from the other? What's its history? Where did it come from? What function does it serve? What other countries or peoples have them or use them? How do they differ in those other places?

What do they use in place of your collection item? Why did you choose these to collect rather than the other items collected in the class?

Ask all of the students to bring samples of their collections to class, to explain them, to share their progress, and to compare differences to their own people differences. Where are these made? Where were you born? Who makes them? What's it like where they come from? What's it like where you come from? What are your parents like? How are they like you? Exploring diversity in people and things and being able to describe and value those differences are continuously encouraged with this long-term activity.

Adapted from an exercise by: Wanda Russell, Teacher, Ford Greene Elementary

---

SMORGASBORD

Set aside portions of every week to deal with human relationships, ethnic studies, and self-concept development . . . show

MULTI-CULTURAL EDUCATION IS MORE THAN STRUCTURED ACTIVITIES—IT'S THE WHOLE ENVIRONMENT THAT HELPS STUDENTS LEARN ABOUT OTHERS.

films . . . study songs from other countries and how they developed . . . introduce Handy and other Black musicians influential in pop music . . . teach folk dances . . . play records of different kinds of music . . . make tapes of different kinds of music . . . discuss how children feel about the different types . . . rank each type of music according to how each student liked it (boys want lyrics, girls just instrumentals, all like pop?) . . . read a book about boys in the ghetto to the class . . . explore how we differ in what we would take with us to the moon, what we would leave . . . tell what we each do best on earth—all are ways of helping students learn about cultural diversity, human relationships, themselves. You can take a smorgasbord approach and find it most successful in developing a multi-cultural climate in your classroom.

Adapted from an exercise by: Linda Dunlap, Teacher, Ford Greene Elementary

---

LOTS OF LIFE AND LIVING

If you believe, as many educators do, that people who know "where they're at and where they are going" are healthier, happier, and more productive, this is right up your alley. You can help your students realize what they like about themselves and their accomplishments, what they want to do in their lifetimes, and how they differ; relate more effectively to others; and appreciate others' ideas as well as their own. (What more could you want?)

First, explore the song, *Turn, Turn* (". . . for every time there is a season . . ."). Direct the children to make collages of important moments, events, and feelings in their lives. Put these up together on part of the ceiling or wall of your classroom (which could probably use some decorating anyway). Follow up with each student writing a poem or statement concerning his/her own collage . . . What do the pictures represent? Which are their favorites? Why? Then comes the sharing time . . . students sharing their past successes and important moments. You decide the best way.

Next, ask each kid to make a list of the things (new vocabulary lists!) he or she *expects* will happen to them during their lifetimes, including what they *want* to have happen to them . . . the hopes and dreams aspects. Include lifestyles, homes, travels, re-

79

lationships, occupations, belonging; but don't forget the futurism considerations of what might it be like in the year 2000. Now back to collage-making: turn those lists into picture representations. Fill another wall or part of the ceiling with these masterpieces. Compare past and future collages.

Pair off your students and ask each to take turns as interviewee/interviewer to assist each other in articulating what they are going to do between now and the future. The class could help each student, one at a time, think of ways to accomplish his/her goals. List the step-by-step plan they have for achieving their pictured hopes and dreams.

Don't forget to ask the class to look for differences and unique ideas, and remember, "we are all pulling for one another!" Ahhhh . . . leave up the collages for purposes of checking out student behavior for consistency between what one wants in his/her future and classroom behavior patterns.

Adapted from an exercise by: Loretta Green and Joan DuChane, Teachers, Wharton Elementary

---

MULTI-CULTURE SCIENCE

Here are just *some* avenues a teacher takes in enriching her science classes in a multi-cultural manner:

"We get into the nervous system, the human body in depth . . . we do several activities and have many discussions on factors that affect perception."

"We study ant colonies and other life forms . . . and talk about different ways of living . . ."

"I ask the kids about Hindus who do not believe in killing anything and Hopi Indians who have only present-tense words . . ."

"I believe that if you come from a different culture and language, your perceptions are different; so, I wonder, can you make the same discoveries?"

"I took a drug prevention course at the teacher center on values clarification . . . I use many such class activities."

"I use a Time-Life sound filmstrip series. It is an open-ended, problem-solving approach . . . subjects are family, dating, sex . . ."

"I do a blood typing activity where everyone has their blood typed and we discuss our blood groups."

"We compare Indian cultures' respect and reverence for nature with our culture and pollution."

"I use resource people from the medical school . . . especially in the work on genetic diseases like sickle-cell anemia."

Adapted from exercises by: Lolita Hutton, Science Teacher, Wharton Jr. High

---

THE PEOPLE MACHINE

A major issue destined to face the United States Supreme Court revolves around the philosophical question of who controls or decides the creation of life. Science is rapidly moving through DNA research to develop the ability to produce people. Your students may see the day. It is imperative that they learn to value cultural pluralism.

Ask your students to work in small groups and come up with as *many* answers as possible to the following questions:

—Who are your five favorite people (outside of your immediate family)?

—What makes them so special to you?

—What do you like about their looks? What do they look like?

—What do you like about their personalities?

—What do they do with you that you enjoy?

Then, as a total class group, compare the similarities and differences of answers discussed in the small groups.

The next task for the small groups would be to respond to the following: If your group had the ability to make people like you want, how would you make them? First, draw a picture of the people you would make—What colors would you make them? Would some have black arms and white legs? Stripes? Polka dots? All the same? How would they differ? Second, list the

abilities and personalities of the people you would make—
Should they all be the same? Should they all be able to do everything? How do the people you are creating compare with yourselves, and your parents, friends, and teachers?

Put the completed pictures on the walls along with the lists of ability and personality characteristics. Follow up with discussions including:

What would it be like if the people we made were real? Who should decide what people will look like, be like, and be able to do? If someone could remake you, what would you like to look like? Should we become people makers? What would our society be like if we were all alike? Isn't it far more fun and pleasurable that we have differences as well as similarities?

Additional activities might include reading and reporting on some of the scientific work in the DNA areas—evolution, the creation of humanity, the universe, Earth.

Adapted from an exercise by: Lolita Hutton, Science Teacher, Wharton Jr. High

---

CAPITAL PUNISHMENT

Different groups hold conflicting value-based viewpoints. Understanding how to agree and disagree successfully are important learnings. The conflict over capital punishment has been so much in the news that recent issues of periodicals and newspapers are filled with pro and con arguments. Information, viewpoints, and positions differ with group identification, customs, and geography.

This complex activity represents the opportunity for any of the typical disciplines to be touched upon . . . reading, writing, science, political science, math, art, music, drama, etc., any one of which may be the focal point. Multi-cultural understandings are many as you work through the following with your students.

Ask your students to conduct opinion surveys on their neighbors, parents, and other students in the school concerning their attitudes toward capital punishment. Compare results by neighborhood, ethnic identification, and age. Ask the students to request that their relatives and friends in other communities do the same and mail the results to your class for comparison.

Each child should be involved in additional research on the

> *"After a group activity I will often ask for discussion of how well the groups worked. I have the groups make a list analyzing their group processes: Who were the blockers? Was someone 'goofing off'? Was there someone who deviated from the group? Supportive? Helpful? Did one person do all the work? How can we do it better next time? With whom can I be better friends?"*

subject. Find out by phone how the legislators and clergy in their area stand on the issue and why. Identify which states have legalized capital punishment and make a map. Make a chart identifying reasons pro and con, which groups support and oppose, and what crimes are specified.

Are there regional differences in our country? What customs are represented by group differences? What are the highly emotional questions, such as: Why are more minority members executed? Would you press the button knowing it's possible the person may be proven innocent some day? Do you think capital punishment stops people from killing? How would you feel about it if someone murdered one of your loved ones? Why is it that some states without the death penalty have crime rates lower than others with it?

Ask the students to write the embassies or U.N. representatives of other countries to find out if they have capital punishment and for what reasons. Each student should formulate an opinion and write a position paper of his/her ideas related to the issue. A class debate can be organized . . . representatives of opposing groups invited to speak to the class . . . discussion of the differing opinions . . . presenting the history in the U.S. and related questions of crime increase, penal institutions, and whether humanity is basically good or evil. Explore how art and music represent death; create a court room drama skit with multiple endings.

This activity is an extremely high-interest and thought-provoking one, so it is important to ask the kids how they feel about what they are doing. Be aware of anyone not able to express his/her doubts, concerns, anxieties. It is worthwhile to have each child make a for or against choice on a secret ballot at the end of the activity. No indecision allowed: it enhances the value clarifying at "that" moment in time. Tell the kids they may someday change their minds.

Adapted from an exercise by: Karen Roach, Teacher, Washington Jr. High

BE YOUR THINGO

This exercise is designed to explore uniqueness among your students—to help them to know others in the classroom better.

Give each student a dittoed grid portioned off like a bingo card. Put a master card with directions on the overhead so that students know what to write in each space. Have students write in the appropriate term to describe their characteristics. Next, ask the students to write each characteristic on a small square of paper so that it could be placed in the "draw pot." Give out very small squares of construction paper or dried butter beans to use as counters. Then play bingo!

The filled-in columns on the sample card below are only sug-gestions—create some others!

B I N G O

Colors	Name	Place	Family Members	Likes
Your Clothes	Yours	Now Living	Me	Bike Riding
Your Hair	Your Mother	Born	Mother	Playing Guitar
Your Eyes	Your Father	Like to Go	Father	Reading
Your Favorite	A Friend	Wouldn't Like to Go	Sister	Cooking
Your House	A Favorite	Have Visited	Brother	People

Adapted from an exercise by: Jane Bandy Smith, Multi-Cultural Instructor

---

SOUND OFF

This activity engages students in an examination of the instru-ments people have developed to make music. It is designed to support the common bond music establishes as it stretches across cultures. It also provides an opportunity for students to explore how people make use of materials obtainable from their surroundings.

Explore with the class the different ways to make sounds, by using items common to our culture. Try blowing across the top of a small-necked bottle or tapping with a spoon on glasses filled with varying amounts of water. Tap pencils against one another. Ask your students to engage in divergent thinking and come up with a variety of sounds. You might develop a "culture-based band" by having the students "play" their culture-oriented instruments, accompanied by a popular recording.

Expand this class project into a study of the history of instruments, beginning with the early wind instruments made from dried hollow bones or bamboo. Also investigate the development of the drum. People have used this instrument since primitive times for communication as well as musical enjoyment. Some suggested types of instruments to explore are: the Japanese bamboo shakuhachi, bagpipes, panpipes, Japanese temple drums, and African talking-drums. Larry Kettelkamp has written several basic, easily absorbed books on instruments.

Have students invent ways to make drums by using items from their culture. What will provide a base? What will provide a top? How will they secure the top to the base?

You can further develop this activity into an exploration of the use of instruments and the country of their origin, for example:

Instrument	Development	Country
French Horn	Used for hunting purposes	France

Or you can develop this activity as a personal exploration of feelings. Provide the class with pictures of orchestra instruments accompanied by a recording of their sounds. Let the class complete sentence stems like:

I feel like a drum when . . .
I feel like a picolo when . . .
I feel like a guitar when . . .
I feel like a tuba when . . .
I feel like a cymbal when . . .

Discuss the feelings that are associated with certain instruments. Limit the instruments to five or six that express their emotions. For example, a drum or bass horn for anger. A french horn or violin for sadness. Put each instrument's name on a set of 3" x 5" cards for each student. Have the students form an "emotional orchestra" by holding up the card with the instrument that best reveals the way they are feeling that day. Since instruments in a band are grouped together, let all those that feel like a drum (anger) get together and talk about what has happened to make them angry.

When the class holds up the cards, the teacher will have an indication of what the class attitude is that day and can adjust lessons accordingly.

Adapted from an activity by: Kay Vaughn, Teacher, Wharton Jr. High

---

OPERA—MORE THAN UGHH!

This activity has the objectives of helping students gain information about a music form and using that form to explore common human characteristics that exist across cultures. Initially, briefly discuss operas with your class, or ask your students to investigate the subject and report back to the class. Be certain to point out to the students how operas represent the cultural characteristics of the peoples and countries portrayed in their performance. Emphasize the story aspect of operas, and compare the themes of jealousy, anger, etc., to other story forms.

Obtain recordings of many different operas representing different countries either in music style or story setting. Some suggestions are:

Wagner's *Lohengrin* (German music)
Puccini's *Madame Butterfly* (Japanese setting)
Bizet's *Carmen* (Spanish music)
Gounod's *Romeo and Juliet* (French author)

Let the students listen to brief selections from the variety of musical sounds, then focus on the stories told by the lyrics.

Follow the classical opera with exploration of "modern opera" or Broadway musical productions. Compare these presentations in regard to setting, costuming, customs, dialogue and lyrics, and story line. Some suggestions are:

Porgy and Bess
Anna and the King of Siam
South Pacific
My Fair Lady (English)

Bubblin' Brown Sugar (Black American)

Fiddler on the Roof (Russian-Jewish Culture)

West Side Story (Inner-city life with the Romeo and Juliet theme)

Students will probably want to learn some of the songs from these shows. In the process, they will be learning about many cultures.

Adapted from an exercise by: Kay Vaughn, Teacher, Wharton Jr. High

---

"YOU BETTER BELIEVE IT"

Human beings have attempted to explain happenings in the world which they did not comprehend by attributing them to gods. Let students explore religions of the world by examining the stories connected with them. For example, Greek myths, Christian parables, Confucian sayings, and similar legacies of the religions of African tribes, Buddhists, Muslims, Jews, American Indians, and so on.

Are there parallels among these stories? What standards are established through these stories? What does man's religion provide? Why do people worship in different ways? Why do people worship gods by different names? Is one religion better than another? Would where you live probably affect the religion you practice? Locate, on a world map, the centers of different religions.

Have students study and discuss the religious practices of the world of today and of past eras. What religious holidays are celebrated and how? What are the differences in these practices and what are the similarities? For example, Moslems are forbidden to smoke, as are some Protestant Christian groups.

As an alternative activity, ask students to select a religion that is different from their own and write a manual or handbook explaining that religion. This book could include the history of the religion, some stories, sayings, or laws associated with the religion, descriptions of ceremonies, and drawings of the symbols used.

Ask each student to select one belief from each of the religions being studied. Make a list of these beliefs on a ditto master so that all students have their own copy. As the individual

87

students examine the list of beliefs, they can *individually* identify for themselves the ones they value. Ask them to think about the following (to themselves): Have they acted in accord with the beliefs they value? What would they like to improve? Discuss whether it is easier to live up to beliefs when they are held privately or when "everyone" knows. Are we more concerned with the judgments of others or how we see ourselves?

Ask students to write a story or poem titled, "To Thine Own Self Be True." What situations have they seen that made it difficult for them or others to be true to what they believe?

This activity is designed to help students understand the religions and related lifestyles peoples have believed to be valuable. Be certain that you support the diverse qualities of all the religions so that no student believes you are endorsing one or another. It is possible to make this too sophisticated for your kids by "making" them "question" their own religion. Don't do it. Also, remember not all families practice or believe in a religion. Children from such families should not come away feeling something is wrong with them, and no children should feel their religion is not being respected.

This activity does not have to be conducted in a controversial fashion. Rather, it can be a tremendous vehicle for multi-cultural understandings and support.

Adapted from an exercise by: Linda Molteni, Teacher, Ford Greene Elementary

---

ONCE UPON A HAPPY EVER AFTER

Folktales are common to all cultures. They provide teachers with entertaining, yet enlightening, mechanisms to encourage class discussion of many social problems. For instance, folktales give many examples of the value of not judging people by their looks, but by their character. The false maid in "The Goose Girl," the powdered fox in the "Fox and Seven Kids," and the frog in "The Frog Prince" are some examples of mistaken looks. These kinds of stories are opportunities to make analogies to humans who are misjudged because of their looks. Discuss how people are sometimes wrongly "lumped" together because of the color of their skin, or their dress, or hairstyle. Examine advertisements and story illustrations to find examples of exterior characteristics that are supposed to represent good or bad character (like the black leather jacket). Use some examples from the television productions *Good Times, Happy Days,* and *Welcome Back, Kotter.*

Another activity relating to common elements found in folktales involves the similarity of story plot. There are over three hundred variations of "Cinderella." The story of a runaway is depicted in "Henny Penny," "The Pancake," and "The Gingerbread Boy." The mischievous imp in "Tom Tit Tot" is the same as in "Rumplestiltskin." Let your students explore possible causes of these similarities. Have them find other examples of stories from different cultures with common themes. Why would Anasi, the Spider Man, have a similar experience to B'rer Rabbit and the Tar Baby? Anasi is a storyteller found in Jamaican lore and B'rer Rabbit evolved through Joel Chandler Harris in the Georgia lowlands. What common human characteristics are indicated by these and other stories?

For a different approach, let your class write a story from the viewpoint of the outcast or evil character. For example, write the wolf's story as he would see the three pigs, or the evil characters on T.V.'s *Charlie's Angels,* or the witch and her problems in "Hansel and Gretel." You could expand this activity into a "Meeting of Misfits" in which the class discusses how the misfits could improve their public image—perhaps through a media campaign. Let the class brainstorm.

A variety of related activities that enhance ethnic understandings for children can be developed. Select a culture and children can learn about it through the folktale approach. A good resource for this activity is Funk & Wagnall's *Dictionary of Folklore, Mythology and Legend, Index to Fairy Tales.*

Adapted from an exercise by: Jim Hartman, Teacher, Ford Greene Elementary

---

ORIGINAL FILMSTRIPS

"WOW" your students with the unbelievable news that they are going to be the writers, producers, and directors of their own filmstrip festival. They can do it, y'know. The general theme of the filmstrips should reflect that all people can live side by side in peace and harmony, regardless of how different we are. The kids may want to depict something from their personal experiences (previous activities you've done together to foster better understanding of our differences, sports where team members play side by side, integrated neighborhoods, etc.) or use their imaginations to capture the concept of what might be if we were to care for one another as fellow humans.

Divide the class into four or five heterogeneous groups of five or six students and give each group a blank filmstrip and markers (washable small point felt tip pens, like those used on overhead projector transparencies, work fine). Explain that the group's film may be accompanied by a narrative, music, poetry, sound effects, or a combination of any of those. Provide necessary equipment such as tape recorders and record players.

It might be fun if awards were presented, but be sure you have enough categories so that each filmstrip gets an award (e.g., Most Original Idea, Best Art Work, Best Musical Score). Try to arrange for the students to go to other classrooms in the school and show their masterpieces!

Not only is this activity fun, it also challenges the creative abilities of students, provides an experience of working cooperatively together, and gives them incentive to think about how they can best demonstrate the value of cultural diversity. You might want to follow up with a Super 8 film festival focusing on their communities, neighborhoods, and leisure activities—make some popcorn and invite the school.
P.S. There's lots of reading and writing to this one.

Adapted from an exercise by: Mary Buerger, Teacher, Ford Greene Elementary

---

MULTI-ETHNIC FAIRY TALES

One way to examine labeling is through the use of the story, "Master of All Masters" where the master tells the maid-servant what she must call everything. The story carries labeling to extremes and is a humorous way to begin a discussion of how we name groups as well as things. Your class could develop a dictionary of words that are used as labels. Explore the different connotations that result from differences in age, culture, or ethnic background. For example, how do different groups use the words chicken, yellow, cracker, trash. This list can be an on-going activity that is used from time to time throughout the semester or year. As words are brought to the class' attention through television, newspapers, or texts, add them to the list and discuss how and why we label people and things.

Use folk and fairy tales to instigate activities about how people change. The prince was changed from a frog into a handsome character because someone cared for him and showed him love. Cinderella became a princess because she was given an opportunity. The animals in "The Bremen Town Musicians" were able to perform an exciting task and found acceptance and acclaim, even though their masters thought them old and not serviceable any longer. Ask your class to find examples in real life of people who overcame great odds but found success and acceptance. How many of these examples represent minority members? Do minorities have better opportunities today? Do students feel better when they are accepted as themselves? Does it change their feelings and, thereby, their actions when they are loved?

As an alternate activity, examine family relationships through the use of folktales. Why did the father and mother leave Hansel and Gretel in the woods? Are step-daughters generally treated like Cinderella or Snow White? Was Pinocchio loved by his father, even though he was adopted? Or Tom Thumb loved by his family, even though he was small?

As you can see, stories, tales, and legends potentially provide many opportunities for kids to learn about and to support ethnic diversity.

A good story source to use is *The Arbuthnot Anthology of Children's Literature,* revised edition, 1961, published by Scott, Foresman and Company. This book is generally found in school or public libraries.

Adapted from an exercise by: Jim Hartman, Teacher, Ford Greene Elementary

---

THE EYES AND EARS OF THE WORLD

The saying "One picture is worth a thousand words" is well accepted by teachers. Why not structure a class activity around pictures? This activity will provide an opportunity to encourage

"Whenever we rent movies we try to pick one that has an impact on the kids as well as one that's entertaining. Brian's Song is a super example of a beautiful friendship and understanding between a White man and Black man . . . it does happen . . . it can happen to you and me . . ."

group interaction as well as creativity—make a documentary multi-cultural film!

First, develop a class discussion of problems facing people in the school, the community, or the world. Make a list of these problems on the blackboard. Ask the class to consider these problem areas and decide on one topic for the subject of a documentary film. Some suggestions they might make include: problems of new students, barriers that handicapped people face, how to get along in a game without arguing, or a study of an ethnic group.

After your class has decided on a topic (or several topics, if to be done as group projects), search for information. Be prepared to suggest books, encyclopedias, and newspapers for students to read for background information. If possible, have students conduct interviews with people who have experienced the problem. Let everyone in the group make a list of the ten most important things they learned about the problem. Compile the student lists, make ditto copies, and distribute them to the class.

Have the class create an outline on the chalkboard of how they see the film unfolding. The students will take the facts they have selected as important and organize them so that they lead one into the other. Ask a group of students to volunteer to write a complete script that is developed around the class-originated outline. The writing group will have to decide how to present the subject matter—as one person's point of view, as an actual experience, in flashback, or some other way.

When the script is completed, the next step is deciding what visual image will best demonstrate the flow of the script. This is a time for role selection . . . director, set manager, actors, art work, background music managers . . . also an opportunity to recognize each student's special talents and capabilities. There should be a role for everyone.

If possible, film the production with videotape first. This medium is desirable because it is easy to re-do if you mess up. You might even want the videotape to be the final production. Be certain to plan a time for the class to critique the production, even rehearsals. Remind the class that it is the *product* that we criticize, not the people. Did the film achieve its purpose to inform or inspire? As a follow-up, lead the class in a discussion of the process—e.g., Did the group work together? Finally, give a preview for other classes. The preview is an opportunity to "show off," as well as to share. Make it a really big show!

Adapted from an exercise by: Kathy Bryant, Teacher Corps Intern, Washington Jr. High

---

IT'S A GOOD DAY

Boxing Day is the first weekday after Christmas, observed as a holiday, when Christmas gifts or boxes are traditionally given to household employees and other service workers. This British holiday is celebrated in the United Kingdom and countries that either remain or at one time were under British control. These countries include: Australia, Solomon Islands, Cyprus, Gambia, Jamaica, Kenya, Malawi, Nigeria, Sierra Leone, Swaziland, Tonga, and Zambia. However, other countries have celebrated this day; these include Greece, Hungary, Iceland, and Liechtenstein.

An interesting activity could include grouping the class to locate places on a map that celebrate common holidays. For instance, students that select Boxing Day would locate the countries or island groups on a world map and use a symbol to indicate their observance of Boxing Day. Other student groups could select one of the following holidays: Independence Day, Corpus Christi, Epiphany, Eid-ul-Fitr, All Souls' Day or All Saints' Day, Mardi Gras, or Constitution Day, to mention just a few possibilities.

This activity will provide an opportunity for students to learn more about other cultures as they work together. Encourage students to analyze the reason why the holiday is celebrated in one country and not in another. There are many influences responsible for holidays, such as the history of a country, the dominant religion, and birthdays of famous people.

The study of holidays is a good initiator for other activities such as map study, religions, anthropology, dress, and customs. Since holidays are exciting to students and can be used to generate art and music activities, they can be an enjoyable method of

93

finding out more about other cultures. Use an almanac as a resource, since it usually has holidays listed by countries.

Adapted from an exercise by: Jane Bandy Smith, Multi-Cultural Instructor

---

OUT WITH THE OLD, IN WITH THE NEW

New Year's Day is celebrated throughout the world. Most countries celebrate this day on January 1st because they use the Gregorian calendar. However, there are New Year's celebrations held on different days and this fact can develop into an interesting classroom experience to promote acceptance of differences.

Some examples of New Year's celebration that are different from the United States:

Afghanistan . . . . March 21 or 22
Burma . . . . April
Ethiopia . . . . September 11
Hong Kong . . . . January-February
Iran . . . . March 21-25
Israel . . . . September (first and last days of Rosh Hashanah)
Korea . . . . January 1-3
Lebanon . . . . March
Malaysia . . . . January-February
Nepal . . . . April 14
New Zealand . . . . January 1-2
Rumania . . . . January 1-2
Somalia . . . . March
Thailand . . . . January-February (Chinese New Year)
United Arab Republic . . . . April (Moslem New Year)

In some instances, celebrations are set by the government of a country but are observed at a different time by some of the people. For instance, in Korea the government decreed that New Year's Day would be celebrated on January 1st, but the older people still adhere to the Lunar or Chinese New Year.

Even more interesting than when holidays fall is how they are celebrated. Koreans, as an example, celebrate this day by honoring their ancestors. All the offspring of a family gather at the house of the oldest brother for a feast. Hung above the table are pictures or letters representing the family ancestors. Following the feast is a Bowing ceremony to the ancestors. Another practice followed in Korea is a unique Bowing ceremony that is similar to our "Trick or Treat." Young people "bow" to older people and are given small sums of money. The money is kept in a pouch tied around their waist. However, the bow is more elaborate than just bending at the waist. Discuss with your class the body movements we use in this country to demonstrate respect or friendship . . . handshakes, waves, standing up . . . many more.

Have your class find out more about other practices followed by other people when they celebrate New Year's. If there are Jewish students in your class or school, let them share information about the celebration of Rosh Hashanah. Have a class celebration of this day by asking a Rabbi as a guest speaker. Rosh Hashanah (ros-has-a'-na) is a solemn, yet festive occasion that lasts forty-eight hours. This day is considered to mark the creation of the world and is the Jewish "Day of Remembrance." The ram's horn (shofar) is blown to hail the new year and call for repentance. This day is a day of judgment when God reviews the deeds of human beings. It is also a custom to eat apple dipped in honey for a sweet and happy new year. This custom would be easy to enact in the classroom and would add a dimension of reality to a class investigation of the Jewish New Year's celebration.

Students could make their own Book of Judgment wherein they write unfair or unkind things they had done. Discussion of these books should strictly be left open for individual desire— respect privacy. If the class wants to, this would be a good time to discuss "saying you are sorry," "forgiving others," and "why we sometimes do things we know are wrong."

The New Year's celebration in China is the most important day of the year. Everybody celebrates their birthday on New Year's Day, regardless of when they were really born. So, plan a big birthday party for the day on which the Chinese New Year's Day falls; each year's almanac should give you the date. Remember, too, that the Chinese believe that you should have paid all your debts and cleaned your house in preparation for New Year's Day. What a great idea for cleaning the classroom and encouraging everyone to get in all their work! The Chinese end their celebration with a Feast of Lanterns—take this as a suggestion for crafts.

India's celebration of New Year's also involves bright lights. They are used to welcome the souls of the dead. The New Year observance in India lasts for the last four days of the year. It is called Diwali.

In Japan, everyone gets new clothes before beginning a celebration that lasts three days. During these three days, the custom is to visit with friends. Children in Japan play a New Year's game called "Henetsuki." This game is similar to badminton where you hit a shuttlecock back and forth with rackets called "hogoitas." In ancient times, Japanese children played the game to keep away evil spirits. Compare this custom to those that can be found in the United States, such as the jack-o-lantern.

Adapted from an exercise by: Janice Klein, Music Teacher, Washington Jr. High

---

CALENDAR CAPER

Holidays may vary because of the calendar that is used in that country. The four principal calendars used today are: Gregorian, Hebrew, Moslem, and Lunar. The Gregorian calendar is used by most nations, including the United States. All the calendars are based on time cycles, but they began at different times; for example, the Lunar calendar began in 2397 B.C., the Hebrew in 3761 B.C., the Moslem in A.D. 622, and the Gregorian in A.D. 1582.

Some holidays, like Christmas Day, are celebrated on set days; but others, like Easter, are established according to the calendar. The holidays that depend on the calendar are sometimes called movable holidays.

Some movable holidays that are celebrated around the world include: Prophet's Birthday in Afghanistan, Carnival in South American countries, Water Festival and New Year's Day in Burma, nearly every holiday (except New Year's Day and Independence Day) in India, Rice Growing Day in Laos, Eid-ul-Fitr in Pakistan. Many other movable holidays are generally based on religious history.

It is interesting to let students make the four different calendars, or to mark a Gregorian calendar with the dates of celebrations throughout the world. Holidays give you an opportunity to see that although we may celebrate differently, the cause of the celebration is common to all men—freedom, beliefs, and respect for leaders.

Give your class the opportunity to plan a holiday. It can be an occasion to celebrate or commemorate anything they wish. Let them plan the customs, appropriate dress, activities, and foods that will be used in the celebration. Let them select one school day for the celebration and lead the other class members in appropriate songs, skits, or art activities. This activity can instigate a discussion of symbols, beliefs, other cultures, and common characteristics of people everywhere.

Adapted from an exercise by: Tom Sloan, Teacher, Wharton Elementary

---

SAME WORDS BUT DIFFERENT

Words have come into the language of our country from every nation of the world. A true multi-cultural experience for your class is to make a dictionary of words that we use but which originated in other cultures. For example: kimono, canoe, sabbath, ski, chauffeur, dachshund, menu, sauerkraut, waltz, and garage. Many more can be discovered by examining the dictionary for derivatives or looking through books on etymology. It will interst students to discover that many words in various languages are similar. Our word mother is mere in the French language, mutter in German, madre in Spanish, mati in Russian, and mader in Persian. It is beneficial to point up the commonality of people through similar word spellings and uses. You might want to add a section that focuses on the slang words your kids use and their origins.

It might be fun for your class to make a map of word origins. They could draw a very large world map on butcher paper and then write in the words that we have "borrowed" from other cultures. For instance: we have tea, as well as its name, from China; khaki from India; and ukuleles from Hawaii.

Students enjoy looking into how names derived and what they originally meant. This activity can foster greater understanding among people because it stresses how names are related. There are probably several students in your school named John. John came from the Hebrew Yohanan, which means Gift of God. Today, variations of that name are found throughout the world— Jean in France, Johann in Germany, Juan in Spain, Giovanni in Italy, Jan in Holland, and Ivan in Russian. By the same token, your class can explore surnames. These names derived from personal characteristics, occupations, offices held, terms of affection, and locations where people lived, as evidenced in the surnames of Smart, Hill, Goldsmith, Duke, Davidson, and Peterkin.

Where did the names of your students originate? Ask them to find out and to share their findings.

Adapted from an exercise by: Jane Bandy Smith, Multi-Cultural Instructor

---

MULTI-CULTI-CARTOONS

Everybody enjoys cartoons. Young and old relate to a story told or a point made by a simple line drawing. One of the most popular features of the newspaper is the political cartoon. Good cartoons require use of the imagination in simplifying a complicated idea. Cartoons sometimes use symbols to help simplify ideas. For example, death is represented by a skull; peace, by a dove; justice, by a set of scales; and the U. S. government, by Uncle Sam.

Encourage your students to have an exercise in imagination by drawing a cartoon that represents people of a culture or subculture within our own country. For example: "Little Chief" is a comic strip drawn by a Pawnee Indian, Brumett Eclshawk. Perhaps they would like to draw a comic strip consisting of many frames. Remind them that cartoonists usually exaggerate the features or characteristics of people. Also, ask them to include themselves in the cartoon.

Or, as an alternative, cut figures out of comic books, comic strips in the newspaper, or magazine cartoons. Mount these figures on 3" x 5" unlined index cards. Let students select several figures and see if they can create a funny story. Perhaps the story could involve one culture meeting another, such as Snuffy Smith meeting Mary Worth. What problems might they have in relating to one another? Would there be a problem in understanding each other's language? Would it be easier for Li'l Abner to relate to Snuffy? Why?

Another characteristic of cartoons is that people and animals often talk to one another. It would be interesting to see how your class would depict themselves or others in animal form. This activity could provide you with some insights about the attributes they see in others and allow you to plan a good discussion period.

Cartoons make effective bulletin boards, especially those from *The New Yorker Magazine.* By projecting the cartoon on a large piece of paper with an opaque projector, you can create a giant cartoon for your board.

Adapted from an exercise by: Pamela Lusthaus, Teacher, Wharton Elementary

---

B. Activities Generated in the Multiple Talents Inservice Seminar

---

Introduction

by John Lifsey

The activities contained in this section are examples of those developed by teacher and community participants in a Multiple Talents Seminar. The activities have been adapted to enhance multi-cultural emphases beyond those originally intended.

In 1977, Multiple Talents was a new inservice area for the Nashville Teacher Corps program. This inservice opportunity was offered as a result of the needs expressed by teachers during the first year's multi-cultural education program. Of the more than eighty participants in the multi-cultural foundations seminar who were surveyed, the number one priority cited for further inservice programs was "more training opportunities focusing on a multi-talented approach to learners' growth and development." The survey followed the introduction of the multiple-talents approach and its relationship to and/or within multicultural education in the multi-cultural foundations seminar. A later needs assessment further indicated multiple talents as a high priority among teachers and community participants.

Leslie Horowitz and I (of Tennessee State University and Metro Schools, respectively) designed and implemented the instructional opportunities for multi-talents inservice training. A seminar format where classroom activities and concepts were developed was used. We utilized small group discussions, peer teaching, demonstration teaching, self-evaluation, and instructor classroom observation and support. The instruction focused on five talent areas: divergent thinking, convergent thinking, evaluative thinking, creativity, and planning. The activities in this section help to develop multi-cultural understandings and also enhance at least one of these talent areas.

The instructional process included four steps. The first was gaining knowledge of the concepts. Here participants were asked to read materials pertaining to the talent area under consideration. They were then administered a criterion-referenced test to be certain that they acquired the necessary knowledge. Having completed the knowledge step, the participants moved on into planning. Activities in a talent area were modeled in a seminar session by the instructors. The participants then worked in small groups to develop activities of their own. Next, classmates were selected to peer teach one of their activities. Each participant then planned three activities for the talent area under study and for the subject area and grade level of his/her choice. These were duplicated and a copy of each was distributed to everyone in the seminar. Thus, each participant received approximately 375 planned activities for multiple talent instruction upon completion of the seminar.

In the instruction phase the participants chose two of the three activities they had planned and used them in a classroom situation. They kept a log in which they made notes of successes, problems, conclusions, and suggested changes for the activities they had taught.

Evaluation was the fourth step: the evaluation included both a teacher self-evaluation and an evaluation of student performance. The teacher self-evaluation was designed to assist teachers in looking at their own instructional techniques. The pupil evaluation was an attempt to help teachers identify children who had strengths in the talent areas under consideration.

The instructional materials used in the seminar were:

—*Igniting Creative Potential,* Project Implode, Salt Lake City, Utah, 1971

—Criterion-referenced tests developed by the instructors

—Packets developed by Leslie Horowitz of Tennessee State University (these included a summary of information about each talent area, a teacher self-evaluation checklist, log forms, and pupil evaluation forms)

—Activities developed by the participants

Teachers involved in the Multiple Talents Seminar reported that they were able to find many unique and heretofore unrecognized abilities in their students. Many reported that they began to look at students in a new way as they recognized the potential talents students displayed in completing the activities. Many participants were also pleased to find in themselves abilities and talents which they had not previously recognized. The recognition and support of this diversity certainly enhanced multicultural learnings. It provided avenues to help children and adults develop new understandings of ethnic and cultural differences and to support such pluralism. Both instructors were astounded at the amount of enthusiasm the seminar generated and the amount of creative potential obvious in the work of the participants.

SPACED OUT

In past years American and Russian astronauts and cosmonauts have joined their space capsules for orbits around the earth. Pretend the U.S.A. and the U.S.S.R. are going to send one astronaut and one cosmonaut on an entire space mission together. What arrangements will have to be planned so that persons representing two cultures can live in space for a period of time? Types of food? Music? Communication?

This exercise necessitates that students gather information on space flight procedures, food during space flights, control of the send off and splash down. What does each person need to know about the other's culture?

Ask the students to pretend they are in charge of the training program to ready the astronauts for space travel. Ask the students to create a training plan for them that will help the astronauts know and feel comfortable with one another.

Design some activities and try them out in a role play. Explore the question, "How do you help people from different cultures get to know and feel good about their differences?"

As an alternative or extension of this approach, have several groups in the classroom select other countries with make-believe astronauts. Ask the groups to compare the preparations and conditions for their space flights.

Ask the students to design space suits, flags, menus, etc., for themselves (as individuals) as if they were astronauts . . . *and* their designs should incorporate their own cultural and/or ethnic background.

Adapted from an exercise by: Ann Robertson, Teacher, McKissack Elementary

---

"BECOMING" . . . CULTURAL INVENTIONS

Something we create—conceived in our own minds and actualized by our own talents—is probably the strongest statement we can make about who we are and how we are unique. We help children develop healthier self-concepts as well as greater appreciation of others' differences when we encourage them to be creative and support them as their own uniqueness emerges. The activities listed below were developed by teachers who, by asking students to invent, were ready to help them realize their own creative potential. The fun part for you will be your saying to children, "Be crazy, be wild; if it sounds outlandish, do it" and watching them stretch and grow and experiment until they find all things are possible. Here are some ideas . . . but remember, identify and support the students' individuality.

—Ask children to invent a machine that would recover used rocket stages from the bottom of the ocean.

—Give each child the same amount of clay and ask him to make as many different things as possible. After he makes an object show it to the person sitting next to him. Tell him/her to guess what it is. Each individual should keep a list of everything he makes. At the end of twenty minutes ask each student to remake whatever he/she liked best and allow each one to share his/her creation with the rest of the class.

—Ask students to invent something that will be added to their bodies that will make life easier for them (for example, an adjustable back scratcher).

—Ask the children to invent a fast, efficient transportation system for a city in the year 2000 (for example, atomic powered pogo stick, computerized car).

—Ask the students to think about an invention that would make the world better. Ask them to defend their inventions.

—Ask students to invent an animal that could have lived on earth millions of years ago and draw a picture of it.

—Read Sendak's *Where the Wild Things Are.* Explain that it is a picture book for young children. Tell the students that you want them to create a "wild thing" that could be used in a book for young children. Give them paper, cardboard, scissors, string, egg cartons, egg shells, straws, and anything else that is available. Show them how to make movable parts using brads. Each "wild thing" should be given a name and a description should be written about its lifestyle, what it eats, where it lives, number of offspring, etc.

—Using the book *Kites* by Downer as a guide, ask the children to create and make their own kites.

—Copy the verse "A Tutor Who Tooted the Flute" by Carolyn Wells (found in the book *A Little Laughter* compiled by Katherine Love) on a chart and read it to the class. Encourage the students to create their own humorous poems. This can be done as a class, giving individuals the opportunity to contribute a line, or individually and allowing the students to read their verses to the class.

—Tell the students to think of something they think needs to be invented for the kitchen on the order of a kitchen appliance. Ask them to think of tasks in the kitchen they dislike the most and then invent a machine or appliance to do that job. Ask them to describe (complete with drawings) how it would operate.

—Share the book *Creating with Found Objects* by Lother Kampmann with the class. Then go on a scavenger hunt around the school grounds. Come back and ask the students to create something with the objects they found.

With each of the above activities watch for opportunities to relate the students' creations to those of cultural groups that may exhibit similarities.

Adapted from an exercise by: Donna Barr, Lynda Burton, Lois Jones, and Ann Robertson, Teachers, McKissack Elementary; Johnny Thompson, Teacher Corps Intern, Washington Jr. High; Linda Therber and Claire Carter Baker, Teachers, Ford Greene Elementary; Barbara Egel, Teacher, Wharton Jr. High; and Joyce Blair, Community Participant

---

YOUR SCHOOL . . . AS YOU SEE IT

Even though all of your students experience and share in the culture of their school, they may not be aware of how differently individuals within the school perceive that environment. The purpose of this activity is to help students take a look at how others feel about schools and how those feelings differ from their own. They will delve a little into some of the reasons for these differences, looking specifically at the roles ethnic and cultural stereotypes and biases play. Do they think the school provides for and supports uniqueness? This activity is most successful when group trust has already been established.

Ask your students to list individually their ten favorite experiences and ten worst experiences in school. Share the completed lists with the whole class. Ask them individually to think of new names for their school; each name should reflect the student's feelings about those school experiences previously listed. Encourage them to be honest about their choices. When the new school names have been selected, divide the class into small groups (four or five) and have each student share one school name and the reasons for choosing that name. Have a group recorder list the reasons, avoiding duplication. Ask the children to discuss the following questions:

—Does everyone have the same experiences and feelings about school?

—Why do you think some students' experiences are so different from others'?

—Do you think everyone at school is treated fairly?

104

—Do you (as students) expect certain people or groups of people to have a more difficult time at school? Who are these people? Why do you feel that way?

—Do you think teachers and principals expect certain students or groups of students to have a difficult time at school? Why do you think that?

—Do you think people in schools are prejudiced toward certain groups, children who behave differently, children who dress differently, children who don't learn easily, or any other group you can think of?

Have the class make a list of suggestions that could be given to the teachers and the principal which would support diversity and make the school a place where *all* children could have good experiences and happy feelings.

Adapted from an exercise by: John Culley, Community Participant

FOLLOW IN THE FOOTSTEPS

This activity will encourage children to examine the lifestyles, times, and feelings of other people. It is a good idea for a story-starter to initiate a creative writing activity. It is also a good example of how something as simple as shoes relates to culture.

The Indians have an expression that you should never judge a man until you have walked two days in his moccasins. Begin an activity by writing this expression on the board and letting the students discuss what it means. What are some things that might have happened if they had worn Indian moccasins . . . a hundred years ago . . . today? Why did the Indian wear moccasins? What were they made of?

Ask the students to imagine that they are a pair of moccasins belonging to an Indian who lived during the time that the Pilgrims came to America. Next, each one should write a creative story as experienced by the moccasins. Ask the students to share their stories by reading them aloud, exchanging and reading silently, grouping in small groups and selecting one to act out, or by placing them in a notebook in the learning center.

> "It's important to stress that Columbus was not the first person in America. Let's explore the contributions of the Indians and Asians who were here first."

Alternative activities could include searching for other sayings and stories that relate to shoes, for instance:

"The Shoe's on the Other Foot"

"The Red Shoes" by Hans Christian Andersen

"Cinderella"

"Twelve Dancing Princesses" by the Grimm brothers

Find pictures showing different kinds of shoes, boots, and sandals from other countries (and subcultures within the USA) and mount each picture on construction paper. Give half-pictures to students and have them find the students holding the other halves of their pictures. Each pair of students will comprise a research team to discover what kind of life the people in those shoes lived. What did they eat? What did they do for fun? What dangers might they have faced?

Sports shoes are interesting to kids and can provide an alternative activity that permits inclusion of both sexes and all ethnic groups. Various types of shoes—tennis, boating, basketball, golfing, skating, bowling, etc.—have certain characteristics that fit them for that sport. You can easily lead into a discussion of how much better it is to have differences in people too, because then we are suited for different activities.

Adapted from an exercise by: Donna Barr, Teacher, McKissack Elementary

---

ETHNIC/CULTURE MAPPING

Divide the class into groups of four or five students, being certain you have a multi-cultural "mix" in each group. Tell the students that they are going to have an opportunity to create their own country. Three major areas of emphasis in this project will be creativity, geography, and cultures.

To assist them in developing a geography for their countries, a brief lesson in map making will be necessary. Explain that the country can be any shape or any size they desire. Look at some maps together and determine what kind of a legend everyone is going to use to indicate roads, highways, rivers, lakes, railroads, mountains, towns, and the like. Any special features they want to include are left strictly up to them.

106

STUDENTS CREATING A GROUP PICTURE OF THEIR "TURF" AND ITS CULTURAL CHARAC-
TERISTICS.

Introducing the concept of culture requires a more sophisticated kind of thinking. Raise these questions:

—What is culture?

—What makes "American" culture different from Spanish or
German culture?

—What about cultures within a culture, i.e., the subcultures of
Blacks, Chicanos, Native Americans?

The kids will quickly realize that they will have to consider
language, dress, housing, foods, art, music, dance, government,
and much more if they're going to come up with a culture for
their country. The members of different subcultures in each student group should be a built-in safety system to see that the new
culture reflects the possible diversities of its people.

After each group has finished creating their own country, complete with map and cultural description, have them share it with
the total class. This may be done by drawings, charts, student-
made filmstrips, etc. A few of the pertinent topics of discussion
which should arise from the activity are:

107

—Did the cultures created actually reflect an understanding and appreciation for diversity?

—As your groups decided about the culture, were there ever any conflicts of interest among the group members? If so, how did you resolve them?

—What were some of the other things you found that have a bearing on culture?

—Are there other cultures you would like to learn about?

—Do you think it's important for your country (or any country) to support cultural differences within its borders? Why?

—What advice would you give to the leader of a country to help support diversity within that country?

If interest is high, this activity could be expanded by having the student groups do sand or salt maps of their country and accompanying illustrations, collages, etc., depicting the culture.

Adapted from an exercise by: Ann Robertson, Teacher, McKissack Elementary

---

PERCEPTIONS AND CULTURES

Begin by discussing with your students the fact that we know the world through what we smell, taste, hear, see, and feel. Ask them if they think we would all receive identical data through our senses if we were placed in the same environment. Propose the following experiment to find out.

Each day, for five consecutive days, send the students to the lunchroom with a paper and pencil. They will choose one sense for that day and try to record what they perceive through that sense. For instance, if the sense of smell is what they are concentrating on for the day, everyone will write down what they smell. Encourage the students *not* to share their perceptions with other students; they should record them privately.

Collect the lists each day and compile a master list. After the five days have the class take a look at the lists. Include the following points in your discussion:

—Did everyone perceive the same environment the same way?

—What do you think contributed to the differences?

—Is someone "right" and someone else "wrong" in their perceptions if they are different?

The purpose of this is to help students realize that although we may share an experience with someone, our perceptions of the experience may be very different. If you've attempted to create an environment in your class that values diversity, you might explain that this is the ultimate in uniqueness. It is also probably the most challenging concept to deal with as students come to grips with living in a society filled with differences. For although perceptions are often influenced by culture, they more often than not cross cultural boundaries; in a way, each person's sensory perceptions become a culture unto themselves. Discuss the implication of this with your students as it relates to communication, interaction, and understanding between human beings.

Adapted from an exercise by: Ann Robertson, Teacher, McKissack Elementary

WISH UPON A CULTURE

This activity is designed to help students evaluate their own desires as well as those of differing cultural groups. It also helps kids to establish priorities, to rationalize, and to form convincing arguments.

Draw a genie on the chalkboard or bulletin board. Ask each student to think of three wishes they really want. Have everyone post their number one (most desired or important) wish on the board. After the class has had time to examine these wishes, it's time to discuss them. Give each student thirty seconds to justify why the wish should be granted and why it is so important. Following each student's presentation the class can ask questions if they wish. At the completion of everyone's presentations and justifications, ask the class to discuss which wishes seemed most justified. Do the wishes fall into categories? What criteria for judging should be used?

Ask the students to write down and turn in the one wish, other than their own, they would grant. Determine the top three selections.

The following day, select one article for each of your students from newspapers and magazines (like *Time, Newsweek, U.S. News and World Report*) that focus on certain problem situations

> *"We watched the James Baldwin film,* Harlem, *for creative writing purposes. I asked the students to place themselves in the story as Harlem inhabitants and to react in some form of creative writing. Our reactions evidenced our own individual cultural differences and likenesses . . . we talked about them . . . we now understand and like each other more."*

that people of differing cultural groups or countries are experiencing; for instance, situations involving earthquake disasters, political riots, trade relations, starvation, discrimination and intolerance, poverty, and injustice. Ask your students to read them and write down a wish for those people involved in the problem situations. The wishes should be written from the oppressed or distressed person's point of view. Request that the kids give a brief descriptor of the article's story, explain their wish, and put it up on the board.

After each student has taken his/her turn, examine and discuss these wishes in comparison to those expressed the day before. No doubt, most of the individual wishes reflecting personal desires will not be as important as those created for people in the problem situation. Discuss how the day before, if they had been in touch with world problems, they could have stopped a war, poverty, or disease instead of wishing for something for themselves. Discuss the reality of how none of us can wish major problems in our world quickly away, but by being aware and doing something about them, together, we can help others. Oops . . . and suggest they continue to wish for themselves and others, too.

Adapted from an exercise by: Johnny Thompson, Teacher Corps Intern, Washington Jr. High

---

WRITE ON

This activity is designed to encourage divergent thinking, increase awareness of individual differences, and heighten student interest in multi-cultural books. It also focuses on the unique characteristics of different regions of the world.

Ask the students to develop a history of books from the clay tablets of the Egyptians through the use of papyrus, sheepskin scrolls, hornbooks, and the development of the printing press.

"Sounder, Queenie Peavy, Christmas Present . . . I ask students to read books about people . . . their happy and disappointing relationships. I ask them to transfer these feelings to themselves. Have you ever felt like that person felt? Did the story help you learn about others and their feelings?"

Stress that people use materials indigenous to their areas and the technical development of the time span. Stress the interrelatedness shown by paper from China, ink from Spain, and the printing press from Germany.

Share information by having each stage in the development of books written on a circle of paper by the students. Connect these circles at the edges and make a "bookworm" for your bulletin board. Or make an oversized book with each student's contribution on a separate page, and place it in the room or a learning center for individual students to examine during free time.

Use the bulletin board or book activity to lead into the "write-on." For this exercise, ask each student to make up a book title. It should be a title that they originate—not a published book title—and consist of several words. Ask the students to think about why they chose their particular title. Have they had an experience that the title suggests? Did they use a word that is a symbol? Does their title reflect something found in their lifestyle? Does the title reflect a special interest of theirs?

Or, alternatively, you can take up the book titles developed by the pupils and drop them in a hat. Draw them out one at a time and have the class try to identify who wrote each title as it is read aloud or written on the board.

This is a good opportunity to demonstrate that authors usually write from personal experience. For example, Mark Twain, as a boy growing up on the Mississippi River, had many experiences similar to those of his character, Tom Sawyer.

Another alternative exercise on the theme of multi-cultural books is to use book characters to expand the students' awareness of cultural variations and lifestyle differences within our own country. Ask students to select a book that features the life of a boy or girl.

After they have read the book, ask them to compare their lifestyle and culture with that of the book's character. For example:

111

Myself	Book Character
Name	Name
Dress	Dress
Family Members	Family Members
House	House
Food	Food
Play Activities/Leisure	Play Activities/Leisure
Favorite Expressions	Favorite Expressions
Concerns/Problems	Concerns/Problems

—Among books featuring girls, graded for the upper elementary and middle school student, are these:

Anderson	*Hai Yin, The Dragon Girl*	Harcourt, Brace, Jovanovich
Bennett	*I, Judy*	Messner
Calhoun	*Honestly, Katie John*	School Book Series
Carlson	*Ann Aurelia and Dorothy*	Dell
Cornett	*Alaskan Summer*	Avalon
Farjeon	*Maria Lupin*	Abelard
Gates	*Blue Willow*	Viking
Gates	*Poor Little Rich Girl*	Abelard
Rose	*Brooklyn Girl*	Follett
Sorenson	*Around the Corner*	Harcourt, Brace, Jovanovich

—Among books featuring boys, graded for the upper elementary and middle school student, are these:

Bradburry	*Andy's Mountain*	Lothrop
Corbett	*One by Sea*	Little
Donovan	*Wild in the World*	Harper Row
Durstine	*Monty of Montego*	Bobbs
Fox	*Portrait of Ivan*	Bradbury Press
Hill	*Ramon's World*	Herald Press
Hurd	*Follow Tomas*	Hale
Kalnay	*It Happened in Chichipica*	Harcourt, Brace, Jovanovich
Kipling	*Kim*	Airmont
Lenski	*Project Boy*	Lippincott
Merrill	*Song for Gar*	Hale
Meyer	*Me and Caleb*	Follett
Starr	*Rufus*	Gambit
Vance	*Willie Joe and His Small Charge*	Hale

—Other books can be located in *Subject Guide to Children's Books in Print,* 1971, published by R. R. Bowker Co., New York. Look under the headings: Girls—Fiction; Boys—Fiction. This reference indicates the recommended grade level for each title, which allows you to select a book that is "readable" and enjoyable for students of all reading capabilities.

Adapted from a suggested exercise by: Lois Jones, Teacher, McKissack Elementary

---

YOU ARE "IT"

This activity will provide an opportunity for your students to react to problem situations in a non-threatening environment; it will aid evaluative thinking; and it will help them understand that "human rights" are for all cultures.

You will need a series of cards with descriptive phrases that elaborate personal problem situations. Prepare at least one card for each class member. Let each student draw a card from a box and pantomime what they would do in that situation. Each may use other students to act out parts, but the student drawing the card must act out the role of the decision-maker. Let the class see if they can guess the situation and solution. Discussion should follow each episode.

Some suggested situations:

1. You are in a store and you see someone pick up an object and put it in a sack from a different store.

2. You do not have any thumbs, yet you must learn to write your name.

3. You are the only witness to a car accident and the driver at fault is your best friend.

4. During a fight between a good friend and a boy you do not like very much, your friend picks up something heavy and it looks as if he is going to hit the other boy.

5. Your next door neighbor is trying to push the car (out of the snow) or (to get it started).

6. A new student in class asks directions to the library; your best friend indicates the wrong way on purpose.

7. The mother of a classmate brings a tray of cookies to your teacher. Since the teacher and the rest of the class are out of the room, she leaves them with you. It is just before lunch and you are really hungry.

8. This is the day to buy tickets to the musical production and you really want to go but you do not have enough money. The student next to you, a real fat person, has left lunch money on the desk top while in P.E.

9. You really want to make a good grade on this test because you have been promised a horse if you make an "A". Your teacher is talking to another teacher and has the answer sheet in her hand. The answers are in full view to you.

10. The student sitting next to you has asked to borrow a pencil for about the fifth time. You know that the student's father is laid off from his job and that the mother is sick. But the student is always borrowing pencils and paper and does not repay you.

Set a limit of time for discussion of these situations. It is easy to vary the situations by changing the character from someone very poor to very wealthy, from a good friend to someone not liked, from someone of a different ethnic group to someone of the same. Variations provide an opportunity for students to examine the effect relationships may have on how they react to situations. They furnish a grand opportunity to explore the concepts of justice and morality. "Right" is not determined by who is in the situation. It is what a person does or does not do in relationship to what is "just." Discuss with your kids when some rights must be above others . . . that the rights of life, liberty, and the pursuit of happiness sometimes have different meanings for different people. All people are entitled to "human rights" . . . explore with your students what that means . . . regardless of ethnic background . . . and that differing backgrounds make us even more special as a country.

Adapted from an exercise by: Johnny Thompson, Teacher Corps Intern, Washington Jr. High, and Cheryl Williams, Teacher, Gower Elementary

NAME CALLING!

Show your students some representative works of famous artists. Make certain that you have examples from different countries, time frames, and styles. Tell the students something about the artist and the style but not the titles of the works. Encourage them to choose the ones they like best and talk about how differently a single piece of art can appeal to people. Ask the students to give each of the paintings a title reflecting what they think each painting is all about. When they are through, let them share their titles with the entire class. Ask them to consider the following questions:

—Which titles expressed similar feelings about each painting?

—Which titles were very different from the others suggested?

—Were they surprised to find someone very different from themselves express the same feelings about a painting?

—Did they expect certain classmates or groups of students to respond to the art work in a certain way because of a stereotype based on cultural or racial bias?

—Did anyone look at a painting differently as a result of listening to someone else's point of view?

This activity will not only encourage students to appreciate differences among people but also help develop creative thinking skills. Variations of this activity could use: short stories, essays, instrumental music, poetry, vocal music, or pictures/photographs.

Remember to provide time to relate the works of art to their cultural backgrounds. Explore the cultural differences represented. The students will want to know why the artists did what they did. That's the best moment to get into the people, places, times, and how they relate to today!

Adapted from an exercise by: Katie Williams, Lois Jones, and Karen Catignani, Teachers, McKissack Elementary, and Linda Walker, Community Participant

"MAN, THAT'S THE MOST"

This activity is designed to improve the development of evaluative thinking and prioritizing and to increase self-awareness and knowledge of others. Watch for the opportunity to point out ethnic/cultural characteristics as they become apparent. Many will emerge.

Ask your students to respond to the following questions, in writing:

—What was the largest thing you saw on the way to school this morning?

—What was the smallest thing you saw?

—What do you do that makes your parents the most angry with you?

—What is your most fun thing to do?

—What makes you most angry?

—What has happened recently that made you most happy?

—What would you most like to eat?

—What friends do you like most?

—Which people in your class are most like you?

—Who in the school looks most like you?

—What would you most like to change about yourself?

Ask the students to make up some more "mosts."

Use variation in having the class share their responses. The following processes are often successful:

1. Take up the responses and list all answers (anonymously) on a ditto sheet.
2. Head up a separate sheet of paper for each question and pass them from person to person for responses. Then mount them on the bulletin board.
3. Compare responses through oral discussion.

This can be a continuous activity to be used at least on a weekly or bi-weekly basis.

Adapted from an exercise by: Johnny Thompson, Teacher Corps Intern, Washington Jr. High

---

COLOR IT GRAY MATTER

The objective of this activity is to help students develop evaluative thinking about the thought process and to explore individual and common patterns in thinking. It is an example of how to utilize evaluative-thinking classroom activities for multi-cultural purposes.

Begin this exploration with a classroom discussion concerning thinking. Some possible questions are:

—When do you do your best thinking?

—Where do you do your best thinking?

—What things happen in the classroom that help you think?

—What things happen in the classroom that keep you from thinking?

—What advice would you give a teacher to help him/her have a classroom in which students do their best thinking?

—Describe how you act or look when you are thinking.

—Have you ever seen your teacher think? If so, how does he/she act when he/she is thinking?

—Is it easier for you to think when it's quiet?

—Do you like to have music playing when you think?

—Does whether you want music depend on how difficult the material is that you are studying?

—How do you feel you learn best: seeing a movie? reading a book? listening to someone? watching someone? working through trial and error?

Now is a good opportunity to use the tangram game. Focus on how someone's experiences determine their mental responses by playing a word association game. Read a list of ten words that have multiple meanings and uses. Ask the students to write down their first thought upon hearing each word. Some suggested words are (call out only once):

pop	sorry
hustle	beat (beet)
grass	cell (sell)
cool	sees (seize, seas)

Ask students to discuss their responses and examine their past experiences to see if they are aware of a connection. What are some of the unique experiences the children have had? Would their parents have a different response? Their friends?

Follow this class session by asking the students to work in

pairs or small group to devise other word lists. Do the lists reflect their differing cultures (lifestyles, behaviors, values, languages, etc.)?

Adapt this lesson by using descriptive words frequently applied to subgroups of people—e.g., dumb blondes, fiery redheads, and irresponsible teen-agers. Do we use stereotypes in our thinking as a result of experiences or biased information?

Adapted from an exercise by: Linda Therber, Teacher, Ford Greene Elementary

---

YOU'VE COME A LONG WAY, BABY!

This activity is to generate information concerning past times and conditions. It can be used to establish a data base as well as to examine beliefs and customs.

The teacher should begin a discussion of women's roles 100 years ago. Let the students brainstorm ideas of what activities women undertook, jobs they held, dress they wore, and items they used in the home. Record these ideas on the board, overhead projector, or by using a class recorder.

Let the class divide into interest groups to determine the accuracy of their ideas. Some students can explore dress, others the home, etc. Ask students to plan a reporting session later in the week. Encourage students to bring in comparative pictures of "then" and "now."

Laura Ingalls Wilder's books present an honest portrayal of life in the Mid-West 100 years ago. These books have been popularized in the television production, *Little House on the Prairie*. Another appealing book is *Caddie Woodlawn*. This story features an active girl and warm family life of the time period.

Additional activities could include the following:

1. Students can research biographies of women leaders in the Women's Movement like: Gloria Steinem, Kate Millett, Betty Friedan, Mary McLeod Bethune, Jeanette Rankin, Carrie Chapman Catt, Julia Ward Howe, Lucy Stone, Susan B. Anthony, Elizabeth Cady Stanton, and Lucretia Mott. *Ms. Magazine* and *Current Biography* should be good resources for this project.
2. The class could invite grandmothers and/or great-grandmothers to visit in the classroom for a talk or panel dis-

cussion concerning how women's roles have changed.

3. Ask the class to check on a list of varied occupations, those occupations they think are suitable for women to hold. Tally the responses and display, using the blackboard or overhead projector. This should provide an opportunity for a class discussion. As a follow-up activity, the class could create a montage mural for the classroom wall that features the names of women in previously all-male roles along with pictures from current magazines.

4. Invite visitors to class who are persons from other countries to tell about customs toward and/or restrictions on women in their countries. Good resources are: Ireland's *Index to Women of the World* (Faxon, 1970) and *Reader's Guide to Periodical Literature.*

Adapted from an exercise by: Barbara Egel, Teacher, Wharton Jr. High

---

FOOD FOR THOUGHT

Foods have always been an avenue by which one can approach culture. This activity begins with individual perception and sense experiences and expands to include possible new cultural awarenesses.

Ask your class to begin by creating a list of interesting spices characterized by their unique smells. The kids can look up in the encyclopedia the origins of the spices. An initial selection (you add more) could be:

curry	dill
onion salt	chives
dried orange	ginger
oregano	cinnamon
garlic	nutmeg
white pepper	parsley
basil	sage
thyme	allspice

Collect the spices on your list and display them in class. Ask students to volunteer to "experience" the spices through the sense of smell. Blindfold your students and have them smell the

EXPERIENCING "STRANGE" FOODS LEADS TO EXPLORING THEIR BACKGROUNDS AND THE
PEOPLES WITH WHICH THEY ARE ASSOCIATED.

spices according to a fixed sequence. After each experience,
have the students note their sense reactions and share them with
others. Identification of the spices will yield interesting percep-
tual differences. Lead a discussion about the backgrounds of
certain spices and their individual cultural associations.

Afterwards, shift the focus of the activity from individual
awarenesses to cultural awareness. This stage begins with students experiencing types of basic vegetables prepared in a variety of ways from unique cultural recipes. A good resource here
is the "International Vegetables" line from Birdseye Food Company. Some examples reflecting diversity are:

Birdseye Vegetable Recipes
1. Mexican Style Vegetables
2. Bavarian Style Vegetables
3. Mediterranean Style Vegetables
4. Parisian Style Vegetables
5. Oriental Style Vegetables

Each recipe may be prepared, experienced, and discussed by
groups of students. Use the unique recipe ingredients to serve

as a class discussion starter about cultural differences in vegetable (or food) preparation.

Adapted from an exercise by: Barbara Egel, Teacher, Wharton Jr. High

---

READY, SET, GO!

This activity gets students to generate problem-solving information based on specific problems. It also encourages value assessment.

Ask the students to pretend they are hikers getting ready to make a trip from California to Tennessee. The year is 1977. Have each student make a list of the things they would carry with them. Provide an opportunity for classmates to compare their lists in small groups.

Afterwards, ask the pupils to consider what values were established by the lists they made. Are the items to be carried mostly practical in use? Are some items to be carried mainly for their sentimental value? Are pets included or left behind? Are there differences between lists made by boys and those made by girls? How would the lists differ from ones made by their parents? What item would you carry if you were limited to one?

On another day, ask the students to analyze their lists to determine what human need each item meets. Put each heading on a large sheet of newsprint:

> Physical Needs . . .
>
> Mental Needs . . .
>
> Emotional Needs . . .

and list the students' items under the appropriate heading. Does the length of the list tell what we value the most? Would the list be different if the students lived in Japan, Egypt, Norway, or some other country? This focus would permit the students to conjecture what students in other cultures would put on their lists, and then read about those countries and their cultures in order to generate the necessary information.

121

Another alternative activity would be to mount each student's list on a bulletin board without the name of the student. Let the class figure out which student wrote each list. This could be conducted as a contest.

Adapted from an exercise by: Katie Williams, Teacher, McKissack Elementary

---

AS YOU LIKE IT

This activity could become a super language arts lesson focusing on similes. It is a creative and divergent thinking activity for promoting self-understanding, classroom relationships, and cultural awareness.

Explain to your students the idea of simile development: "a figure of speech by which one thing, action, or relation is likened to or compared with unlike things." The word *like* or *as* usually is included in the expression. Discuss simile construction and write some examples on the blackboard. Stimulate students to contribute their own or perhaps complete some stems which you have listed, such as these:

Sly as a fox, _____
Soft as _____
Bouncy as jello, _____
Like kites in the air, _____
_____ as a kitten

Ask your students to discuss and evaluate their responses.

Your explanation of similes should include comments about how some similes are culturally related or culturally stereotypical. Examples being:

As brave as an Indian, _____
_____ as an Eskimo

Discuss the dangers and failures of stereotyping. One extension of this activity may be the acting out or demonstration of similes (as in the game of charades). Viewers of simile demonstrations would attempt to identify the idea.

Another extension would direct students to write similes about themselves. The writers would then choose a friend and write a simile for them. All similes could be shared with the entire class at this point.

122

The activity initially stimulates creative and divergent thinking as similes are created. Group reactions, individual or group responses, demonstrations, etc., are used to reinforce and reward individuality, class cohesiveness, and diversity in thinking.

Adapted from an exercise by: Cheryl Williams, Teacher, Gower Elementary

---

WE'VE GOT YOUR NUMBER

This activity will help the student relate symbol systems to different cultures. It will stimulate their awareness of the symbols around them.

For example, give each student a copy of a ditto sheet showing the symbols used by the Egyptians for their number system. Discuss the symbols and let the class try to figure out what the symbols represent. What can we learn about people's lives from understanding the symbols they use?

What are symbols that we recognize in our culture? Examples that can be mentioned include McDonald's golden arches, skull and crossbones, stars and stripes, arrows for direction, red lights, and the four-leaf clover.

Adapted from an exercise by: Mary Pagan, Teacher, McKissack Elementary, and Thelma Johnson, Teacher, Head Elementary

---

I WAS THERE . . . WERE YOU?

How we react to a surprising or frightening event depends on personal characteristics. This activity will encourage students to examine their own reactions and to explore the differences and similarities in their reactions to other people.

During the first part of your class, have another teacher storm into your room spouting parts of nursery rhymes and numbers, then pretend to cry or laugh, and leave. Ask the students to write down exactly what they saw and heard . . . what the teacher was wearing . . . what you, their teacher, did. Share the students' observations in discussion. See if you can group them. Did most students see and hear the same thing, or was there a lot of variation? What happens to people's observation powers when they are startled or frightened? Have you ever awakened in the middle of the night and mistaken something in the room for a person?

—Have your students pretend to be newspaper reporters at the scene of a crisis and write articles describing the scene. What questions would you ask by-standers? What would you ask those involved? Some examples of crises that could be used are a presidential assassination, a plane crash, an earthquake, or a kidnapping.

—Secure copies of several newspapers and news magazines that have articles of the same event. Let the class read them and discuss their similarities and discrepancies.

—A further activity is to examine words that have emotional content like an *irresponsible* act; a *faulty* decision; an *aggressive* man. Political speeches are good sources of emotional content. These words affect our feelings and prejudices. Have your students rewrite sentences and ads to make them less emotional. What are the facts that are left when emotional words are removed?

Adapted from an exercise by: Lynda Burton, Teacher, McKissack Elementary

---

C. School and Community Activities Focused on the Multi-Cultural Climate of the School

---

Introduction

by Martis M. Okpalobi

Family life culture provides the basic foundation for the development of a child's personality, characteristics, beliefs, values, self-attitudes, lifestyle, and other diverse but individually unique human behaviors. Sometimes, as a result of a community's cultural diversity, the purposes and goals parents have for their children are in direct conflict with those of the school. At other times, the purposes and goals of parents and schools are congruent, but the procedures and strategies for attaining them seem

124

to be in conflict. Such disharmony often happens when school and community people do not understand the "other's" culture. Without proper communication processes, the goals of both the school and the parents may be misunderstood and without support. Children become the losers.

The Nashville Teacher Corps implemented a number of practices to improve communication processes in the schools, and between the schools and the communities sending their children to the schools. Some of the most successful practices included weekly newsletters and student progress reports to parents *(Happy News Notes);* the involvement of teachers and parents on the Community Advisory Committee; visits to parents' homes; phone visits; and a school Handbook for Parents and Kids. The role of parents in the schools changed from that of infrequent visitor or chaperone at an annual party or field trip. Home visits became a successful means of enlisting parental interest and support. Parents became more involved in the schools. Contacts with parents outside the school also occurred more often. For example, in one school a parent worked with teachers over the summer in helping to develop useful supplemental mathematics and reading materials. At the end of the experience, the parent commented: "I got to know the teachers really well, and I grew more interested in what's going on at (my child's) school. . . . This will be a growing involvement."

At other schools, different kinds of school improvement practices were tried. Parents and teachers successfully planned and implemented all-school covered dish suppers. At each school, parents were volunteers in the classrooms. Their responsibilities ranged from tutoring students, including their own, to helping teachers make supplemental teaching aids. Two schools successfully implemented an "exploratory activities program" that provided the opportunity for teachers and parents to share their creative abilities with children. Expertise of parents and teachers was tapped in such areas as art, music, drama, culinary arts, photomaking, and anthropology. Related activities included Indian jewelry making, cultural songs (singing and writing), cooking from culturally different recipes, aerial photography of the immediate community, and many others.

In some situations, teachers planned and taught as a team. Parents were encouraged to participate with the teaching team by visiting the classroom, working in the classroom, helping to locate and contact other community resource persons, and participating in work of the Citizen's Advisory Committee. Some other ways teachers and parents worked together to improve the climate of the school were to circulate library books from the public library system, create a new P.T.A. image, initiate subsequent P.T.A. membership drives, and establish a school-community "resource club." The "teamness" involved the identification of each member's (teacher's and parent's) unique and individually different function in order to help all participants unite their best efforts toward common goals and a common philosophy for the work of the team.

One school in particular capitalized on the strengths and talents of each teacher and openly encouraged teachers to truly share their ideas with one another. These teachers attempted to create an atmosphere conducive to building healthy human relationships among adults and children. As a result of their commitment, the teachers and parents participated in a one-week summer preplanning work session. At the workshop, using a group consensus decision-making process, they established priorities, purposes, and a philosophy for the operation of "teamness" within the school. The immediate outcomes of the session reflected a plan for their new type of school—a plan to help each child realize his/her individual uniqueness and potential; a plan to encourage flexibility and trial and error. More and more parents are finding themselves teamed with their kids in the schooling process.

Activities designed to enhance healthy school-community relationships must take place or the classroom learnings will be forgotten or ignored outside of school. The activities described on subsequent pages are a series of related approaches which were designed in the Nashville Teacher Corps program to improve the multi-cultural understandings between school personnel, parents, and students. Many of these activities support and encourage two-way communication between the school and the home, between teachers, and between students and teachers. They also increase cultural literacy, develop supportive relationships, and enhance the valuing of human differences. Generally, each activity in this section was designed with one or more of the following purposes:

—Improving the all-school multi-cultural climate (i.e., the positive, happy feelings that children and adults have about

126

each other; how well they interact; how fully they value their differences).

—Improving the multi-cultural climate between the school and community (including school activities, field experiences and practica which explored the communities of the school in order to understand multi-ethnicity, multi-culturalism, and multiplicity of talents of its residents and citizenry; their economic life, their government, and the workings of their planning groups—official and unofficial; public agencies whose work related to the lives of students and their families; and relevant communication media with their positions and patterns of influence).

—Team planning approaches (such as building healthy working relationships among adults, developing healthy teacher concepts of self and appreciation of self, and a trusting school climate).

—Increased communication (although languages, beliefs, lifestyles, values, and behaviors of adults differ, they have mutual understanding of what is important in order to help children grow and develop. Also, adults can work together through common approaches to enable students to learn better and teachers to teach better.)

Some guiding principles which functioned to improve the multi-cultural school and community climate were these:

1. Problems are precipitated and aggravated by a lack of clear communication between school and home, and by lack of a positive school climate.
2. Community members and school personnel should be sensitive to the mutual dependence of school climate and school-community communications, and other relationships involving the communities of the school and the school's organizational characteristics.
3. In order to resolve problems interfering with maintaining a positive school climate, the planning and operating of all school projects should include the active participation of parents, kids, and teachers.
4. In order to develop good feelings about the school's role in helping kids learn, grow, and develop, parents should be informed about and included in developing and improving the school program.

Inservice education opportunities provided the teachers with the support necessary to develop new strategies on the job. They created new ways of improving communication between the schools and the communities of the school, and in all-school activities and in-class activities. The multi-cultural climate of the schools was enriched and this resulted in more comfortable schools for learning by children and teaching by adults. The following are selected activities designed to serve as examples of how to improve the multi-cultural climate of a school.

THE "ALL-SCHOOL" FESTIVAL

Amazing excitement and high-level morale among teachers, kids, and parents are generated when the school and community are involved in a multi-cultural festival! Such an activity can be based upon historical holidays, sports events, community celebrations, or significant accomplishments. For example, you might want to create, as we did, a multi-cultural celebration of the Christmas holiday season. First, get the teachers and community folks together and sort out your purposes. These were ours:

—To develop everyone's awareness, appreciation, and understanding of different cultures and the contribution each has made to the growth and development of our world.

—To develop this awareness through the study of selected countries and their customs during celebration of the holiday season.

—To understand lifestyles of these countries through media, such as art, music, foods, etc., as they relate to the holiday season.

—To become aware of, and to examine, the Christmas trees of other cultures and countries in order to see that the celebration of Christmas is unique and distinctive, depending on where it is celebrated.

Ask each class to participate in the study of a different country and the significance of their unique celebrations of the holiday season. Students should make decorations unique to the selected country or culture, and use them to decorate their classrooms, a tree displayed in their room, and the school hallways. Each class could contribute to the decoration of a multi-cultural auditorium.

128

Have the musical groups in the school and community practice and present a multi-cultural music festival which would include the music and dances from the many cultures celebrating the season. Parents and other citizens could be invited. The kids will also enjoy making cookies and other refreshments to serve each other and their guests. These goodies should also reflect the many cultures represented by the classrooms. Let each class and your community guests move from room to room to learn from each classroom the ways that country or culture celebrates Christmas (students in each classroom take turns being tour guides). Thinking up skits, plays, pantomimes, slide shows and other presentations for these touring groups will be a challenge to each classroom.

Here are some of the topical trees for classrooms that you might want to include in your celebration:

George Washington	Mexico
Pioneer American	Tree of Jessee
Germany	Ukraine
China	Bicentennial
Lithuania	U. S. Community
African (numerous styles)	Denmark
Finland	France
Holland	Moravian
Old Russia	U. N. Tree
Festivals at Chanukah and Christmas	

For information on how to decorate cultural trees write: Tennessee Botanical Gardens and Fine Arts Center, Cheekwood Botanical Gardens, Cheek Road, Nashville, Tennessee 37205.

This activity provides students and adults with an opportunity to become involved in many different ways in the study of other cultures and traditions. The emphasis on Christmas could serve as a base for continued study and foster other understandings throughout the year. A holiday such as Thanksgiving could initiate a cultural festival. Between the Thanksgiving and Christmas season a great deal of time could be spent through art, music, discussions, celebrations, etc., sharing with kids and adults the customs unique to the season. The universal symbolism of light in pagan, Hebrew, and Christian cultures may be explored, or the festivals of Chanukah, Christmas, and the winter solstice.

"One example of the activities initiated by the community program that helped improve the multi-cultural climate of the school was a Halloween Party which brought together 400 participants. It generated some enjoyable communications between students and parents—Black and White. We also held an Ecumenical/School Open Meeting . . . where Black ministers, the Director of Metro Schools, and others met in the community and discussed concerns of mutual interest."

Whether you celebrate the coming of spring, summer, fall or holidays, multi-cultural festivals are grand opportunities for your students and community folks . . . and teachers, too!

Adapted from an exercise by: Aldorothy Wright, Principal, and James Hartman, Paul Cotton, and all other teachers at Ford Greene Elementary

---

POT LUCK TOGETHERNESS

If you are looking for activities that bring parents, teachers, and students together, here's one that everyone seems to enjoy. A school-wide covered dish supper provides an informal, relaxed atmosphere for teachers, students, and their families to spend an evening getting to know one another better. The result can be a heightened feeling of trust between school and community.

After securing the permission of the principal, identify several teachers who support the idea of a covered dish supper and are willing to serve as the planning committee for it. Their first responsibility should be to identify several parents to assist in planning the supper. Using whatever means (telephone calls, notes carried by students, letters mailed out) is most feasible, notify all parents about the supper. Get the students in on the act by having them draft letters, make centerpieces, design placemats, and so on.

If you want to go a step further than just bringing people together for a nice evening, then give the supper a multi-cultural emphasis. Ask all parents to bring a dish that reflects their culture. If there is some doubt that the dishes will be recognized, have the students make signs for the dishes their parents are bringing. In this way, people will know they are eating German potato salad or Indian spoon bread.

Some multi-cultural entertainment might also be fun. Do a little research and locate parents who have a talent they would be willing to share with the group. Kids also usually love a chance to join in with friends for an evening of "hamming" it up. Let your imagination go—you're bound to "come up with something." Your multi-cutural covered dish supper may be such a hit that you'll want to do it again and again. Don't be surprised to hear such comments as, "it worked," "a smashing success," and "I wouldn't mind making this an annual event."—We did!

Adapted from an exercise by: Doris Adams, Donna Barr, Karen Catignani, Pamela Craig, Jean Elchesen, Mary Pagan, and Ann Robertson, Teachers, McKissack Elementary

A CASE IN POINT

An example of the impact parents and community folks can have on the educational opportunities of children in an ongoing fashion is described in this selection. We choose it because it is simple and to the point. Adults coming into the school to work with children help kids *and* adults enrich their understandings of others. Often we overlook these opportunities. For our kids it opened multiple doors.

In any school you will probably find that although some students have public library cards, most do not. In fact, many children have never even visited a public library and are unaware of the resources available to them.

Identify several parents and/or community members who are willing to help you with this project. For best results, have one parent per every four to six students. Hold a meeting with the parents in which you explain that you would like to have kids really discover the library—not just for reading, but for exploring hobbies and interests in greater depth; for discovering different kinds of music; for looking at films; and for attending and/or participating in puppet shows and story-telling sessions.

The parents' role is to volunteer about a half a day every couple of weeks to take their four to six kids to the library. Once there, they can help the children use the card catalog and locate materials. They may also want to read a story to the students, show them a film, or watch a play and talk about the plot and characters. They should also keep abreast of the activities sponsored by the library so that their groups may attend such events should they be things the students would enjoy.

The students should be encouraged to read one another's books, to share an interesting point with the rest of the class, or to suggest group and/or class projects that result from a "find" at the library. To make a long story short—parents often rediscover the library, get involved with kids, and feel good about themselves because of it. Kids (who otherwise might not ever see the library) get turned on to libraries, learn to use their facilities, and have a rich experience as a result of their association with a parent.

Adapted from an exercise by: Donna Barr and Jean Elchesen, Teachers, McKissack Elementary

---

EXPLORATORY COMMUNITY PROGRAMS

This all-school activity will provide almost unlimited opportunities for kids, teachers, and community members to enrich the multi-cultural climate of the school. It is based on the assumption that kids want to explore new skills and understandings and that the school is the place for such exploration.

Begin by doing a survey of teachers and students. Ask what they would like to teach and learn that is not normally a part of the school program. Make your list and distribute it to the kids to explore the demand. Of course, the length and time involvement will have to be decided. (One of our schools schedules two mornings per week for these activities, with each exploratory activity lasting nine weeks, then a new list is created and kids switch to a different activity reflecting their choice.) A letter to parents and other community folks can bring them into the school to teach or assist teachers on a regular schedule. This activity is ideal for the community member who would like to work with kids one or two mornings or afternoons a week.

Be certain that each student is able to participate in at least one of his/her top three choices. You might want to arrange the switching of students into new choice-based activities every three, six, nine, etc., weeks to respond to interest and need. Every exploratory activity can be designed to emphasize multi-cultural learnings. After a while you might want to select some of your students to teach in the exploratory offerings.

Selected examples of exploratory activities several Nashville Teacher Corps schools implemented were:

Folk Dancing	Macrame
Pottery	Guitar
Independent Reading	Coin/Stamp Collecting
Jigsaw Puzzles	The American Musical Theater
Jewelry Making	Needlepoint
Baby Sitting	Stitchery
Poetry	Sign Language
Crocheting	Arts and Crafts
Plants and Plant Care	Cooking
Table Games	Drawing
Knitting	Typing
Beginning Piano	Industrial Arts
Microscopes	Band
Hunting and Fishing	Spanish
Athletics	French
Advertising	Baking
Newspapers	Classics
Media	

Remember . . . every exploratory activity can be designed to increase cultural literacy and develop healthier human relationships and self-concepts among the participating children and adults.

Adapted from the faculties of: Ford Greene Elementary and Washington Jr. High

---

CREATING A MULTI-CULTURAL TEAM

This idea is based on the assumption that several people sharing the same purposes and working together in a supportive fashion can enhance the multi-cultural climate of the school. You may not believe in teaming in your teaching, but this activity is the result of it in Nashville. It briefly reports what happened and suggests that you might want to try some aspect of it, in your own way, with your colleagues and/or community members.

Identify several teachers who understand the cultural diversity and individual uniqueness of students served by your school.

Pull together a small group and develop a process for exploring middle school concepts relating to alternative approaches to teaching and learning experiences. Help may be found in the library, your school administration, or a local college. They might consent to provide a workshop to serve your specific interests. Similar groups of teachers in your school might become involved.

In the beginning, the group should set the purposes they are committed to achieve. Use a process to help the group reach a true consensus. An outside facilitator can be really helpful to the group as it tries to set a reasonable and clear set of purposes and goals for your multi-cultural teaching team. Here's an example of such purposes and goals:

—To create a non-threatening atmosphere for learning which will help students explore creative activities and succeed in school.

—To develop a learning environment conducive to the students' response to decision making in responsible and independent ways.

—To teach basic skills in content areas and to integrate various areas of learning across disciplines.

—To identify and work toward meeting the diverse cognitive, affective, and psychomotor needs of individual students.

—To promote development of positive concepts of self and healthy human relationships among students and adults with whom they come in contact.

—To apply basic skills from content areas to everyday life.

—To help children become more culturally literate.

Once you have set similar directions, your team of teachers, kids, and parents should assume new roles in planning and implementing school experiences. Teachers can develop a climate wherein they accept and support others' ideas even though different from their own. This kind of teaming will help everyone understand that "it's okay" for kids and parents to assume classroom leadership roles. It does not usurp the teachers' command in the classroom, but strengthens it. Of course, developing a process to have student input on a systematic basis into curriculum decision-making is imperative. Representative elections to pick kids to take part in the teacher planning sessions is one way. Bringing community people and parents into those decisions will enrich the team. A weekly newsletter will help the kids, teachers, and parents interact more. Together, they plan for the reporting of what goes on in the team; they can write, edit, type, print, and publish the paper as a group effort. Parents will enjoy sharing the paper with their kids.

Many of the interdisciplinary multi-cultural activities described in this book can be implemented and broadened throughout the teaching team. These and others like them can be used more often because of the increased energies and commitment of the group.

Adapted from an exercise by the Mini-School Instructional Team at Washington Jr. High: Liz Bivens, Wayne Betts, Janet Szczypien, and Bob Rice, Teachers; Johnny Thompson, Sheila Patterson, Kathy Bryant, and Esther Wright, Interns; and John Lifsey, Team Leader

---

SCHOOL CLIMATE IMPROVEMENT PROJECTS

Multi-cultural school improvement projects can be designed to focus on the communications within the school; to identify, examine, and improve the school's belief and value system (philosophy, purposes, and goals); to broaden the school's performance expectations; and to humanize the classroom and/or school's reward and punishment system. Such projects which focus on the modification of the basic nature of the school itself will, in turn, help provide the necessary climate for a multi-cultural school. Here are the kinds of projects you and your colleagues might develop to improve the multi-cultural nature of your school:

—Study and revise the school's reporting systems so that it is possible for everyone to feel that she/he is succeeding every day.

—Design and develop a new organizational plan to encourage decentralized decision-making which includes parents and students.

—Develop projects to include students in the direction and evaluation of their own work.

—Replace the present achievement recognition system with one that emphasizes more immediate and widespread rewards for tasks well done.

—Develop student and teacher retreats, or form in-school dis-

". . . a series of early morning teachers' meetings prior to the school day . . . (were conducted by) the school systems' human relations department. These helped us to question the appropriateness of our perceptions; examine the strengths and weaknesses of our individual communication systems; examine causes for people being untruthful; and support strong feelings of concern for the human community. Some insights expressed were: People are different . . . Words have many meanings . . . People can be cast in roles based on the assumptions of others! Some of our activities were adapted for use with our students."

cussion groups, designed to foster open communication, mutual respect, and understanding.

—Ask the parents, teachers, and students to become involved in an ongoing process of studying the inconsistencies which exist between what the school's philosophy statement says and the manner in which the school's programs operate. This could lead to a revision of school purposes and curriculum workshops to organize more responsive programs and grouping patterns.

—Form a task force to talk with some of the students really "turned off" by school. Listen carefully to their description of how school affects their attitudes toward themselves and others. On a regular basis, create a plan to do something about at least one of the concerns expressed by the group.

The above list is only suggestions, but does advocate a number of practices that have worked to enhance the multi-cultural climate of a school. In an improvement project undertaken by one Nashville Teacher Corps school, the faculty spent an entire week during summer break working carefully to establish their purposes and goals. A process approach helped them reach consensus on purposes, goals, school philosophy, and program. Notice the support for implementing a multi-cultural climate and program for their school in their list of purposes ranked according to priority:

1. To provide an atmosphere of equal opportunity for all children (success).
2. To provide opportunities that will foster self-discipline and self-responsibility ("group" decisions, "individual" decisions).
3. To provide for individual learning differences.
4. To provide a climate in which children can develop a positive self-concept.

5. To develop positive relationships and respect for others' opinions (understand and appreciate others).
6. To develop reading skills.
7. To offer life-related learning situations.
8. To create an atmosphere which will stimulate the desire to learn and will foster an appreciation for learning itself.
9. To ensure a climate which is conducive to creative, positive learning at all times.
10. To develop math skills.

Adapted from an exercise by: Michael G. Pasternak, Associate Professor, George Peabody College

---

PARENTS AND CITIZENS ARE "IN"
(The Schools)

This activity is based upon the assumption that the more you bring diverse people together, the richer everyone will become. Begin by exploring with your students what parents and other community folks could offer your classroom. Could they help students learn about careers by explaining their occupations? Help learn about new skills and understandings related to music, arts, crafts, leisure activities, hobbies? Assist in classroom activities related to science, language arts, or mathematics? Take class members on field trips? Do a thorough brainstorming with your students and make a list of areas that you and the class would like to invite community members to help you with. Next, devise forms of communication that will bring in the helpers. Sometimes a simple note to parents and others requesting specific assistance will get the ball rolling. Be certain to open the door for volunteers in areas not included on your list. You may find community people coming up with good ideas that your class did not think of.

Here are several ideas the Nashville Teacher Corps teachers have used to increase parent/community involvement:
—Identify a few teachers and community members to act as recruiters for teachers seeking volunteers in the schools. Even though all of the teachers can become involved in recruiting, it will help to have assistance from those who are really good at it.

A STUDENT INTERVIEWS A PARENT IN A SCHOOL PROJECT TO LEARN ABOUT THE COM-
MUNITY AND ITS CULTURAL CHARACTERISTICS.

—Make phone calls to colleges, local sport teams, local in-
dustries, religious groups, youth groups, and state historical and other associations to ask for assistance in your
room.

—Organize family night field trips for your whole class,
friends, students, relatives, and anyone else that wants to
enjoy an evening of fun.

—Regularly make telephone calls to the parents about the
"Good News" progress of their children.

—Ask parents to come to school and work with their children
in skill development and other activities. If the parents
both work, hold regular evening game nights where learning games for parents and kids could be shared.

—Involve parents in your classroom advisory council. Make
all of your parents official members. Ask parents to meet
with you once a month to plan new activities for your classroom for parents, kids, and other community participants.

—Initiate a classroom newsletter that both adults and kids
would create and share on a weekly or bi-weekly basis.

—Develop a feedback questionnaire and ask parents to fill it out on a monthly basis to indicate how they feel their children are progressing, how the class might be improved, and what they might be able to do to help.

—Develop a pupil progress reporting plan that will express to parents how well their children are doing at school.

—Create a class trip that requires parents and children to take a train or bus trip out of state to visit a unique cultural setting. The fund-raising and chaperoning activities will pull together your parent group. Kids will find that the trip provides them the opportunity to interact with each other in new ways outside of school. You might want to do this activity combining several classrooms and parent groups.

—Hold a school mascot contest (or classroom contest) where students and parents nominate mascot ideas (animals, cars, heroes, etc.) and then vote. Ask kids, parents, and community members to design the insignia representing the new mascot and then make flags, shirts, stationery, bumper stickers, etc. Sell the product and lift the spirit of your classroom and school. A happy classroom/school "self-concept" can be developed through such spirit-building activities.

Your kids will learn through many of these activities how they can use the community as a resource for their learning . . . especially from those culturally different from themselves.

Adapted from exercises by: Approximately 50 Teacher Corps Participants

---

SCHOOL-COMMUNITY COMMUNICATIONS

Probably the greatest threat to positive school-community relations is a lack of communication. Teachers claim that parents *aren't* interested in their kids' schools, *won't* come to conferences, *don't* understand what the school is trying to do and so on. Parents say they are *not* welcome at school, teachers *don't* tell them what's going on, and the only time they hear from school is when their child is in trouble. Here are some suggestions that do not require a great deal of time and expense but show fantastic "pay off"—just by using the school duplicating machine and the talents of students, parents, community members, and teachers to create school-community publications.

139

A classroom newsletter is one idea to keep parents in touch with "what's happening" in their child's classroom. This is different from the traditional all-school newsletter which generally focuses on business and administrative matters. The classroom newsletter may include some all-school business, but its primary function is to provide a means of letting parents know about their child's classroom. Be sure to include a section for parent contributions, a section for student contributions, current areas of study and new student needs generated by them, newsworthy items (like who has a new baby in the family, who has kittens to give away, etc.) and anything else you feel is pertinent. As you explore cultural differences with your students, your most valuable resource could be parents with their diverse range of experiences and backgrounds. Parents must sense that you are sincere in your appreciation of the contribution they make and of their presence in the classroom. Before long the word will get around and you will have all kinds of parental support!

Another school publication that can result in better school-community understanding is a handbook distributed to parents. The purpose should be to provide a guide to parents for better understanding the school's purposes and goals and how they, as parents, can best support those goals so that their children will receive the maximum benefit from their school experience. The handbook should not be full of educational jargon, but rather should provide simple guidelines in laymen's terms. Include such basics as the importance of regular attendance and sufficient rest, and asking the child about his school day, and the more complex matters of communicating with your child ("listening" to what he's telling you non-verbally as well as verbally), dealing with behavior problems and so forth. It is not difficult to find parents who are willing to work on this endeavor with you. A caution: don't get "preachy." Your parents represent a diverse group and any handbook must reflect a respect for those differences. But almost all parents, regardless of their differences, will support a teacher and school they believe truly represents the best interests of their child.

After you have a firm support base from parents, you may find some who are interested in helping compile a directory of resources available in the community. This publication would be a great service to the community as well as to the teachers in the school. It should include such things as charitable agencies and

STUDENTS INTERVIEW A BANKER ABOUT LENDING REGULATIONS THAT PROTECT MINORITY GROUP MEMBERS.

their services, medical clinics, special education services, adoption facilities, mental health facilities, legal aid, and so on. If you are in a school where children are bused from different areas, be certain you include the resources from *all* areas. It is possible someone might find a needed service in another part of town. The directory should include: name of agency, address, phone number, and a brief statement describing services available and fee (if any).

Adapted from an exercise by: Twenty-one teachers at McKissack, Wharton, and Ford Greene elementary schools

---

THE MEDIA PROGRAM FOR PARENTS

Want to bring parents into the school to become involved in multi-cultural activities and at the same time give kids feedback about how well they are doing in school? If so, you and your kids create a slide-tape presentation as a media overview of your

141

"An example of how we used community resources was the green circle program. It consisted of stories about outcast animals (representing individualism). Actually any story may be created wherein the main character does not "fit in" with society. A green circular flannel board was erected to represent society and individuals within it. Discussion focused on the "whys and hows" behind the animal character's struggle with his environment and society. Analogies were drawn between the animal's experiences and how we, as people, react toward others and wrongly 'place' them outside of our circles of relationships and interaction. Some of the examples we explored were the 'unpopular' individual and his/her classmates, Chinese Americans in our community, relationships—adult-child, black-white, and student-teacher. The whole thing supported our multi-cultural program. Kids related to supporting diversity through how it could affect them." (Ford Greene Elementary Teacher)

multi-cultural activities. The goal is to get students interested in recording things they do and parents interested in seeing their products and being supportive and involved.

Ask some of your students to be the photographers to share a series of your multi-cultural activities by capturing some of the products on film. Have other students make a cassette tape to go with the film in order to describe its significance and meaning. If you have a video-tape recorder and Super 8 camera you might be able to use all three processes to develop a media production. Ask the parents to an evening production, or show it at parents' night or P.T.A. Draft yourself some helpers and supporters.

Adapted from an exercise by: Kathy Bryant, Teacher Corps Intern, Washington Jr. High

Part II

Identification and Communication of Multi - Cultural Resources

Developing a Resource Center for Multi-Cultural Education

by Jane Bandy Smith

Jane Bandy Smith was responsible for the success of the Nashville Teacher Corps multi-cultural resource center. Planning, coordinating, and improving every aspect of a responsive instructional center was an enormous task. She also worked as an instructor with teachers who requested assistance in developing multi-cultural activities. All of these accomplishments she related to her doctoral studies in Curriculum Leadership at George Peabody College. The following is her description of how to develop a multi-cultural resource center. It reflects her outstanding efforts.

A primary goal of the multi-cultural program is to integrate multi-cultural activities into the existing curriculum by means of teacher-initiated plans. Therefore, the aim of our resource center was to support the Nashville program's efforts to facilitate and foster classroom activities that explore cultural diversity and individual uniqueness.

One of our first decisions was to develop the center as teacher-oriented and not for student use. We saw the role of our resource center as auxiliary to the school library. In order to promote this partnership, we actively sought a cooperative relationship with all the librarians in the Teacher Corps schools by providing copies of our bibliographies and offering access to any materials within the resource center.

Next, we decided that our collection would focus on free or inexpensive materials, although we wanted to be aware of the commercial materials available. Our intention was to become informed about commercial materials so that we could aid teachers in obtaining the materials they would need in their multi-cultural lessons. We planned to build our collection of multi-cultural films, books, and tapes from the free or inexpensive materials available.

Since many variations in developing a multi-cultural resource center are possible, it was important for us to set priorities regarding our center's use of money, time, and effort. Our staff discussed a list of proposed activities for our center and established priorities. This interaction and discussion is extremely important to the success of a resource center because it clarifies goals, increases understanding of the program, and analyzes possible problems.

In setting the parameters and priorities for our center, we were able to define our purposes as:

To provide access to relevant holdings of other institutions that would relate to the school's multi-cultural program.

To act as an impetus for production of teacher-made materials and as a collection place for those materials.

To serve as a clearinghouse for human resources that would enrich multi-cultural activities.

To collect professional materials that would increase faculty awareness and knowledge.

To provide facilities and a meeting place that would stimulate professional development.

Simply stated, our objective was to encourage and aid the classroom teacher, through any means available, to implement lessons which incorporated multi-cultural implications.

We prepared written descriptions of our objectives, priorities, parameters, and proposed methods of meeting our objectives. This written account is serviceable when you need to orient a new staff member. A detailed plan also aids in evaluating the effectiveness of the center, since it provides a blueprint of objectives with which you can compare your activities. Such a plan should be filed in the center for easy access and frequent reference.

THE PROCESS

Though we wanted our center's appearance to reflect the program, we planned a minimum outlay of money on the physical aspects of the center. A room in one of the schools, adjacent to the Teacher Corps offices, was designated as the resource center. The furniture consisted of whatever could be found; although quite a mixture, it proved to be effective. We discovered that we needed filing cabinets, portable bookshelves, a large table, and a number of chairs. This equipment was used to provide storage and display for our materials. In order to make our center more attractive, we put up some colorful posters, prepared a multi-cultural bulletin board, developed a "notes and news" center, and added some green plants.

It was important to design the center so that it would interest people in the program and the materials housed there. One good idea is to borrow materials from public libraries and create displays in the resource center. A local travel agency is a possible source for posters to use in decorating the center. Health department brochures on diseases common to ethnic groups, magazine articles about lifestyles, news clippings, and human interest stories are some possibilities for bulletin board displays to help make the center an interesting place.

Our search for information and materials began with a visit to the local public library. Most libraries are on a film circuit, a network of cooperating libraries that share film purchases, and they have 16mm films which can be borrowed without charge. Sometimes it is even possible to borrow a projector from the library. During our initial visit to the public library, we secured a list of available films having multi-cultural applications and put a chart in the center outlining the correct procedures for obtaining the films. Users need to know how to reserve films, the length of time they may be checked out, and how to fill out the viewer information slip for the library.

We made lists of relevant records, tapes, pictures, magazines, and services that were available from the public library. We also discussed the goals of our program with the librarian and obtained a bibliography of the holdings related to ethnic groups.

As a second step in locating information, we went to the local college and university libraries where we followed a similar procedure of checking the card catalog for multi-cultural books, magazines, and records. Colleges which have teacher education programs may also have a curriculum laboratory where copies of texts, games, filmstrips, and other teaching materials can be obtained for use or display in a resource center.

School systems usually have a central media collection in addition to the individual school libraries. This central collection is an excellent source for materials with which to enrich your program, and it is wise to establish a good relationship with the central director. Occasionally, classroom teachers do not know the process to use in securing items from this centralized collection and are not aware of relevant materials that be obtained from this source. Your teaching resource center can facilitate use of the centralized collection by compiling bibliographies of available books or media and educating teachers about the procedures to use in obtaining these materials.

The State Library and the State Department of Education are also sources to explore for multi-cultural materials. You should write a letter to the director of each or visit these institutions to explain your program and determine what resources are available.

Visit the local school supply houses and become acquainted with their stock. If possible, arrange for a display, examination, or trial use of the materials that support your program. Organize a group of faculty and staff members to examine and discuss the materials you have located. This group process will result in a greater understanding of which materials are desirable and worthwhile as teaching aids for your program. It is especially important to obtain the opinion of minority members on your staff and faculty about materials which deal with their ethnic groups. Materials have been produced that promote stereotypes and are either insensitive or incorrect in their treatment of minorities. Asking for an evaluation of materials by a minority staff member is a means of eliminating this problem.

The business community is a fruitful area to search for materials that focus on diversity and uniqueness. The utility companies in many sections of the country offer 16mm films on a free loan basis. Films you order can be returned by library rate mail, which is very low in cost. Look for other businesses in your area that might have published or pictorial materials to use "as is" or to convert into effective teaching resources. The Yellow Pages of the telephone book is a good source list of businesses.

Media is an area that should be constantly monitored and explored for multi-cultural programming. Television stations have advance information on national programming and are also informed about locally-produced programs that may be relevant. Local programs reveal interesting resource people, places for field trips, and facts about people's lifestyles, roles, or cultures

—good multi-cultural materials. Acquaint the management of these stations with your resource center's aims and ask their co-operation in securing information about multi-cultural programs.

Public television provides offerings that can be used in a multi-cultural school program. The Public Television Library (PTL) is a-department of the Public Broadcasting Service and has a number of videotapes that may be rented or reduplicated for a small fee. PTL will send you annotated brochures of their programs. Send your request to: The Public Television Library, Video Program Service, 475 L'Enfant Plaza, S. W., Washington, D.C. 20024. The categories for their 2,000 videotapes include: "Public Affairs and Current Issues," "The Arts, Health and Science," "How-to/Instructional," "Sports and Recreation," "Children," and "Coping with the 70s."

Marvelous sources for up-to-date information and activities are the following magazines: *Teacher, Instructor, Learning,* and *Media and Methods.* The latter is a publication that contains complete information on national television programs, including lessons and follow-up suggestions for teachers. These magazines have many reviews, articles, and advertisements that provide ideas and information.

Newspapers are an inexpensive, yet timely way to gather materials that deal with the diversity and commonality of people. Articles taken from newspapers can be used on a bulletin board, duplicated for additional reading material, laminated for use in a learning center, or serve as initiators for lessons or books. Material for multi-cultural lessons can be found, for example, in an article describing food or fashion from other cultures, an in-depth study of foreign-born people living in an area of the United States, a reporter's exploration of ethnic problems, or a biographical study of a current figure. For additional ideas of effective classroom use of newspapers, you can order *Newspaper in the Classroom Project,* a 68-page teacher's guide from *The Tennessean,* 1100 Broadway, Nashville, Tennessee 37203 ($3.25 plus postage).

In an effort to find out what others in the field of education were doing in multi-cultural education, we searched the ERIC system (Educational Resource Information Center) in college and university libraries. These reports can be ordered in microfilm or printed form from ERIC Document Reproduction Service (EDRS). These materials are inexpensive, but special equipment is needed for reading those in microfilm. For a list of ERIC entries that relate to multi-cultural education, see the resource list in the next section (pp. 164-165).

Our staff wanted to know what available commercial materials had multi-cultural education implications so we could be more aware of instructional possibilities they provided. Therefore, we sent a form letter to commercial suppliers to request a copy of their current catalog. We located the names and addresses of publishers and media producers in the second volume of *Books in Print, Education Media Yearbook,* and *Materials and Human Resources for Teaching Ethnic Studies* (Social Science Education Consortium, Inc.) Copies of *Books in Print* and *Education Media Yearbook* are available in local public libraries or in college libraries. Be certain that your letters to these companies are written on your organization's letterhead stationery.

We also sent form letters requesting free materials to organizations and associations. For each letter sent, we made a card listing the name and address of the company and compiled a master card file of requests. As the organizations and associations responded, we made notations on the corresponding cards of the items that were sent. Names and addresses of organizations producing multi-cultural materials can be found in *Materials and Human Resources for Teaching Ethnic Studies* or *The Directory of Associations,* which are available in a public or college library.

Two of the best sources for multi-cultural materials that are well prepared and reasonable in cost are: the Anti-Defamation League of B'nai B'rith (315 Lexington Avenue, New York, New York 10016; North Carolina-Virginia Regional Office: Suite 202, 4615 West Broad Street, Richmond, Virginia 23230; Southeast Regional Office: 805 Peachtree Street, N.E., Atlanta, Georgia 30308) and, the Council on Interracial Books for Children (CIBC Resource Center, Room 300, 1841 Broadway, New York, New York 10023). The Anti-Defamation League (ADL) provides materials for teachers and students that include publications, audiovisuals, simulations, songs, and inservice programs. The Council on Interracial Books for Children (CIBC), which has been in existence for about eleven years, publishes *The Bulletin,* which reviews books and learning materials for racism and sexism. The CIBC Resource Center publishes books and teaching materials that are designed to develop pluralism in schools; and, in addition, it conducts inservice workshops and training programs for schools. Some of the materials that are available from these two organizations are listed in the resource section following this article. If you were planning to contact only two sources, these two are highly recommended from our experience.

It is always important to have correct facts before you teach, and multi-cultural education is no exception. Perhaps it is even more critical to be accurate in the case of multi-cultural education because of the feelings and emotions of people involved. It is, however, more difficult to acquire dependable bias-free materials in this area than in others. Some guidelines can be offered that might be useful when you are selecting multi-cultural materials.

Since writers effectively write about life that is known and significant to themselves, you will find that writers of authority in multi-cultural materials are frequently part of these cultures, religions, or ethnic groups. For illustration, James Banks is a Black American who has written prolifically about that ethnic group. Jack Forbes, Professor of Native American Studies at the University of California, is of Powhatan Indian descent and has written numerous books and articles about Native Americans. Carlos E. Cortes, in addition to his teaching responsibilities, is a contributing editor to the Mexican-American periodical *Aztlan* and has written extensively about the Chicano experience. This is not to say that a writer must be a member of a minority in order to write effectively about that group, but it does follow logic that interest is heightened through first-hand experience and that accuracy is more easily obtained.

It is helpful to investigate an author's background in order to understand why that author has chosen to deal with certain topics or subcultures. Frequently, you find authors who write repeatedly about a culture or subculture. If the information about the author cannot be found inside the book jacket or in the book preface, you can probably find it in one of the following reference sources which are generally available at public or college libraries:

Bibliography Index: A Cumulative Index to Biographical
  Materials, Books, and Magazines
Contemporary Authors: A Bio-bibliographical Guide to
  Current Authors and Their Work
Current Biography
Twentieth Century Authors

You can also use these reference tools to gather information about minority figures to develop biographies suitable for your instructional level. Teachers frequently request biographical information to supplement textbook information, since texts and curriculum materials have been guilty of slighting the contributions of minority members. A resource center can prepare biographies of ethnic leaders as a service to teachers.

A list of reference books usually available at public or college libraries which will assist you in finding sources of information relating to multi-cultural education are given in the resource section following this article. Reference to the bibliographies given in books and at the end of journal articles can also aid you in locating professional reading for faculty members who are involved in implementing multi-cultural activities. In the *Forty-third Yearbook of the National Council for the Social Studies* there are informative articles and excellent suggestions for multi-cultural programs and curricula. This book was printed by the National Education Association and should be available in any college library.

THE RESULTS

In this section, we will specify some of our resource centers' outcomes and relate them to its purposes in the Nashville Teacher Corps's multi-cultural education program. Our first purpose was to provide access to relevant holdings of other institutions that would relate to the multi-cultural program in the schools. Thus, we established a relationship with the librarians in the participating school libraries and requested that they watch for relevant materials to bring to the attention of the teachers. Though we purchased some materials, most often our center's holdings were obtained by loan from other institutions. Frequently, we provided the teaching staff with a list of materials available from various institutions and outlined the procedure for them to use in securing these materials. To facilitate utilization of these materials, we compiled a list of places where audiovisual equipment could be rented or repaired and posted this list of equipment sources in the resource center.

One of our staff's tasks was to compile bibliographies on different subjects. We thought these lists of books and media would be invaluable to teachers who wanted material to supplement a textbook, to initiate individual projects, to meet individual needs for materials, to interest or motivate a child or a group, or to furnish a remedial reader with material on an appropriate level. It is desirable to have these lists readily available so you can provide the materials or suggest applicable titles when they are needed rather than have to initiate a search after a request has been made. An excellent source for bibliographies which focus on ethnic groups is George D. Spache's *Good Reading for the Disadvantaged Reader* (Champaign, Ill.: Garrard, 1975). Another source is Bowker's *Subject Guide for Children's Books in Print.*

The bibliographies we developed consisted of three classifications: 1) personal problems faced by all people (death, divorce, mental handicaps, physical handicaps, and social development); 2) subcultures and ethnic groups (inner city life, religions, American Indian background and history, Eskimos and Alaska, Orientals, Puerto Ricans, Mexican-Americans and migrant workers, and Black Americans); and 3) non-sexist materials.

Our center's primary purpose was service to teaching personnel. In fulfilling that purpose many specific requests for assistance passed across our desk. One example of the service we rendered was locating and ordering professional publications for a staff member who was developing original human relations activities. In another instance, we located and listed publications for a teacher's classroom project in values clarification. Our center's personnel spent many hours locating supplementary materials to enrich an all-school winter holiday program. We previewed materials relating to multi-cultural education and made recommendations for purchase to the central office for the Metropolitan Public Schools. These are just a few examples of the variety of services a center can provide, but the possibilities are endless and depend upon your program aims. Since our primary aim was to encourage teachers to plan and implement lessons with multi-cultural teachings, we tried to be open and flexible in meeting their professional needs.

The second objective of the resource center was to act as an impetus for production and collection of teacher-made materials. We discovered that most of the cooperating teachers, because of convenience, preferred to use their individual school facilities rather than to work in our center. However, we provided space and production supplies when requested. A center that is used as a production room would provide an opportunity for the center staff to communicate ideas and to generate enthusiasm among faculty members while they worked on projects.

Our center used pictures, slides, cassette recordings, 8mm film, and videotape to record multi-cultural activities being implemented in the classroom. Some teachers used these visual and sound recordings of class activities as learning resources to examine classroom interaction. These resources were effective in initiating student discussions.

The center's third objective was to serve as a clearinghouse for human resources that would enrich multi-cultural activities. The local newspaper and its files are a good starting place for development of a "community resource file." Countless human interest articles are written about different nationalities, lifestyles, religions, and talents. Frequently, reports are published about people's visits to other lands, or projects that are being done in the inner city, on a reservation, or in a rural community. These articles provide resources for the examination of many subcultures. Also, the entertainment section features artists and musicians that represent various cultures. These people who live in your geographical area are possible human resources for a multi-cultural program.

When developing a human resource file, be consistent in your system for card entries. Our resource center uses a card format like the one shown in the sample below. We suggest that you type a profile for each person on a separate card, after taking

---

(subject heading)

Name   Phone
Address
Area of Interest:
        Talent:
        Travel:
Availability:
Date:
Source: Lib.:   Other:
Limitation Re Class Size, Age, Etc.:

Source: "Card for Community Individuals," *Libraries: Center for Children's Needs. A Practical Guide for Developing A Community Information File.* (Chicago: American Library Association, 1974).

the time to verify the information by writing or phoning the individual. Find out if the individual is willing to visit in a classroom and, if so, what time and days are convenient for the visit and make a note of that scheduling information on the card. File the cards according to subject headings that are descriptors which relate to your program.

A marvelous source of people for a multi-cultural community file is foreign students who are attending local colleges. These people make interesting and informed classroom visitors or consultants about other cutures. Since many teachers are middle-class Americans with limited exposure to foreign and minority cultures, they should be encouraged to check the validity of curriculum materials with individuals who are knowledgeable and foreign students can help with this problem. Do not assume that materials, merely because they are commercially prepared, will be accurate in depicting other cultures. Check the validity of these materials as you would any others. A school that wants to implement a multi-cultural curriculum should see that all cultures and ethnic groups are accurately depicted.

Another human resource that is a multi-cultural activity which has great appeal for students of all ages is pen pals. There are several agencies currently in the business of furnishing names for correspondence; these are listed in the resource section which follows this article. Most of these agencies require a fee for their service but an exception is "The Big Blue Marble," a program sponsored by International Telephone and Telegraph (ITT). This non-profit agency matches students between the ages of six and seventeen as correspondents. Matching is on an individual basis which considers their sex, age, and interests with the children of ITT employees. Students in the United States are matched with foreign students abroad whenever possible, but if foreign students are not available they are matched with other North American children.

When students wish to correspond with a pen pal through this program, they should send the following information: name, address, sex, age, interests, or hobbies. A student may request a pen pal from a particular state or country, but there is no guarantee that this request can be met. If a total classroom wants to participate in this correspondence program, the teacher should ditto a short form for each child to fill out and should send the forms jointly to: Dear Pen Pal, P. O. Box 4054, Santa Barbara, California 93103.

Some effective letter writing tips have been prepared by Robert Carroll of the Afro-Asian Pen Pal Center. These suggestions are free upon request by writing the Information Center on Children's Cultures, 331 East 38th Street, New York, New York 10016.

An adaptation of the pen pal program is to arrange conference calls to different parts of the United States (contact your local phone company to arrange this). This activity enables students to hear different speech patterns or dialects and to obtain information from direct sources about different areas of our country. These conversations can be audiotaped to provide a new dimension for the collection of the resource center.

One of our center's most meaningful purposes was to facilitate and foster professional development of the faculties and Teacher Corps staff by collecting professional materials with which to increase awareness and knowledge. Fortunately, we had access to several college libraries, particularly those texts with ideas that could be used as classroom projects. These classroom suggestions were photocopied, filed, and made available for checkout by our teachers and staff members.

The Teacher Corps resource resource center served the faculty and staff of the participating schools in many ways during the year. However, future activities are anticipated. For instance, the center should develop a picture file of minorities because this will be a useful teaching resource. Also the center could develop an index of local businesses, listing the stock items they have that are common to foreign cultures. Since games and simulations are frequently too expensive for a single classroom to buy, a collection of teaching aids could be purchased to provide a valuable loan service for teachers.

Possibilities for service in a resource center that is designed and dedicated to serving the needs of teachers are endless. Since the teaching program is constantly changing, new demands are presented for teaching materials—and this provides new opportunities for service by a resource center.

Materials and Information Sources for Human Relations and Multi-Cultural Resource Centers

by Kate Williams and Jane Bandy Smith

AUDIOVISUALS BY NON-PROFIT GROUPS

AGENCY FOR INSTRUCTIONAL TELEVISION, Box A, Bloomington, Indiana 47401. Each film and videocassette has a Teacher's Guide; can be purchased in either format. AIT publishes a quarterly newsletter and a mailing list about materials available for educational use. These items are sent to individuals and institutions.

Everybody's Different 15 min., #01605, film $180; videocassette $125. Explores special problems, such as blindness and deafness. Emphasizes self-reliance and self-acceptance.

Friends. 15 min., #01203, film $180; videocassette $125. Children describe what it means to have friends and what it's like not being friends.

How Did I Get To Be Me? 15 min., #01401, film $180; videocassette $125. Process of becoming an individual, interaction between what happens to a person and the things he tries to make happen.

Lost Is a Feeling. 15 min., #03502, film $180; videocassette $125. Theme of uniqueness of the individual, self-acceptance, and self-respect.

People Need People. 15 min., #04012, film $180; videocassette $125. Stresses interpersonal relationships and friendship.

Talking Round the World. 15 min., #01104, film $180; videocassette $125. American children visit and share the lives of other children from Ghana, India, and Japan.

ANTI-DEFAMATION LEAGUE OF B'NAI B'RITH, 315 Lexington Avenue, New York, New York 10016.

Black Odyssey: A History of the American Negro is a filmstrip in two parts: 16th century to Civil War, and Civil War to the present. Each part: $7.50.

Ecidujerp introduces children to how prejudice affects our lives and includes poems and short stories. Sixth grade and up. Hardbound, $3.95; softbound, $2.95. Catalog #C536 and C536s.

Italians in America is a two-part filmstrip with discussion guide and record included. With record, $35; with cassette, $40.

155

Jews in America is a two-part filmstrip with discussion guide. With record, $35; with cassette, $40.

Just Like You is a film that studies the universality of the human experience. Rental: $7.50.

Mexican-Americans: An Historic Profile is a film that emphasizes the last 100 years of Mexican-American history. Rental, $10; purchase, $125.

What We Know About "Race." By Ashley Montagu. 50¢. Catalog #JF101.

INDIAN HISTORIAN PRESS, 1451 Masonic Avenue, San Francisco, California 94177.

Give or Take a Century is written and illustrated by an Eskimo educator and artist. Paperback, $6.

Legends of the Lakota are old stories, myths and legends of the Sioux told in a modern context by a Lakota Storyteller. $10.

The Only Land I Know is about the little-known Lumbee Indians of North Carolina. Hardbound, $9.75; paperbound, $6.50.

The Pueblo Indians is a history of the Pueblos, and contains culture and current situations of this Indian group. It is written by a Pueblo educator. $6.50.

The Weewish Tree is a magazine of Indian America. Seven times a year. Annual subscription, $6.50; reduced rates on bundle orders.

NATIONAL GALLERY OF ART, Extension Service, Washington, D.C. 20565. Audiovisual material is lent free of charge except for postage and insurance on return mailings.

The Far North: 2000 Years of Alaskan Art. Slide lecture with recording. No. 042.

Crafts of the Spanish Southwest. Slides and lecture notes. No. 024.

NEW JEWISH MEDIA PROJECT, 36 West 37th Street, New York, New York 10018.

Bashert. A 17 min. film that provides insights into customs and rituals of Jewish life. #23. Rental $30.

Shalom Israel: A Cinematic Kaleidoscope. This 10 min. film shows Israel without words, but with a background of music. #14. Rental $20.

PUBLIC TELEVISION LIBRARY, Video Program Service, 475 L'Enfant Plaza West, S. W., Washington, D. C. 20024 (202/488-5000). The Public Television Library, a department of the Public Broadcasting Service, has over 2,000 color television programs for individual or group use. All are available on standard videocassettes, and some on 16mm film. The videocassettes may be purchased, rented, leased, or reduplicated. The Public Television Library offers, when possible, immediate access to current Public Broadcasting Service programs. If you see a program on your local PBS station that you would like to use, call the station of the Public Television Library to check its availability. The following sampling is some of the programs available that could be used in a multicultural program.

Carrascloendas. A bilingual series aimed at fostering cultural understanding between Anglos and Latins, and self-pride.

Everyday People. Helping children develop understanding and respect for individual differences.

Indian Arts. The folk art, architecture, music, and dance of the Indians in the Southwest United States.

Our Street. A fictional drama of an inner-city Black family in Baltimore.

Villa Alegre. A bilingual program in English and Spanish, which emphasizes human relations, natural environment, nutrition, energy, and man-made objects.

AUDIOVISUALS BY COMMERCIAL GROUPS

Afro-American Contributions to Science. Bulletin 123, $2.00. Department of Curriculum, 4100 Turo Street, New Orleans, Louisiana 70122.

Black History: Lost, Stolen or Strayed. 54 min., CBS News, 1968. Bill Cosby discusses Black contributions to history that are usually overlooked, also focuses on Black self-concept and Black stereotypes in movies.

A Brief Visit to the Hsin Hua School in Peking. 16 min., color film. Purchase $220; rental $30. Lawren Productions, Box 1542, Burlingame, California 94010.

Can of Squirms. Elementary Squirms (B-S401), Intermediate Grade School Squirms (B-S4-1A), Junior High Squirms (B-S5-1). Available from Arthur Meriwether Education Resources. $6.50 plus postage; five or more games are each

157

$6.00 plus postage. Encourages communication and creativity in role-playing situations.

Checklist to Rate Your School for Racism and Sexism. #D-3. Council on Interracial Books. $2.50.

Children of Che. Available from Ms. Karen Wald, 549-62nd Street, Oakland, California 94609. A documentary of the revolutionary changes in Cuba.

Culturecontact II. Kit $35 plus $1.50 for shipping and handling. A simulation designed to heighten awareness and acceptance of cultural differences. Grades 7-12. From Games Central.

Discovering Music Together. Book 8. Chicago: Follett Publishing Co., 1966. Section, "Man Expresses His Feelings."

Feelin'. #K206. Argus Communications, $8.50. A game based on recognition of one's own feeling and others' feelings. Grades 5-12.

Feelings and Thoughts. Filmstrip and record #F48, $20; filmstrip and cassette #F49, $20. Explores the difference between feelings and thoughts, and how each influences decision making. Grades 5-12.

Folk Dance in American Life. Instructional Planning Division, P.O. Box 307, Los Angeles, California 90051. 75¢. Set of cards with dance instructions.

Free to Be You and Me. 42 min., color. McGraw-Hill, 1973. A three-part film that examines the stages in people's lives and considers character traits and ideals.

Friendly and Hostile. Filmstrip and record #F48, $20; filmstrip and cassette #F49, $20. Argus Communications. Explores how an individual communicates his feelings.

Indian Story Kit. #B-99. Arthur Meriwether Education Resources, $7.50. Seven Indian stories written for a story teller.

Interviews with Black Leaders of American History. A four-part cassette set that "interviews" Booker T. Washington, Marcus Garvey, and W. E. DuBois. Includes discussion guide and suggested bibliography. #B-C 21. $8.50.

Learning About Others (No. 550,011) and *Learning About Me* (No. 550,001) are filmstrips from ACI Media.

Magic Circle. An effective education program related to the student's awareness of feelings, personal effectiveness, and understanding of social awareness. Activity guides for grades 1-6. From Human Development Training Institute.

Picture-Pac Activity on Racism. For fifth grade up, stimulates discussion. From Council on Interracial Books, No. D-1, $2.50.

Rainbow Game. A simulation game designed to help children understand race relations and bureaucracy. Grades 7-12. Kit: $30 plus $1.50 for shipping and handling. From Games Central.

Through Arawak Eyes. A stereo record album by David Campbell, who is of Arawak Indian descent and is from Guyana, South America. The songs deal with people of the Caribbean and Latin America.

Unfinished Stories for Use in the Classroom. Presents values situations for students grades 4-7. No. 1306-9-OJ. $1.25. From the NEA Order Department.

A Unique Experience. #1909-1-OJ, NEA Order Department, 2 tapes. Grades 6-12. $12. Alex Haley tells how his ancestors came to the United States and how he traced his family history.

We Are Black. 120 different reading cards about Black people on reading levels from grades 2-6. From Science Research Associates.

You Never Hear About Any Struggles. A guidebook to teaching oral history. Suggests ways to use the local community as a source of material. $1.50. Charles H. Kerr Publishing Co., 431 South Dearborn Street, Chicago, Illinois 94087.

NON-SEXIST MATERIALS

A World for Women in Engineering. Designed to acquaint young women with engineering as a career. It includes a 20-minute color film, a Leader's Guide, and Student Books, and a Bell System woman engineer is available to speak to the group after the film. Student Book I for junior high, Student Book II for senior high. From the Bell System.

Canadian Women's Educational Press. 280 Bloor Street, West, Suite 305, Toronto, Ontario, Canada. Write for publication lists and order forms for non-sexist children's literature.

Cinderella Is Dead! Color filmstrip with sound. A study of women in the labor market. No. 0571-6-OJ. $16.00. NEA Order Department, Academic Building, Saw Mill Road, West Haven, Connecticut 06516.

Feminist Packet. CIBC Racism and Sexism Resource Center, 1841 Broadway, New York, New York 10023.

Feminist Resources for Schools and Colleges. 19 pages, $1.00 plus 25¢ postage. Feminist Press, Box 334, State University of New York, College at Old Westbury, Old Westbury, Long Island, New York 11578.

Hey! What About Us?, *I Is for Important,* and *Anything They Want To Be* are three films in the Sex Role Stereotyping in the Schools series available from the University of California Extension Media Center, Berkeley, California 94720. A handbook, *In All Fairness,* is included with the films. The films study sex roles in schools in the areas of physical activities, social interactions, emotional experiences, intellectual endeavors, and career preparation.

Interviews with Famous Women of World History. Arthur Meriwether Education Resources, Contemporary Drama Service, Box 457, 1131 Warren Avenue, Downers Grove, Illinois 60515. "Interviews" with Catherine the Great, Jezebel, and Marie Antoinette. Catalog No. B-C 16. Four-part cassette with teacher's guide: $8.50 plus postage.

The Labels and Reinforcement of Sex Role Stereotyping. A two-part color and sound filmstrip for students. Leader's Manual included. No. 0572-4-OJ. $24.50. From NEA Order Department.

Lollipop Power. P. O. Box 1171, Chapel Hill, North Carolina 27514. Write for publication lists and order forms for non-sexist children's literature.

New Seed Press. P. O. Box 3016, Stanford, California 94305. Write for publication lists and order forms for children's literature which breaks down stereotypes.

Non-Sexist Education for Survival. For students grades 7-12. NEA Order Department, Academic Building, Saw Mill Road, West Haven, Connecticut 06515. No. 0582-1-OJ. $2.25.

Picture-Pac Activity on Sexism. For fifth grade through college, stimulates discussion. From Council on Interracial Books, CIBC Resource Center, Room 300, 1841 Broadway, New York, New York 10023. No. D-2. $2.50.

The Presence of Women. By Carol Hymowitz and Michaele Weissman. Women in American History. Junior high level (No. B155). Anti-Defamation League of B'nai B'rith, 315 Lexington Avenue, New York, New York 10016.

Resource List for Nonsexist Education. NEA Order Department, Academic Building, Saw Mill Road, West Haven, Connecticut 06515. No. 0590-2-OJ. 75¢

Sing to the Dawn. By Minfong Ho. Lothrop, Lee & Shepard, 1975. Grades 3-8. 160 pages. $5.95.

BOOKS ABOUT HUMAN RELATIONS

Black is Brown is Tan. Arnold Adoff. Harper & Row, 1973. $4.95. 32 pages. A story of an interracial marriage with parents not restricted to the traditional sex roles.

Blue Trees, Red Sky. Norma Klein. Pantheon, 1975. $4.95. 57 pages. Grades 3-6. Shows children in non-stereotypic roles and deals with growing up and society's changing values.

Christmas Present. Robert Burch. Scholastic Book Services, 1968. A selfish boy comes in contact with those poorer than he.

Grandpa & Me. Pat Gauch. Coward, McCann & Geogegan, 1972. A young boy's account of his relationship with his grandfather.

Grownups Cry, Too. Nancy Hazen. Lollipop Power, 1972. Discussion of the sad and happy experiences that make people cry.

Long Way to Whiskey Creek. Patricia Beatty. William Morrow & Co., 1971. Grades 5-9. A book which is humorous but deals with death as a natural part of the pattern of life.

The Queen Who Couldn't Bake Gingerbread. Parents Magazine Press, 1975. A new version of an old German tale; focuses on self-reliance and consideration for others.

Queenie Peavy. Robert Burch. Viking Press, 1966. Queenie is a girl whose father is in jail and who fights with other children and constantly gets into trouble at school.

The Red Jaguar. Alison Prince. Atheneum, 1972. 126 pages. Grades 4-6. This book follows the friendship of two boys, one from a traditional family and the other who lives with his mother only.

Thanksgiving Treasure. Gail Roth. Bantam Books, 1974. A girl is friends with a man who a reclusive divorcee.

The Witches of Worm. Zilpha Keatley Snyder. Atheneum, 1972. 183 pages. Grades 5-8. A young girl is lonely and depressed following her parents' divorce.

The Beggar and the Blanket and Other Vietnamese Tales. Gail B. Graham. Dial Press, 1970. Grades 4-5.

The First of the Penguins. Mary Q. Stell. Macmillan, 1973. Grades 6-7. An adventure story involving a Black and a Javanese boy in the inner city.

Black Fairy Tales. Terry Berger. Atheneum, 1974. Grades 4-5. African folk tales.

Chicano Roots Go Deep. Harold Coy. Dodd, Mead, 1975. 210 pages. $5.95. Grades 7 and up. An introduction to Chicano history.

An Eskimo Birthday. Tom D. Robinson. Dodd, Mead, 1975. 39 pages. $5.25. Grades 2-5. Gives a believable and interesting picture of contemporary Inuits, with the main character a girl whose feelings and interests will appeal to the reader.

Four Corners of the Sky. Theodore Clymer. Little, Brown 1975. 47 pages. $6.95. Grades 1-4. Anthology of North American Indian folklore.

Heroes of Puerto Rico. Jay Nelson Tuck. Fleet Press, 1970. Grades 5-6. Biographies of famous Puerto Ricans.

I Cry When the Sun Goes Down: The Story of Herman Wrice. Jean Horton. Berg, Westminster Press, 1975. 149 pages. $6.95. Grades 6 and up. Biography of a Black Philadelphia youth organizer.

Indian Patriots of the Great West. Edited by Bennett Wayne. Garrard Publishing, 1974. Biographies of four great Indian warrior chiefs.

Ludell. Brenda Wilkinson. Harper & Row, 1975. 170 pages. $5.95. Grades 3-6. Believable and sensitive story of a young Black girl growing up in the South.

Michael Naranjo: The Story of an American Indian. Mary Carroll Nelson. Dillon Press, 1975. 66 pages. $4.95. Grades 6 and up. A true story of a young Indian man who was blinded in Vietnam, returned to the U. S. and eventually became a sculptor.

Nilda. Nicholasa Mohr. Harper, 1973. Grades 6-7. A girl's attempts to adjust to life in Spanish Harlem.

Small Hands, Big Hands. Sandra Weiner. Pantheon, 1970. Grades 5-6. Subtitled "Seven Profiles of Chicano Migrant Workers and Their Families."

A Snake in the Old Hut. Sylvia Sherry. Thomas Nelson, 1973. Grades 5-6. A 12-year-old Kenyan boy has to take his uncle out of the country because of his anti-government activities.

Sounder. William Howard Armstrong. Harper & Row, 1969. Grades 6 and up. The story of a young Black boy in a life of prejudice and poverty.

ETHNIC PERIODICALS

Akwesasne Notes (monthly), State University of New York at Buffalo, Program in American Studies, Buffalo, New York 14214.

Amerasia Journal (twice annually), Asian American Studies Center Publications, Box 24A43, Los Angeles, California 90004.

American Indian Culture Center Journal (quarterly), 3231 Campbell Hall, University of California, Los Angeles, California 90024.

Aztlan: Chicano Journal of the Social Sciences and the Arts (quarterly), Chicano Studies Center, Campbell Hall, University of California, 405 Hilgard, Los Angeles, California 90024.

Black World (monthly), Johnson Publishing Company, 820 South Michigan Avenue, Chicago, Illinois 60605.

Commentary (monthly), American Jewish Committee, 165 East 56th Street, New York, New York 10021.

East/West (weekly), East/West Publishing Co., 758 Commercial Street, San Francisco, California.

Ebony (monthly), Johnson Publishing Company, 820 South Michigan Avenue, Chicago, Illinois 60605.

Ethnicity (quarterly), Academic Press, 111 Fifth Avenue, New York, New York 10003.

The Greek American (semimonthly), Greekam Publication, 251 West 42nd Street, New York, New York 10036.

Indian Historian Quarterly, Indian Historical Society, 1451 Masonic Avenue, San Francisco, California 94117.

International Migration Review (quarterly), Center for Migration Studies of New York, 209 Flagg Place, Staten Island, New York 10304.

Journal of Negro History (quarterly), Association for the Study of Negro Life and History, 1407-14th Street, N. W., Washington, D.C. 20005.

Phylon (quarterly), Atlanta University Review of Race and Culture, Atlanta University, 223 Chestnut Street, Atlanta, Georgia 30314.

Rican (quarterly), Rican Journal, Box 11039, Chicago, Illinois 60611.

Slovak Americans (weekly), 313 Ridge Avenue, Middletown, Pennsylvania 17057.

Source: *Encyclopedic Directory of Ethnic Newspapers and Periodicals in the United States.* Littleton, Colorado: Libraries Unlimited, 1972. Lubomyr R. Wynar, ed.

ERIC MATERIALS

Note: Copies of the documents listed may be ordered in microfiche (MF) or hard copy (HC) from EDRS, P.O. Box 190, Arlington, Virginia 22210, or from an alternative source where such is cited. Orders to EDRS must include ED number, payment (if less than $10.00) and postage (25¢ for first 60 fiche or pages, 10¢ for each additional 60).

American Diversity: A Bibliography of Resources on Racial and Ethnic Minorities for Pennsylvania Schools. (ED 054 031) Compiled by Elizabeth S. Haller. Pennsylvania State Department of Education, Harrisburg. 1970. 250 pp. EDRS: MF 65¢, HC $9.87.

Annotated Bibliography of Multi-Ethnic Curriculum Materials. (ED 114 378) Midwest Center for Educational Opportunity, Columbia, Missouri. 1974, 165 pp. EDRS: MF 76¢, HC $8.24.
First Supplement (ED 114 379) 1975, 71 pp. MF 76¢, HC $3.32. Second Supplement (ED 114 380) 1975, 24 pp. MF 76¢, HC $1.58. Third Supplement (ED 114 381) 1975, 83 pp. MF 76¢, HC $4.43.

Directory of Data Sources on Racial and Ethnic Minorities. (ED 114 442) Earl Mellor, Bureau of Labor Statistics (DOL) Washington, D.C. 1975. EDRS: MF 76¢, HC $4.43. Or, Superintendent of Documents, U. S. Government Printing Office, Washington, D.C. 20402. Stock No. 029-001-01777-4. $1.50.

Human Values in the Classroom: A Handbook for Teachers. (ED 110 884) Robert C. Hawley and Isabel L. Hawley. Not available from EDRS: order from Hart Publishing Co., Inc., 15 West 4th Street, New York, New York 10012. 1975. $8.95 hardcover, $4.95 paperback.

Local Library Resources for a Multi-Ethnic Curriculum: A Model Program in Multi-Ethnic Heritage Studies. (ED 115 633) Man-

kato State College, Minnesota. 240 pp. EDRS: MF 76¢, HC
$12.05.

*Many Peoples—Shared Dreams: A Curriculum Guide for Multi-
Ethnic Studies. (*ED 117 033) Genevieve Schillo and Mary
Sarah Fasenmyer. National Catholic Education Association,
Washington, D.C. 1973. 51 pp. EDRS: MF 76¢, HC $3.32.

Minorities in the United States: Guide to Resources. (ED 080 133)
Jessie Carney Smith. George Peabody College for Teachers,
Nashville, Tennessee. 1973. EDRS: MF 65¢, HC $6.58.

*Minority Experience: A Basic Bibliography of American Ethnic
Studies.* (ED 111 902) Ron Caselli, Comp. Sonoma County
Superintendent of Schools, Santa Rosa, California. April,
1975, 106 pp. EDRS: MF 76¢, HC $5.70.

Multi-Ethnic Approaches to Teaching. (ED 115 612) Connie Earhart. October 20, 1975, 22 pp. EDRS: MF 76¢, HC $1.58.

*Multi-Ethnic Handbook, Volume I, Later Elementary and Middle
School. Lesson Plans for Teaching Concepts Dealing with
Racism, Contributions of Blacks, Latinos, Native Americans.*
(ED 115 724) Michigan Education Association, Division of
Minority Affairs, East Lansing, Michigan. 1973, 102 pp. EDRS:
MF 76¢, HC $5.70. Or, Michigan Education Association, 1216
Kendale Boulevard, East Lansing, Michigan. $2.25.

Multi-Ethnic Media Selected Bibliographies in Print. (ED 118 114)
David Cohen. Not available from EDRS; order from American
Library Association, Publications Department, 50 East Huron
Street, Chicago, Illinois 60611. 37 pp., $2.00.

*Red, White, and Black (and Brown, Yellow): Minorities in Amer-
ica. A Bibliography.* (ED 039 283) 1970, 32 pp. EDRS: MF 25¢,
HC $1.70.

*Selected Films and Filmstrips on Four Ethnic American Minorities
(Afro, Indian, Oriental, Spanish-Speaking).* (ED 116 702),
Harry A. Johnson, Stanford University, California. January
1976, 58 pp. EDRS: MF 76¢, HC $3.32. Or, Box E, School of
Education, Stanford University, Stanford, California 94302.
$2.00 check payable to "Box E" must accompany order.

Resources for Teaching of English: 1974. Second section, "Multi-
Ethnic Literature in America." (ED 083 049) Edited by Ste-
phen Judy. National Council of Teachers of English, Urbana,
Illinois. 1974, 105 pp. Not available from EDRS: order from
National Council of Teachers of English, 1111 Kenyon Road,
Urbana, Illinois 61801. $2.00.

Note: References cited below are from the U. S. Office of Education publication, *Aids to Media Selections for Students and Teachers* (Rev. 1976), compiled by Kathlyn J. Moses and Lois B. Watts, and available from the Superintendent of Documents, U. S. Government Printing Office, Washington, D.C. HEW No. OE 76-21002. 128 pp. $2.00.

Africa: An Annotated List of Printed Materials Suitable for Children. New York: Information Center on Children's Cultures, 1968. 76 pp. $1.

Compiled by a joint committee of the ALA Children's Services Division and the African-American Institute, this list includes approximately 300 titles in English, published in nine countries. Arranged by regions and countries of Africa; indicates books which are "not recommended for use in American public and school libraries for children," but which, because of their special content or style, will be "of interest chiefly to the African school"; some adult titles are included and designated as such; an author-title-country index.

Africa, South of the Sahara. Barry K. Beyer. New York: Thomas Y. Crowell, 1969. 138 pp. $6.95; paper $3.95. Resource and Curriculum Guide.

An Annotated Checklist of Children's Stories with Settings in Cities Outside the United States, 1960-1971. Unpublished Research Paper. Washington: The Catholic University of America, 1972. 50 pp.

Designed to aid librarians looking for reading materials about foreign cities, the list annotates about 100 fiction titles in English for elementary age children. Arranged alphabetically by country with city subdivisions.

Audio-Visual Guidance Materials, and Annotated Bibliography & Directory of Minnesota Sources. Prepared by Truly Trousdale Latchaw. St. Paul: Minnesota State Department of Education, 1970. 484 pp., $8.75.

Four thousand titles of 16mm films, filmstrips, tapes, recordings, and slides related to guidance, listed under one of five categories: Family Life; Personal-Social Development; Careers; Personal-Social Problems; and Education for Each Age Group. Table of contents serves as a functional index arranged alphabetically by title, indicating age group, category, page references, and whether previously reviewed.

Bibliography of Nonprint Instructional Materials on the American Indian. Prepared by the Instructional Development Program for Services and Research. Provo, Utah: Brigham Young University Printing Service, 1972. 221 pp. $2.95.

An alphabetically annotated bibliography of approximately 1,400 filmstrips, 8mm film loops, 16mm motion pictures, 35mm slides, overhead transparencies, study prints, maps, charts, audio recordings, and multi-media kits. Provides subject heading, subject index, and distributors index. Full entries in the title section give suggested educational level, descriptive annotation, and subject headings.

Children's Books in Print 1973. New York: R. R. Bowker Co., 5th ed., 1973. 790 pp. $17.95 in U. S. and Canada; $14.98 elsewhere. Annual revision in December.

Lists 40,000 juveniles representing nearly 500 publishers; provides author, title, and illustrator indexes to books from prekindergarten through grade 12. Also includes information on translator, price, imprint, year of publication, and data as available on binding, edition, number of volumes, and grade range.

Educational Film Library Association Evaluations. New York: Educational Film Library Association. 1965. Membership $35–$100 per year.

Evaluative reviews printed on 8″ x 11″ sheets include a synopsis, suggestions for use, age level, technical quality, running time, price, release date, producer, and distributor.

Educators Progress Service Guides. Published by Educators Progress Service, Inc., Randolph, Wisconsin 53956.
Educators Guide to Free Films. Compiled and edited by Mary Foley Horkheimer and John C. Diffor. 32nd edition. Revised, June 1972. 800 pp. $11.75.

Of the 4,799 titles, listed alphabetically under broad subjects, 828 are new to this edition. Annotation, size, sound or silent, date of release, running time, if cleared for TV, and distributor are given for each title. Indexed by title, subject, source, and availability.

167

Educators Guide to Free Filmstrips. Compiled and edited by Mary Foley Horkheimer and John C. Diffor. 24th edition, 1972. 161 pp. $8.50.

Of the 145 silent filmstrips, 108 sound filmstrips, 198 sets of slides and 1 set of transparencies (a total of 452 titles from 94 sources), 122 titles are new. For each of the titles, arranged alphabetically under broad subjects, the annotation, form, and source are given. Title, subject, and source as well as Canadian availability indexes are included.

Educators Guide to Free Guidance Materials. Compiled and edited by Mary H. Staerstrom and Joe A. Steph. 13th edition, 1974. 327 pp. $9.75.

Classifies and provides information on titles, sources, availability, and contents of 770 films, 73 filmstrips, 25 sets of slides, 137 audiotapes, 375 other materials, a total of 1,380 selected free items. Title, subject, source, and availability indexes. The body of the text gives full bibliographic information and is annotated. Items are arranged alphabetically under Career Planning Materials; Responsibility: To Self and To Others; and Use of Leisure Time.

Educators Guide to Free Social Studies Materials. Compiled and edited by Patricia H. Suttles. 14th edition. 1974. 673 pp. $10.50.

Selected films, filmstrips, slides, audiotapes, videotapes, scripts, transcriptions, charts, bulletins, pamphlets, magazines, maps, posters, and books on the seven social studies recognized by the National Council of Social Studies. This annotated list is arranged by form of media and provides information on titles, sources, availability, and content. Indexed by title, subject, and source.

Elementary Teachers Guide to Free Curriculum Materials. Edited by Patricia H. Suttles, 29th edition. 1972. $9.75.

The 1,671 maps, bulletins, pamphlets, exhibits, charts, magazines, and books included in this edition were selected on the basis of educational appropriateness; timeliness; arrangement, style, and suitability; and freedom from undesirable features. Teacher Reference and Professional Growth Materials were also selected on the basis as those above. Indexed by title, subject, and source. Six sample units.

Free and Inexpensive Learning Materials. 18th edition. Nashville: Office of Educational Services, George Peabody College for Teachers, 1976. 250 pp. $3.50.

Describes more than 3,000 educational aids including pamphlets, charts, maps, and films, under 85 subject headings. Each entry gives a brief description, ordering information, and price. Entries are cross-referenced.

Free and Inexpensive Materials on World Affairs. Leonard Kenworthy. New York: Teachers College, Columbia University, 1969. 65 pp. $1.95.

Annotated practical list including all types of materials.

Folklore: From Africa to the United States. Compiled by Margaret N. Couglan. Washington: U. S. Government Printing Office, 1974. Stock Number 3001-00066. Hardbound. Library of Congress.

Annotates titles judged to be useful source books for students and teachers concerned with the African heritage.

Folklore of the North American Indians: An Annotated Bibliography. Compiled by Judith C. Ullom. Washington: U. S. Government Printing Office, 1969. 126 pp. $2.25.

Annotates 152 titles of which 50 are children's editions and the others source books for teachers and secondary school students. A section of books presenting an overall picture of North American mythology and folklore is succeeded by sections arranged according to the 11 North American Culture Areas, with "children's editions" identified in each section; compiler-title index.

Guide to Free-Loan Films About Foreign Lands. Alexandria, Virginia: Serina Press, 1975. 283 pp. $14.95.

Synopses of more than 3,000 films about 76 foreign countries. Subject and title index.

Guide to Government Loan Films (16mm). The Third Edition (1974-1975). Alexandria, Virginia: Serina Press, 1975. 185 pp. $9.95.

Includes brief synopses of more than 900 films, 600 filmstrips, and slides available on a free loan basis from 48 federal agencies, together with a list of sources for obtaining the films. Subject index.

169

Handy Key to Your "National Geographics," 1915-1971. Subject and Picture Locater. 10th edition. Williamsville, New York: C. S. Underhill, 1972. 41 pp. $2.50, single copy; 20 percent discount for two or more.

Issues biennially and available on a standing order basis. List includes all colored illustrations, paintings, etc., published in *National Geographic Magazine* from 1915 to December 1971. Arranged alphabetically by broad subjects.

Image of the Black in Children's Fiction. Dorothy Broderick. New York: R. R. Bowker Co., 1973. 219 pp. $12.75.

This "scholarly and provocative study" examines past and present treatment of Blacks in juvenile literature, analyzes stereotypes and related manifestations of racism, and considers historical developments. Bibliographies, indexes, and references to standard selection tools provide provocative perspective for the book evaluator.

Instructional Resources for Teachers of the Culturally Disadvantaged and Exceptional. Robert Anderson, Robert Hemeway, and Janet W. Anderson. Springfield, Illinois: Charles C. Thomas, 1971. 320 pp. $11.00.

Latin America: An Annotated List of Materials for Children. Edited by Elena Mederos de Gonzalez and Anne Pellowski. New York: The Center for Inter-American Relations, 1969. 96 pp. $1.

Evaluates 493 titles selected by a committee of librarians, teachers, and Latin American specialists, nationals, or former residents of the countries concerned, in cooperation with The Center for Inter-American Relations. Attempts to evaluate all in-print English language materials on the subject. Full annotations for only those items recommended as the best; limitations are noted for some otherwise recommended items; and books reviewed but not recommended are listed separately, with reasons indicated. A few Spanish language materials are listed which are considered classics in countries of origin. Arrangement is by region, then by country, then alphabetical by author. Bibliographic information and grade levels are indicated; author, title index. (Note: These lists have been updated by individual country list supplied free by the Center.)

Learning Directory, 1972-73. New York: Westinghouse Learning Corporation, 1972. $24.50. Complete set (7,600): $99.50.

Nonselective list of instructional offerings from every major publisher and producer since January 1971. Latest volume of an 8-volume set. Entries are listed alphabetically by subject, with one-line data on type of media, cost, level, and source. No annotations.

Media in Value Education: A Critical Guide. Jeffery Shrank. Chicago: Argus Communications, 1970. 168 pp. $4.95.

Reviews and discussion guide for 75 short secular films, useful for high school guidance and religion classes as well as some social studies areas, are included. Some rock albums also reviewed. Sources and addresses of chief suppliers of media are located in "An Annotated Guide to Media and Other Sources." Indexed by forms of media.

Periodicals for School Libraries: A Guide to Magazines, Newspapers, and Periodical Indexes. Revised edition. Compiled by Marion H. Scott. Chicago: The American Librarian Association, 1973. 292 pp. $4.95. Paperback.

Records and Cassettes for Young Adults. New York Library Association, Children's and Young Adult Services, 1973. $2.50. (Orders totaling less than $5 must be accompanied by payment.)

A selective buying guide for librarians who wish to start a young adult record or cassette collection or to add to an already established collection. Brief annotations for 461 titles under six categories: popular (rock, soul, country, and western); folk; jazz (blues and gospel); musicals and movie soundtracks; classical, including electronic; and non-musical.

Reading Ladders for Human Relations. Virginia M. Reid. 5th edition. Washington: American Council on Education, 1972. 346 pp. $3.95. Paperback.

Prepared with the help of a committee from the National Council of Teachers of English. Nearly 1,500 titles are annotated in this revision, and the "ladders" have been reduced from the earlier six to four: "Creating a Positive Image," "Living with Others," "Appreciating Different Cultures," and "Coping with Change."

Select Audiovisual Records: Contemporary African Art from the Harmon Collection. Still Pictures, 1972. 14 pp. Free.

Arranged alphabetically by name of the artist, the selections are from the "Artworks by African Artists" series. Indexed by country.

Select Picture List: Indians in the United States. 1971. 18 pp.

Pictures portraying American Indians, their homes and activities; selected from pictorial records of 15 Government agencies, including the Bureau of Indian Affairs, Bureau of American Ethnology, and the U. S. Army. Grouped by subject, pictures bear English names of individuals with native or secondary names in parentheses. Name of the photographer or artist and date of the item are cited if available. Indexed by tribes.

Select Picture List: Negro Art from the Harmon Collection. 1971. 6 pp. Free.

Selected representative listing of artists and their styles, arranged alphabetically by artist and thereunder by subject: Portraits of Outstanding Americans, arranged alphabetically by surname of the painting's subject; Negro Art Exhibits, Workshops, and Demonstrations; and Art Activities in the Kenneth Space Series, arranged alphabetically by name of place and surname of person. Prints, transparencies, and slides available.

A Selective Guide to Materials for Mental Health and Family Life Education. Compiled by Mental Health Materials Center, Information Resources Center for Mental Health and Family Life Education. Northfield, Illinois: Perennial Education, 1973, 847 pp. $35.00.

A highly selective bibliography of program aids that bring sound mental health principles to bear on the whole process of human growth and development, with major emphasis on the life of the individual in the family setting and larger community. Alcoholism, drug abuse, suicide prevention, and mental illness in children are among areas treated in depth. For each film and pamphlet, a summary, an evaluation, suggested audience, ordering information, and excerpts from the discussion guide are available. Indexed by title.

Sexism and Youth. Diane Gersoni-Stavn, editor. New York, R. R. Bowker Co., 1974. 448 pp. $9.95.

Contains 47 articles dealing with aspects of the effect of sexism on children and teenagers; foreword by Letty Cotten Pogrebin. Part III ("Books: Propaganda and the Sins of Omission") gives attention to children's literature and also to textbooks.

Subject Guide to Books in Print, 1974. 1974. 4,000 pp. Annual revision each fall. Lists available books under 63,000 Library of Congress subject headings.

Suggested Readings in the Literatures of Africa, China, India, Japan. New York City Board of Education. Curriculum Bulletin, Education, 1968. 124 pp. $2. Paperback.

Annotates about 500 titles selected for their pertinence to New York City's non-Western study programs, primary grades through senior high school. Arrangement is by subject, then by form: Drama, Fiction, Folklore, Nonfiction, Poetry; grade levels are indicated. Introductory section contains guidelines and suggestions for teachers; index is author-title.

What Is a City? A Multi-Media Guide on Urban Living. Rose Moorachian, editor. Boston: Boston Public Library, 1969. 152 pp. $2.

Includes books, pamphlets, periodicals, films, filmstrips, loops, recordings, and realia because of "their usefulness as an interpretation of all aspects of city living," for K-12. In the main, materials dealing with contemporary themes and issues are cited, with historical developments of the city incidentally included. Arranged alphabetically by authors under broad topics as "A City Is . . . People," "A City Is . . . Many Problems, Many Solutions." Provides Index to Authors and Titles and a Key to Publishers and Distributors.

COMMERCIAL SOURCES OF MULTI-CULTURAL MATERIALS

ACI Media, Inc., 35 West 45th Street, New York, New York 10036.

AEVAC Dept., 109 500 Fifth Avenue, New York, New York 10027.

Afro-American Heritage House, 24 Whittier Drive, Englishtown, New Jersey 97726.

American Guidance Service Inc., Publisher's Building, Circle Pines, Minnesota 55014.

Argus Communications, 7550 Natchez, Niles, Illinois 60648.

Arthur Meriwether Education Resources, Contemporary Drama Service, Box 457, 1131 Warren Avenue, Downers Grove, Illinois 60515.

Association Production Materials, 600 Madison Avenue, New York, New York 10022.

Atlantic Productions Inc., 894 Sheffield Street, Thousand Oaks, California 91360.

Audio-Visual Aids Library, Pennsylvania State University, University Park, Pennsylvania 16802.

Bailey Films, Inc., 6509 DeLongpre Avenue, Hollywood, California 90028.

Baker and Taylor Company, P. O. Box 230, Momence, Illinois 60954.

China Society of America, 125 East 65th Street, New York, New York 10021.

Chinese News Service, 30 Rockefeller Plaza, New York, New York 10010.

Coronet Films, 65 E. South Water Street, Chicago, Illinois 60601.

Council on Interracial Books, CIBC Resource Center, Room 300, 1841 Broadway, New York, New York 10023.

Educational Activities, Inc., Freeport, Long Island, New York 11520.

Friendship Press, 475 Riverside Drive, New York, New York 10027.

Games Central, 55 Wheeler Street, Cambridge, Massachusetts 02138.

Guidance Associates, 757 Third Avenue, New York, New York 10017.

Highlights for Children, 2300 West Fifth Avenue, P. O. Box 269, Columbus, Ohio 43216.

Human Development Training Institute, 7547 University Avenue, La Mesa, California 94117.

Indian Historian Press, 1451 Masonic Avenue, San Francisco, California 94117.

Indian Rights Association, 1505 Race Street, Philadelphia, Pennsylvania 19102.

Inter Culture Associates, Box 277, Thompson, Connecticut 16277.

National Education Association, Order Department, Academic Building, Saw Mill Road, West Haven, Connecticut 05616.

National Gallery of Art, Extension Service, Washington, D.C. 20565.

New York Times, 229 West 43rd Street, New York, New York 10036.

Pan American Union, Washington, D.C. 20006.

Science Research Associates Inc., 259 East Erie Street, Chicago, Illinois 60611.

UNESCO Publications Center, United Nations, 801 Third Avenue, New York, New York 10022.

UNICEF, Information Center on Children's Cultures, 331 East 38th Street, New York, New York 10016.

University of California, Extension Media Center, 2223 Fulton Street, Berkeley, California 94720.

SOURCES OF FREE AND INEXPENSIVE MATERIALS

ACT, Action for Children's Television, 46 Austin Street, Newtonville, Massachusetts 02160.

Agency for Instructional TV, P. O. Box A, Bloomington, Indiana 47401.

Aisarema, Inc., 338 E. Second Street, Los Angeles, California 90012. Attention: John Y. Mori.

Alexander Graham Bell Assoc. for the Deaf, John Hitz Memorial Library, 1537-35th Street, N.W., Washington, D.C. 20007.

American Association for Jewish Education, National Council of Jewish Audio-Visual Materials, 114 Fifth Avenue, New York, New York 10011.

American Jewish Committee, 165 East 56th Street, New York, New York 10022.

Asia Society, 112 East 64th Street, New York, New York 10021, Attention: Mrs. Bonnie Crown.

Australian Embassy Library, 1601 Massachusetts Ave., N.W., Washington, D.C. 20036, Attention: J. Frewer, Librarian.

Austrian National Tourist Office, 545 Fifth Avenue, New York, New York 10017.

British Embassy Library and Information Office, 3100 Massachusetts Avenue N.W., Washington, D.C. 20008.

Canadian Government Travel Bureau, 150 Kent Street, Ottawa, Canada.

Center for Migration Studies, 209 Flagg Place, Staten Island, New York 10304, Attention: Sylvan Tomasi.

Center for Urban Education, 1245 S.W. Bancroft Street, Portland, Oregon 97201.

Chamber of Commerce of the U. S., Guide to Foreign Information Sources, 1615 H Street, N.W., Washington, D. C. 20006.

Chinese Historical Society of America, 17 Adler Place, San Francisco, California 94131.

Council on Interracial Books for Children, 1841 Broadway, New York, New York 10023.

Danish Brotherhood in America, 3717 Harney Street, Omaha, Nebraska 68131, Attention: Mr. Don Eversoll.

ERIC Career Education, 204 Gabel Hall, Northern Illinois University, DeKalb, Illinois 60115.

ERIC Clearinghouse, Handicapped and Gifted Children, Council for Exceptional Children, 1902 Association Drive, Reston, Virginia 22091.

ERIC Clearinghouse, Rural Education and Small Schools, New Mexico State University, Box 3 AP, Las Cruces, New Mexico 88003.

ERIC Clearinghouse, Social Studies/Social Science Education, 855 Broadway, Boulder, Colorado 80302.

ERIC Clearinghouse, Urban Education, Teachers College, Columbia University, Box 40, New York, New York 10027.

Ethnic Heritage Study Program, Indiana University, 1825 Northside Boulevard, South Bend, Indiana 46615.

General Education Branch, Office of Instructional Services, Department of Education, Honolulu, Hawaii 96804.

Intercultural Relations and Ethnic Studies Institute, Rutgers University, Graduate School of Education, 10 Seminary Place, New Brunswick, New Jersey 08903.

Israel Embassy Library, 1612-22nd Street N.W., Washington, D. C. 20008.

Japan Publications Trading Center USA, 1255 Howard Street, San Francisco, California 94103.

Jewish Publication Society of America, 222 North 15th Street, Philadelphia, Pennsylvania 19102.

League of Women Voters, The League, 1200 17th Street N.W., Washington, D.C. 20036.

Middle East Institute Library, 1761 N Street N.W., Washington, D.C. 20036.

Minneapolis Public Schools Task Force on Ethnic Studies, 707 North East Monroe, Minneapolis, Minnesota 55413.

National Council for the Social Studies, 1201 16th Street N.W., Washington, D.C. 20036.

National Education Association Library, 1201 16th Street N.W., Washington, D.C. 20036.

National Geographic Society Library, 17th and M Streets N.W., Washington, D.C. 20036.

New Jewish Media Project, 36 West 37th Street, New York, New York 10018.

New Zealand Embassy Library, 19 Observatory Circle N.W., Washington, D.C. 20008.

Norwegian-American Historical Society, St. Olaf College, Northfield, Minnesota 55057.

Prime Time School Television, 100 North La Salle Street, Chicago, Illinois 60602.

PTL Public Television Library, 475 L'Enfant Plaza West S.W., Washington, D.C. 20024.

Radio and Visual Services Division, Office of Public Information, United Nations, New York, New York 10017.

Research for Better Schools, Inc., 1700 Market Street, Philadelphia, Pennsylvania 19103.

Scandinavian National Tourist Offices, 75 Rockefeller Plaza, 15 W. 51st Street, New York, New York 10019.

Scholastic Teacher, 50 West 44th Street, New York, New York 10036.

Social Science Educational Consortium, 855 Broadway, Boulder, Colorado 80302.

South Central Bell Telephone, 179 8th Avenue North, Nashville, Tennessee 37203.

Southwest Education Developmental Lab, 211 E. 7th Street, Austin, Texas 78701.

Southwestern Cooperative Education Lab, Inc., 229 Truman N.E., Albuquerque, New Mexico 87108.

Teacher's Guide to Television, P. O. Box 564, Lenox Hill Station, New York, New York 10021.

Television Information Office, 745 5th Avenue, New York, New York 10019.

PEN PAL SOURCES

Afro-Asian Center, CPO Box 871, Department IM, Kingston, New York 12401. Thirty-six African and Asian nations, for junior high and older, 70¢.

177

Dear Pen Pal, Department IM, P. O. Box 4054, Santa Barbara, California 93103. Include a stamped, self-addressed envelope for information about pen pals. It is specifically for 10- to 12-year-olds, but other ages can be matched. No fee.

International Friendship League, Inc., Department IM, 40 Mt. Vernon Street, Boston, Massachusetts 02108. All age children, 179 nations, $3.00.

Letters Abroad, Department IM, 209 E. 56th Street, New York, New York 10022. Will match teachers with teachers, $1.00 donation.

Letters Unlimited, P. O. Box 35143, Houston, Texas 70035. Arranges pen pals within the U.S.

Pupil to Pupil Program, Inc., 261 Constitution Avenue N.W., Washington, D.C. 20001. Sponsors communication between U.S. children and children in other nations.

Tips for Pen Pals, Source for Pen Pal Agencies, and List of All Lists. From the U. S. Committee for UNICEF, Department IM, 331 East 38th Street, New York, New York 10016. Include a long, stamped, self-addressed envelope.

The Multi-Cultural Newsletter

by Jane Bandy Smith

Anyone who has worked in a school is aware of the problems that result from poor communication. How many times have you worked on a problem that a teacher down the hall had just solved? If there had been better communication, you would have had access to an experienced resource person.

When the Nashville multi-cultural program began, the staff anticipated a need for regular communication within and between the four schools. Such communication could not only inform everyone about projects in progress but also encourage others to try similar activities. Therefore, we planned for a regular newsletter in which the lead item for each issue would be a brief report about classroom projects being implemented by teachers. As we discovered later, there was an element of status connected with teachers having their activities featured in the newsletter. We also found that it was important to spell names correctly and not to include teachers in a teaming activity who had not really contributed to that activity. This positive feedback indicated that the newsletter was being widely read.

We decided to use the name, *Motley Matters,* because one of the definitions of "motley" is many colors; so this word seemed appropriate for a multi-cultural endeavor. Our masthead included the name of the Teacher Corps program so that we could be readily identified within the network.

Some considerations in planning the newsletter format were designed to attract the attention of our readers. We knew from experience that teachers are busy people with multiple items to read every day—homework, texts, and reports, to mention a few. If teachers were to read our multi-cultural newsletter, we had to write brief, to-the-point articles.

Our layout was irregularly spaced for two reasons: to attract attention to items, and to separate them for stop 'n start reading. We could imagine that a teacher might read one item, get distracted, and begin reading a second item at a later time. We used lines, figures, and cartoon-type drawings in the newsletter to emphasize items, as well as to facilitate easy, quick reading. Additionally, the cartoons were intended to introduce a little humor and establish a sense of informality.

179

Since a major purpose of the newsletter was to communicate information, this meant more than just reporting multi-cultural, school-related projects. Therefore, we promoted local cultural activities such as art shows, musical performances, and movies which featured the lifestyles or artistic endeavors of ethnic groups. Sources telling of these activities were the entertainment section of the local newspapers, television commercials, and newsletters from cultural organizations. We informed teachers of performance hours and ticket costs of these featured events.

In addition to classroom projects and local cultural events, the newsletter gave teaching suggestions. Professional magazines were surveyed to locate activities which taught about other cultures or helped develop better human relations. Our resource center obtained copies of curriculum guides from other school systems or agencies, and portions of these guides were reprinted in the newsletter. Using selected sections of these guides through the newsletter was more effective, we believed, than presenting teachers with complete copies of these curriculum guides.

Another type of material we used for informational purposes was articles from newspapers and journals, such as reports on research and notices of commemorative days. Interest items that can be used are limitless.

A primary reason for having the newsletter originate in the resource center was to notify the teachers and staff of the materials that were available there. Although we published a list of our holdings and distributed it to every teacher, we sensed that the newsletter was also a good or better way to motivate the teachers to use our collection of materials.

NEWSLETTER SPECIMENS

Several sample copies of our newsletters appear on subsequent pages 181-187. A publication like our newsletter is highly recommended to give an opportunity for sharing ideas. We are certain that the newsletter supported multi-cultural education through improved understanding of the contributions of others, and greater awareness of program possibilities.

Multi-Cultural Musings

First--apologies on our spelling!! Catherine (Not E L I Z A B E T H) Green is working with Diane Kern at Wharton on the Foods From Various Cultures program. And, Ella Gandy's class is studying the French language and culture at Ford Greene Elementary.

NOW--Other multicultural activities that are taking place in Nashville's Teacher Corps Schools are:

BARBARA EGEL has a group of her students making a Friendship Quilt. What is it? Well, each student was asked to complete a square of their own design for the quilt. Barbara provided the scraps of fabric so the quilts will be color coordinated, one blue and green and the second one, brown and gold. During this part of the project, Barbara will be able to judge each girl (excuse the sexist slip) person's ability to handle a needle and also determine the student's eye for design. When the individual squares are completed, Barbara will piece the quilt together. Quite a Group-building Activity!

An alternate way to carry out this idea would be to create a patchwork bulletin board by assigning each student one portion of the board that they could design and carry out. A discarded wallpaper book from a local paint company will furnish a background paper or let each student select their favorite color from an assorted package of large construction paper. No telling what they will come up with!!

- - - - - - - - - - - -

Meanwhile in Washington (appropriately enough) students are being involved in an election simulation. The polling place is the Mini-School #1 and the voters are being registered by LIZ BIVENS and JOHNNY THOMPSON. You know, seriously, a national election is an event that really makes us aware of the diversity within our nation. It is this variety of cultures that makes America such an interesting country...that said, the editorial is over.

- - - - - - - - - - -

Here is an activity that we spied in MARY BUERGER'S room and it is a great way to begin a discussion of individual differences. Mirror Names..
1. Folding a piece of construction paper.
2. Take a dark (purple or black) crayon and write, in cursive, along the crease.
3. Re-fold the paper, rub hard using scissors or something hard.
4. The name will rub off on the opposite side, trace over the design.

crease →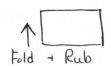
Fold + Rub

 or something like that — ask Mary...

Multicultural Moments

YOU'RE FAMILIAR WITH THE "BICENTENNIAL MINUTES"???

Well, we are going to spend a few moments to try and familiarize you

with things that are happening in Teacher Corps Schools that involve

multicultural education......you know, people learning more about

themselves and others.

You can help by letting us know what you are doing in your class
to help students understand their values and lifestyles---their
similarities and differences, as well as those of other cultures.

BOOB TUBE NEWS!!   The Puzzle Children

October 20th   6:30 p.m.

An hour-long special on learning disabilities.
Followed by a Channel 8 program telling you
of resources available in middle Tennessee.
Mainstreaming brings new importance to this
material.

****

We're getting names of students in other localities that
can be used in a Pen Pal activity. If you would like to
use this information in your classroom, let us know (327-3237).

Diane Kern and Elizabeth Greene (Wharton Jr. High), have planned a
delectable multicultural activity. They are introducing their
classes to foods that are unusual to our culture but common to others.

Ella Gandy has brought a continental touch to her room...you might
hear her students counting in French, mon amie.

              DON'T FORGET THE DISCIPLINE WORKSHOP....FRIDAY.

182

2

We discovered how to make a CHINESE NAME CHOP.......and we'd like to pass it on to you. You know how fascinated most kids are with their initials-- they will write them over and over in many kinds of script or print types. Well, this project should be a natural for them.....

OH! We forgot that you may not know what a name chop is.....neither did we until we saw the article in Chinese Arts, material compiled for Asia House Gallery, The Asia Society. Anyway, a name chop is the way that the Chinese sign their name in China. When they apply their name chop to a document, it is a symbol or pledge of good faith. They don't attach much importance to the signature that is used in the Western world.

The Chinese Name Chop handle is made from precious metals, bamboo, plastic, or rubber. The design on the bottom is pressed into red ink and then applied to the paper. Usually three Chinese characters are combined, sometimes with an animal or other feature, and the design is carved onto the block.

If your class would like to make a Chinese Name Chop-- you will need: art gum eraser, pencil, linoleum cutter, mirror, brush and red poster paint, and paper.

First, let each student make a simple design with their initials--use the mirror so that the initials will be drawn in reverse.
Next, draw the design on the art gum eraser.
Cut the design out (so that the design is recessed), with the linoleum cutter.

Because the linoleum cutter is sharp...use care, maybe a few at a time. Or as an alternative, use potato slices and cut the design out with a potato peeler.

Everyone seems to be afraid of snakes...very few people like snakes....how would you feel if you were a snake...slippery, slithery, slick, sleezey????
Draw a snake that has a design you would like to have on its skin. Is it striped, dotted, dippy?????? If you were a snake and you could only say words that began with "S".....compose a vocabulary of words you could use. REMEMBER, THE WARM WEATHER BRINGS OUT THE SNAKES!!!! In your room?? Compare designs...talk about people not liking you.

183

M OT L E Y ❧ MATTERS

Number 4   1976-77

'TIS THE SEASON....and spirit is running high at Ford Greene Elementary.

Jim Hartman and Aldorothy Wright are heading up an effort by the entire Ford
Greene faculty to have a real celebration. Every room in the building is
decorating a tree following a different theme...George Washington, Pioneer
America, Tree of Jesse, Tennessee, Bicentennial, U.S. Community, U.N., and
many countries: Germany, China, Lithuania, Mexico, Ukraine, Brazil, Denmark,
Finland, France, Holland, Russia, Moravia, and one to celebrate Chanukah. The
students are making most of the decorations during their art periods. Mary
Buerger's exploratory class is ⭐ making cookies to represent many of the
lands represented by the ⭐ trees. These cookies will be served
to parents on December 15th ⭐ when they come to see the program that
will feature music and   skits by the Ford Greene students
who have been filling   the halls with wonderful sounds,
for many weeks now. A   special treat for everyone, will be
the Spanish song by   *Greetings*   the faculty, with the piano being
played by the prin-   cipal, Aldorothy Wright, the
principal musi-   cian in the school..excuse
the pun! This   program will be the culminating activity for *From Michael*   the holiday activities that have
included a trip to   see the lovely trees at Cheekwood. Slides   of present and past trees
were shown,   *robert*   to prepare the students
for this   *Vicki*   extra special field
trip, that every-   one, kindergarten, special classes,
and all got   to see!!!! And everyone
hopes   that you will have a
happy   *Jane*   holiday season that
is   *Martha*   filled with love,
cheer......and most of all..... *Martha* ....a WARM FEELING FOR ALL

MANKIND

184

Systematic Pupil Tutoring: How the Teacher Runs the Show

Pupil-tutoring programs have two precepts: (1) the program must run smoothly enough so that it doesn't "kill" the teacher to manage it and (2) it must effectively contribute to the teacher's main instruction program.

Jane Ogles class at Ford Greene School has a pupil tutoring program in operation and she is currently helping to work the "bugs" out. Mrs. Ogles gets each session started on time and is working to get the tutor consistent at running the sessions. Her trouble shooting has helped to pinpoint two problems so far: (1) the tutor on giving hints to the learner at the wrong time and (2) the record keeping had to be simplified so that the pupil-tutor could keep his own records.

Mrs. Ogles is currently using the program to increase the reading vocabularly of one of her students (the learner) as well as to strengthen the tutor's vocabulary. Actually it's a way of "souping up" drill and practice.

Very early in the year, Mrs. Ogles pointed out the importance of the teacher's role in checking progress through the program and is using the data records to adjust and improve the program.

Although early results are very encouraging, program revision has moved into the next phase, examining ways to ensure that the learner retains the vocabulary s/he has acquired. Every revision moves the program closer to being an efficient and effective demonstration of how teachers like Mrs. Ogles can utilize existing resources. Every revision and tryout confirms the importance of the teacher who, behind the scenes, makes the program work!

IF YOU GET BUGGED BECAUSE YOU DON'T HAVE ENOUGH TIME TO HELP STUDENTS INDIVIDUALLY....YOU MIGHT TRY THIS PROGRAM THAT JOE STOWITCHEK PASSED ALONG TO MOTLEY MATTERS***

A larger proportion of American children are poor today than were poor in 1970 (over 17 million children)..1 out of every 4..are living below the poverty standard. During a gift-giving time such as Christmas, perhaps it would be a good time for a class discussion on the most valuable things we have. Suggestion: have each child write down the ten things they value most..then select the three most valuable and discuss the things they value.

A list of materials in the
Multicultural Resource Center
will be out next week . . .

185

HEARD FROM THE CLASSROOM.......**Ms. Klein's** classes at Washington explore
their individual ethnic backgrounds when they
study folk music...often sing songs in
foreign languages, too.

Jim Hartmann's class at Ford Greene read the Dolch Folk Tales and they
like to find parallels between U.S. folk tales and those from other
countries......they've discovered common characters and plots.

  Mr. Sloan at Wharton Elementary dittoes the words to"The Black Man"
(a song that can be found on Stevie Wonder's new album, Songs in the Key
of Life. The words are provided inside the record album. In this song,
many people and their contributions are mentioned. After using the song
copies in the classroom, Mr. Sloan had each child research a biography of
someone mentioned in the song. This is a super way to build a language
arts lesson that has instant appeal and interest....turn on the record and
turn on the kids!

Coming up on the tube!!!!!!!!!! March 29, NBC 8p.m. ALL CREATURES GREAT AND
                                 SMALL...A veterinarian's life...
                                 in a small English community..a
                                 good chance to discuss the simila-
                                 rities of life, beginning with pts.

April 30, PBS 8 p.m. THE HUMAN ANIMAL
                                 Comparison between human society and
                                 an ant colony. How do we develop
                                 our roles in life?

April 6, PBS 8 p.m. THE WOLF EQUATION
                                 Each year, caribou herds and wolf
                                 packs of the Alaskan Arctic go north
                                 to bear their young. But in recent
                                 years, the severe weather and other
                                 factors have caused a problem for
                                 the wolves.

SEXISMSEXISMSEXISMSEXISMSEXISMSEXISMSEXISMSEXISMSEXISMSEXISMSEXISMSEXISMSEX

  Dr. Floyd Sucher at Brigham Young University says that his research
revealed that during question and answer sessions, boys tried eight
times more frequently to respond.....but that teachers called on
girls ten times more frequently. from Instructor (April 1977, p. 40).

Sadness, sadness--day of sadness for those people who didn't get to the DISCIPLINE WORKSHOP conducted by Bruce Irons from North Carolina. This profitable day ended by playing The Discipline Game.....a fun way to initiate some serious thinking about handling classroom problems... you know, those things you have now and then! If you would like to have a session to play this game, let us know by calling the office or telling your building facilitator. OR, maybe you would like to try playing it with a group of your students. That too, can be arranged.

- - - - - - - - - - - - -

We are building a file of activities designed to promote human understanding within classrooms. One of our favorites is called FIVE SQUARES-- it is a simple, uncomplicated game that works well with all age groups. This game creates events which enable students to observe themselves and others within a group experience. Also, one of the rules of this game is, there must be absolute silence.

☐ 1 2 3 4 5 ☐

Tennessee State University is showing a collection of fabrics, needle-work and accessories from private collections. This show is called, THAT ETHNIC LOOK. You can see it in the Foyer of the Home Ec Building-- on the campus. Monday-Friday, 8 to 5. Great cost,it's free!!!!!!! Just right for our salaries. $$$$$$$$$$

Many teachers have been asking us about new ideas--and creating new ways of integrating multicultural concepts into the pattern of their classrooms and total school. The following is an evaluation sheet for you to use in evaluating your school's multicultural program. It might help you to generate some unique activities. It might be interesting to fill it out as a class activity and let students suggest ways to enrich the multi-cultural program of you school.....................

TRY FILLING IT OUT.

PLEASE.

Part III

Inservice Training:
Leading, Organizing, and Implementing

This part of the book outlines the multi-cultural training program that motivated and supported the development of the multi-cultural activities used in the schools and community. It includes the basic characteristics of the organization, management, and implementation processes. Some descriptors of leadership roles, instructional processes, and participant motivators are also included. Some aspects of the design of the first-year Nashville multi-cultural foundations program entitled "The School As a Culture Approach" are included. Basically, the subsequent articles on the training program concentrate on the organization and implementation of the second-year phase to integrate multi-cultural education into the curriculum of the Teacher Corps schools. Included in this series are pieces by some of the training instructors in which they discuss their roles and instructional processes.

How We Generated All This "Action" . . . *Or*
Organizing to Develop a Multi-Cultural Education
Inservice Program and to Reach the Kids
by Michael G. Pasternak

In the planning stages of the 10th Cycle of Nashville's Teacher Corps project, the need for a multi-cultural education program in the schools was obvious. The teaching of understandings that supported and encouraged multi-culturalism and alternate lifestyles was deficient. The decision was made to begin with a multi-cultural instructional team leading a series of weekly seminars and workshop experience as the basis for a multi-cultural foundations program. Given the tradition of teacher and community involvement in the planning of Nashville Teacher Corps projects, and the preference of the instruc-

188

tional team (George Cox of Tennessee State University and Michael Pasternak of Peabody College—shortly afterwards Martis Okpalobi from Peabody joined the team), teachers and community members were invited to become involved in planning the foundations program. A series of four teacher-community seminar planning sessions were held. Related needs assessment and survey activities sought recommendations as to what should be included in the foundations program. Those polled included teachers, community members, college instructors, students, and school principals. Whatever the design of the program, it was going to begin at least with the support of its participants . . . for they had a major role in designing it. We titled the program "The School As a Culture Approach."

ASPECTS AND ACCOMPLISHMENTS
OF THE FOUNDATIONS PROGRAM

It was the instructional team's belief that the typical multicultural education program was frequently limited to the simple dimension of understanding multiple cultures and ethnic characteristics. We also believed that *simply* knowing about and understanding differing cultural and ethnic groups would *not* influence people to develop school programs that would help children understand cultural diversity, help children develop healthy relationships with others who were different from themselves, or help children feel good about being different. Moreover, we wanted a multi-cultural program that would also improve the multi-cultural climate and relationships in the schools.

Therefore, the foundations program's instructional format, seminars, workshops, and related activities were unique in some ways. First, they were based on an analysis of typical school problems which concluded that these problems were the result of the schools' failure and teachers' inability to propose and develop adequate resolutions. Most of the problems they encountered stemmed from four intertwined factors, namely: cultural diversity, differing educational belief systems, distinctive personal characteristics, and differing leadership styles. Thus, the primary purpose of the program became the support and encouragement of cultural diversity through the exploration of these four related areas:

1. Multi-Ethnicity/Multi-Culturalism—differing languages, beliefs, values, behaviors, lifestyles
2. Social Systems/Organizations — differing roles, norms,

189

power structures, decision-making processes, related beliefs and values

3. Educational Belief Systems—differing values and beliefs
   related to the how, what, when, why, and who in teaching

4. Multiple Talents—the concept that everyone is talented in
   different ways.

The assumption was that these four areas, and the beliefs and
values individuals held related to them, represented the culture of
the school. If we could help the participants in the foundations
program become more aware of their own beliefs and values related to the four areas, and help them become more aware of the
beliefs and values of others in the school, it would lead to consistent and conscious behaviors, clear identification of differences among everyone, and the opportunity to develop new
resolution action plans to support their differences and multi-
cultural purposes . . . and for many participants, that's what
happened.

Second, the focus was on helping people develop the ability
to define the school's problems in terms of a cultural frame of
reference (instead of exclusively in terms of personality differences or moral judgments) and thereby assist participants in
proposing and developing solutions based on and consistent with
enhancing cultural diversity. An example taken from the foundations program would be the session for examining classroom materials being used in the Teacher Corps schools and the multi-
cultural criteria for materials usage. It was found during this
awareness/consciousness activity that sexist/racist/stereotyp-
ing materials were being used. The teachers' beliefs about such
discrimination, once identified and articulated, led them to search
for and adapt new materials to replace the old.

Third, the sessions of the foundations program provided activities to help people become more understanding of the school
organization and of the people living in the school community,
and to capitalize on the diversity of the group itself as healthier
relationships developed. Finally, the program depended on instant (weekly) anonymous feedback from the participants in order
to determine the seminar's direction and their enthusiasm. This
feedback was also shared with all of the participants on a weekly
basis.

At the completion of the foundations program (spring 1976),
the 85 participants were questioned about the future directions of

the multi-cultural program. The following summary indicates the twenty highest priority sub-topics for future training:

- more on multi-talented approach to learners' growth and development
- more on integrating foundations of multi-cultural approach to teaching in all subject, content and/or teaching areas
- working with teachers on identifying, recognizing and incorporating their educational belief systems, values, and cultures into classroom teaching-learning situations
- more emphasis on recommended resource materials and sources for obtaining and developing materials for meeting the cultural and other diversities which currently exist in our classrooms
- developing activities and games for use in helping us to recognize our personal feelings and multi-cultural differences
- information on and strategies for learning kids' jargon, dialects, body language, street language, etc.
- more positive community input for school and vice-versa
- more on kids' lifestyles
- helping students learn more about themselves individually and others and thus better understand, appreciate, and accept individual and group differences
- more on how to get to the "we're all okay" feeling
- how to resolve classroom behavioral problems
- how teachers can facilitate group decision-making
- more sharing of teacher-developed activities
- help in motivating children with whom teachers work
- how to deal with feedback from children
- more emphasis on cultural likenesses rather than cultural differences
- how to make kids more trusting
- break down training into smaller groups by school
- study other specific minority groups, e.g., Puerto Ricans, Italians, Jews
- more from anthropological perspective
- more from psychological perspective, i.e., learning theories

ORGANIZATION AND IMPLEMENTATION

As a result of the wide range of inservice needs expressed by the participants of the multi-cultural foundations program, it was apparent that no *single* instructional process would be responsive to those expressed needs and, therefore, appropriate for the second year of the program. A variety of approaches allowing for individual participant needs but offered in a coordinated fashion by an instructional team seemed to be the answer. Because almost everyone was concerned that the results of their endeavors have an impact on children, the focus of the new instructional training processes emphasized developing action plans, or activities and strategies, to be implemented in the schools.

An interdisciplinary instructional team was formed that linked together all of the facets of the training program. Instructors associated with exceptional children, math, social science, reading, parent education, curriculum leadership and supervision, and counseling recognized the stated needs of the program participants and indicated their willingness to help teachers learn new ways to integrate multi-cultural education into the classroom, school, and community. The instructional management team included a representative group of instructors, the building principals, the Teacher Corps director and assistant director, a team leader, and community coordinators. This team linkage was assisted by a definition of multi-cultural education that was initially broad enough to incorporate everyone's talents into the training endeavor. Therefore, all the instructors identified an instructional process that fit their own style of training and still achieved success in helping kids and teachers learn multi-cultural concepts. The definition included any instructional activity that helped children or adults develop new learnings in any combination of the following three areas: 1) cultural literacy . . . multi-cultural/ethnic understandings; 2) developing cooperative group styles and learning how to develop healthy human relationships; and 3) the students' self-realization and healthy self-concept development. Simply teaching about different ethnic or cultural characteristics of people was only one aspect of this multi-cultural education program. Some instructional needs of teachers and community participants called for either seminars, individual consultation, workshops, individual projects and studies, or some combination of the above. The instructional management team met every other week to communicate problems and progress and to explore new ways of responding to teachers' needs. All instructors and the Teacher Corps staff held at least one large group meeting monthly for the purpose of further ensuring team efforts and effective communication.

An overview of the second year program shows the following training opportunities offered on a credit or non-credit basis:

1. Seminars, workshops, and individual consultation and study in the exceptional child areas which included the diagnostic-prescriptive process and criterion-referenced testing, mini-resource centers for learning disabilities in

192

the regular classroom and for helping special education teachers function as resources to the regular classroom teachers. These areas offered ample opportunity to help teachers create new ways for their students to explore diversity and human relationships, peer tutoring, group dynamics, personalizing instruction, cultural motivators, and successful utilization of community volunteers working with students.

2. The Parent, School, and Community Program which provided boundless opportunities for multi-cultural learnings and applications to activities for kids (see page 204).

3. The multiple talents approach to teaching seminars which included helping teachers develop classroom activities designed to identify, understand, and enhance each individual's talent as well as to help students appreciate each other's unique talents.

4. Seminars and workshops in the area of reading which assisted teachers in helping students learn how to read by using a variety of multi-cultural, multi-ethnic books in the teaching process and which showed teachers ways to use the child's community as a stimulus for language arts activities.

5. Seminars on classroom strategies for teaching thinking and valuing which helped teachers learn new ways of helping children identify values, feelings, and thinking processes. Through these activities children learned about others' values and value diversity.

6. Field experience and practicum opportunities within the curriculum leadership training component which were considered by many as the most unique aspect of the program because it provided for almost any individual teacher training need and for relating it to multi-cultural education. In the field experience, teachers and community participants were assisted by a series of meetings and questionnaires to indicate new teaching skills they would like to develop or to identify a real instructional problem they were experiencing in their classroom or school. The key element was that the teacher identified *his/her* own needs. Thereafter, a resource instructor was assigned to work on a one-to-one basis with each teacher over a 15-

week period to accomplish his/her need-related goals. Weekly progress reports and instructor visits followed. A section of the progress report requested that each participant respond to the following questions each week: "In what ways have your activities related to helping children develop new multi-cultural understandings?" and "How is what you are doing related to multi-cultural education?"

For example, if a teacher needed assistance in helping develop new skills in teaching reading or math and enrolled in the field experience program, an instructor with reading or math expertise would work with that individual to develop the new skills and understandings. No matter what math or reading teaching skill the teacher wanted to learn, he/she would be asked by the instructor to relate it to multi-cultural education in his or her teaching, or to develop additional multi-cultural education activities to use with students in math and reading. If, while working with any individual, the instructor needed assistance in relating multi-cultural education to the particular field experience's purposes, he/she requested such aid from an instructor with more experience in multi-cultural education. In this way, college instructors as well as teachers learned how to integrate multi-cultural education into all areas of the curriculum.

In some instances, teams of teachers requested assistance in the area of team planning. A field experience designed to help them function more effectively ensued. Instructors were assigned to meet with the team on a regular basis and multi-cultural education became a team as well as an individual teacher and/or community participant concern. The practicum experience was designed to train teachers in supervisory skills to enable them to work with other teachers for improving their classroom instruction. As with the field experience approach, the practicum also helped teachers work with others in identifying how multi-cultural education could be implemented in their classrooms.

The interdisciplinary teaming was enhanced by the instructional staff's commitment to utilize multi-cultural education as the basis for improving the total school program. All of the training components and leadership roles integrated multi-cultural education into their objectives. In the instructional staff meetings the instructors began to plan teamed inservice activities. Typical "turf" identifications or specialty teaching areas of college in-

194

structors seemed to be less important than multi-cultural education as they shared expertise in working together.

At the beginning of the second year of the multi-cultural education program, the writer met with all of the teachers in each Teacher Corps school to explain the training and other opportunities available to them. While these opportunities reflected the results of the participants' needs assessments (teachers filled out forms indicating their training and other needs at least twice every four months), a large number of inservice possibilities required face-to-face explanations and communications. These meetings were important involvement motivators. University credit was always an option for teachers, but such enrollment was not necessary in order to receive training opportunities. Other key aspects of the organization and delivery system of the second year program are described in the subsequent points.

1. Advanced degree graduate students were used as co-instructors in the inservice program. Approximately ten doctoral students spent a minimum of six hours per week working as support instructors in the multi-cultural program through the field experience approach. Some took major leadership roles in helping teachers teach multi-cultural understandings through developing a resource center, materials identification, foreign language development, group counseling skills, reading development, teaming, group social skills, and planning and evaluation. Frequently a doctoral student would be directly supervised by an instructor from a different college than the one attended. Expertise was shared in this consortium regardless of institutional attachment.

2. The development of a multi-cultural resource center including materials, bibliographies, and newsletters resulted in a place where teachers received assistance in identifying and creating classroom materials and activities.

3. Financial assistance was available for instructional support. At the beginning of the second year, the multi-cultural program announced that it had a limited amount of seed money for teachers who design and implement new *and* unique multi-cultural activities. "Just write up a brief request and justification and the money is yours!" It was amazing how many super ideas we received—and how few of them actually required any money at all! We dis-

195

covered that most requests fell into existing instructional budgets of the schools and could be implemented with materials and equipment already in the schools or school system, or those which could be borrowed or contributed by people in the community. It became apparent to many teachers that multi-cultural education could be implemented in creative, enthusiastic, yet low-cost approaches.

4. All-school multi-cultural activities were encouraged. School faculties identified several all-school multi-cultural activities that took several weeks or months of involved planning and preparation on the part of teachers, community members, and kids. Activities such as festivals, celebrations, and exploratory programs developed a high level of multi-cultural awareness and enthusiasm within the schools (see pp. 124-142).

5. A leadership support system was maintained. The writer met with a principal almost every Thursday at 7:30 a.m. During an hour or so together we discussed how to initiate new training opportunities for teachers, plan all-school multi-cultural activities, support teachers' good ideas, and share new "seeds" or ideas on school-improvement. New opportunities were planned for the doctoral students working in the schools, brainstormed, and evaluated. These supportive activities also occurred between college instructors and between doctoral students and instructors.

6. Teachers' support to other teachers was built in. Regular meetings of field experience and practicum participants for the purpose of sharing accomplishments increased teacher teaming and supportive relationships. As teachers learned of each other's multi-cultural activities, they began to share, work more closely together, take more risks at trying new "things," and to resolve difficult problems together.

7. An atmosphere of trust was created. Because of the broad definition of multi-cultural education and the willingness of the Teacher Corps staff, principals, and college instructors to support almost any activity that enhanced multi-cultural purposes, teachers had a broad range of means for being successful. Once everyone began succeeding in their own way, many began to take new risks with unfamiliar activities. No packaged or "laid on" les-

sons or programs were required of teachers. All created, selected, or borrowed their own approaches. It was truly a developmental process. It became "okay" for anyone to ask for help.

Another immeasurable factor was the "snowball effect." It is most difficult to set down in print *all* of the instructional processes or aspects of the delivery system. After a while, teachers and others began to help each other develop multi-cultural activities in very informal ways. For example, one day a teacher was putting up a new bulletin board in the hallway. It was supposed to be a series of pictures to celebrate national inventors' week. Shortly after the teacher began hanging pictures, another teacher commented that no minority members were pictured on the board. Realizing his mistake, the teacher began to search for pictures of minority inventors, going about the building asking teachers for assistance. While he was gone, another teacher went by the incomplete board and noticed the absence of women. It wasn't long before that bulletin board became an all-school effort. No one seemed to get "uptight." Making a mistake was okay. Giving and taking suggestions related to improving the multi-cultural climate of that school is now a way of life. It is also a retraining program for teachers. And, it is interesting to watch the kids support diversity in similar ways.

Management of Program Development and Implementation in Multi-Cultural Education
by James M. Yonts, Jr.

Appropriate administrative arrangements are necessary for the successful development of a multi-cultural education inservice program. Without them, the potentially successful program will become bogged down and relegated to a secondary priority. Jim Yonts has managed a successful program. His strong commitment to multi-cultural purposes, enthusiasm, and administrative skills pulled together a team of dedicated practitioners. Nine years as Executive Director of the Teacher Education Alliance for Metro provides the experiential background for his remarks. They are helpful insights for those who want to manage a multi-cultural education program.

To be effective, multi-cultural education must focus on modifying the total school environment of both the institution of higher education and the public school system. Attention must be given to such elements as admission policies, testing programs, decision-making (power), grouping practices, and curriculum modification for teachers and children.

The role of the Teacher Corps Director was to secure institutional commitments that permitted the development of a new system of relationships between the university, the school system, and the community. Thus, Teacher Corps served as a new vehicle for the utilization of resources to develop and implement multi-cultural activities. Had not some college program decision-making power been shifted to a collaborative governing structure (Program Steering Committee and School Community Council) and to the Teacher Corps staff, the commitment of participating institutions would have been questionable. In addition to institutional arrangements, the director was committed to collaboration at all levels of program development and operation. Staffing in this project reflected the diversity of cooperating institutions and the general population served. School system and community personnel were accepted as teacher trainers in parity with college instructors.

Therefore, the primary function of the Teacher Corps Director was to secure collaborations, policy decisions, and administrative arrangements that assured the development and implementation of multi-cultural education at the university and in the school system. The policy decisions and institutional arrangements that provided options and motivators for the teachers included:

—Training was available to all teachers in target schools; graduate credit and degrees from the university were optional.

—Multi-cultural education was a core retraining requirement for all teachers. A commitment to the incorporation of multi-cultural education into the regular university program was made prior to the implementation of the Teacher Corps program.

—Multi-cultural education activities were field-based and referenced to the needs identified by children, teachers, and community personnel.

—For teachers pursuing degrees and university credit, practicum and individualized field work activities were available.

Effective management of program development and the implementation of multi-cultural education for children and adults was the direct responsibility of the director and an instructional management team. The management team included Teacher Corps staff members such as the program development specialist, team leader, and community coordinator. In addition, the lead trainers from the various inservice program components—community, exceptional child, and curriculum leadership—were included. Important members of the team were the principals of the target schools.

Other management responsibilities of the director included:
—Negotiating for adequate instructional staff in terms of quality, numbers, and time.
—Providing adequate time for personnel to conduct needs assessment and subsequent program development.
—Developing an effective and open communication system to include:

> a governing council with parity.
>
> a parity school-community council.
>
> regularly scheduled staff meetings that include the management team.
>
> regularly scheduled meetings with all inservice instructors.
>
> program facilitation at each target school. This was the role of the principal, team leader or another designated person.
>
> a weekly schedule of activities for all participants.

—Providing for periodical review and evaluation of the multi-cultural program.

Role of the Principal in the Development of a Multi-Cultural Education Program

by Aldorothy Wright

Aldorothy Wright is the principal of Ford Greene Elementary School. While some principals relegate instructional leadership to a secondary priority, it is not so with Principal Wright. She is clearly the educational leader at Ford Greene. She has experienced all of the Teacher Corps inservice opportunities (and many more) side-by-side with her teachers . . . at every seminar, workshop, and inservice experience. She has also moved beyond

that role to become a colleague on the Teacher Corps In-
structional Management Team. Wright was involved with
the staff and instructors in designing the teaching/learn-
ing program to respond to teachers' needs. It also was
not unusual to see her take on the role of instructor as she
worked with her teachers. Without a doubt, the multi-
cultural program would have been seriously impaired had
it not been for her leadership, cooperation, and concern.
We seriously question whether any extensive multi-cultural
program can be integrated successfully into the curricu-
lum of a school without such leadership from its principal.
In this selection, Wright briefly describes the principal's
role in the development of a multi-cultural program.

The role of the principal in the development of a multi-cultural
education program is demanding. When I combined the existing
responsibilities of the principalship with the development of a
multi-cultural program, it necessitated far more planning and
preparation. However, if a viable program was to develop, I had
to provide the necessary and supportive leadership.

Multi-cultural education programs do not miraculously occur.
Their development is a result of planned strategies and the cooperative efforts of many groups. The principal is the key person in
this process. As the principal, I became a leader in the development, utilization, and integration of the concept of multi-cultural
education in all phases of the school program. My support and
active involvement in the multi-cultural program influenced many
others in the school to participate.

Obviously, I could not have developed a multi-cultural program independently. I utilized all of the available resources to
accomplish the task. I worked with the Teacher Corps staff, college instructors, teachers, parents, school system personnel, and
all others who would assist in planning the program and the appropriate delivery systems. We decided that the starting point
should be a series of seminars which would serve to help us develop some common understandings of what multi-cultural education meant to us. After this, additional support services were
initiated, such as the following:

1. A resource center was established that contained commercial and teacher-made materials, activities designed
   by teachers for use with students, books, listings of films
   and filmstrips, professional development materials, and

other curriculum materials that could be utilized by teachers for self-development and programs for students.

2. Advanced graduate practicum and field experience students were recruited from Peabody College to assist teachers in planning, developing, and providing a variety of multi-cultural experiences for the classroom that included role playing, values clarification, and simulations.

3. Consultation with a professor in exploring my role as a principal in the process and potential of planning all-school multi-cultural activities. Regular meetings were held so that I might better identify my needs and get a better view of my leadership role.

4. A proposal was submitted for additional funding to promote a school-wide multi-cultural day.

The best starting point for the development of a multi-cultural program is in the planning of the activities along with the faculty. Total involvement of all faculty members is important. Without it, the success of the program is in jeopardy at the outset. I became involved in developing action plans to provide opportunities for teachers to learn more about the multi-cultural education program and what they could do to facilitate related purposes and goals in their classrooms. These plans included the following:

Inservice Meetings. Inservice sessions should be structured to include a variety of activities such as human relations workshops, role playing, values clarification, films that will generate discussion, and exchange of ideas, games, and any other activities that seem appropriate. Opportunities for developing all school projects will almost certainly emerge from sessions such as these.

As a result of one of these sessions, our teachers decided to select a culture to study with their classes and to share with all pupils in a multi-cultural Christmas program. Classes shared these experiences by presenting a Christmas musical, decorating trees of the particular culture studied, and planning a reception for parents where they served refreshments representing foods from different lands. A final activity for all pupils was a field trip to see "Christmas Trees of Many Lands" at Cheekwood Gardens. The enthusiasm generated by teachers, students, parents, and community was well worth all of the time and energy spent in the planning.

201

Seminars. Cooperative planning with college professors and Teacher Corps personnel to provide seminars for the faculty was a priority. The participation of all faculty members in such seminars was encouraged. It is extremely important for the principal to be just as involved in these seminars as the teachers. For example, teacher needs were assessed and high on their list was that of dealing with discipline as related to social literacy. An outside consultant conducted a one-day workshop in this area for the staff.

Use of Outside Agencies. Solicit assistance from agencies such as the Panel of American Women to work with teachers and pupils. This one agency provided three different programs for the entire student body throughout the year. They also provided us with filmstrips dealing with human differences that teachers used with their classes. Many other agencies have programs designed specifically to help teachers and pupils explore ways of dealing with conflict and encouraging respect and appreciation for differences.

Local Colleges and Universities. Educational institutions have many practicum and field experience students who will work with teachers in the classroom or assist them in the development of activities that promote multi-cultural education. One group of practicum students worked directly with students in our TAD (Towards Affective Development) program and trained teachers to use this program more effectively with students. Other students developed activities for role playing and values clarification. Another group used a series of filmstrips on understanding ourselves and others in activities with small groups of students.

Local School System. Resource people and materials were secured through our local school system to promote our program. The human relations department supplied us with a consultant who conducted three workshops for the faculty. Most large school systems have a human relations department with personnel available to assist schools in this area. The system also supplied films, recordings, filmstrips, and other audiovisual aids through their materials center for our use.

Volunteers. Classroom participation from persons in the community should be solicited. They come from diverse backgrounds and cultures and will certainly enhance your program. Through our exploratory program we were able to get a substantial number of persons to help. Again we relied heavily on the colleges and universities to get students representing different cultures to share their customs with us. An African student spent one day per week one semester volunteering her services and sharing her lifestyle with her pupils.

Parents. Many parents are eager to do anything to promote the school program. Not only should they be encouraged to serve in some capacity in the school but also they should have a part in the planning of worthwhile experiences for students. They enrich the school experience because they bring different values and beliefs to the school environment. In one class a German parent spent time with students simply answering questions posed by them ranging from "What kinds of food are eaten by Germans?" to "What kinds of special days are celebrated in Germany?" This was a rewarding experience for both pupils and parent.

Students. Inasmuch as the objectives of the multi-cultural education program were designed to effect change and bring about a better understanding and appreciation of differences, students must be actively involved. They are creative and imaginative and can come up with many ideas that support cultural diversity. Throughout the school there was evidence that pupils were involved. School and classroom bulletin boards reflected the kinds of things they were doing that supported the multi-cultural concept. They became more aware of their feelings and those of others. In some of their rap sessions it was not uncommon to hear them remark that they were proud to be who they were, that they felt they had something worthwhile to offer to their school or that it's all right to be different.

The success or failure of a multi-cultural program is difficult to evaluate, but we tried. There was an ongoing evaluation of what we were doing and constant feedback on what we could do to improve. We observed carefully the reaction of those involved, especially the pupils. We felt good about what we saw happening and what we were doing—and did more of it.

The plan mentioned here constitutes only a small part in the development of a multi-cultural education program. Opportunities for the development of a program are unlimited. However, there must be commitment on the part of all involved to make it work, especially the principal. If the principal is not committed and involved at all levels of the development process, it becomes meaningless.

Parents, the School, and the Community
by Jerold P. Bauch

Jerry Bauch is a Professor of Education at George Peabody College for Teachers. His leadership role in the Nashville Teacher Corps project has been significant. The work he has accomplished in the community program has earned him both regional and national applause. In this selection Bauch briefly describes the approach that was used in the inservice program. The multi-cultural education purposes are quite clear.

How do inservice teachers increase their understanding and skill in relating to the parents of their students and to the larger school community? Why? Some answers to these questions have come from the experiences of teachers and interns in a graduate school offering entitled "Parents, the School, and the Community." This field-referenced inservice experience was one key element in the community-based education of Teacher Corps participants. The purpose of the community activities was to increase the interaction among the key people in a child's education; the parents and the teachers. It served as a stimulus for parents and teachers to know each other as people as well as in the more traditional ways. Teachers learned to do things *with* parents, not *for* them or *to* them. Parents learned that they were listened to, and that their ideas were valued. Where there were racial, cultural, or other differences between parents and teachers, the typical misunderstandings were reduced as the quality of their communication was improved.

The means for accomplishing this took two basic forms. All participants were engaged in presentations, discussions, lectures, and simulations as a part of the instructional plan. Each member of the group also developed a community action project or projects. These projects were planned by the teacher or intern, were reviewed and revised by the instructor (myself), community coordinators, administrators, or other resource persons, and were implemented. The evaluation requirement was met by the submission of a summary evaluative report.

The group meetings and activities where all participants were

204

in attendance were carefully selected to provoke as well as to instruct. All teachers spent *seven* years deeply involved in the role of a low-income inner-city resident during the simulation called "ghetto." They took on the value and personality structure of the under-educated AFDC mother, the high school drop-out, and the family provider. They played with the restrictions of poor education, housing, recreation, and safety conditions in the neighborhood. And they left the "ghetto" with new and personal insights into the lives of the families represented in their classrooms.

Participants viewed and experienced *"The American Family,"* a dramatic multi-media presentation which brought the diversity of family circumstance into sharp perspective. They followed this strongly affective experience with a new twist; they worked in small groups to identify the *strengths* in family situations which are frequently the topic of gossip or sympathy.

To better understand the attitudes, motivation, and behaviors of parents in their school communities, a simulation called "How Visitors See the School" was used. Through filmed incidents, teacher-participants had a chance to see their schools through the eyes of clients. As parents they found school to be an alien, impersonal, and even threatening place. This activity was used to build awareness of how *others* may perceive schools, so that a more accurate understanding of such events as missed conferences and low PTA attendance would develop.

Throughout the planned inservice activities for community-based education, every attempt was made to reduce the stereotypes of race, sex, income level, and other personal circumstances. These stereotypes were replaced by encouragement to gather *real* information about parents and community residents rather than relying on hearsay. This effort was implemented through the second half of the program, the community action projects.

The community action projects were selected by teachers or teams of teachers after an informal needs assessment and consultation with appropriate resource persons and key administrators. Teachers were encouraged to involve parents and other community members in the planning stage as well as the activity itself.

Teachers began sending home newsletters about classroom activities. Some were written by teachers, some by teacher/parent teams, and some with the extensive involvement of the children. One teacher arranged a home visit with a family of another race in a remote neighborhood and found that the family invited themselves to a home visit with the teacher for exactly the same purpose; each wanted to find out more about the other. Many teachers learned that a social setting allows for more parent-teacher interaction than the more formal meetings and conferences. A covered-dish supper dramatically raised parent (and teacher) attendance at a PTA function, and one teacher recruited five parents to serve as instructional volunteers before dessert was served!

As teachers and parents began to know each other better, they tended to work together on ideas rather than be in conflict or out of touch with each other. Two kindergarten teachers wanted to encourage the children to make more use of books. They learned that few families had appropriate books at home, so they helped parents apply for a library card for their child. Fifty young children are now "card-carrying" members of the public library, and books are a new part of the child's life at home and at school.

Teaching activities, instructional materials, community resources, and ideas for action projects all are part of a growing capability to make the match between parents, the school, and the community. They all provided valuable new input to similar inservice opportunities offered to other groups. They constituted the major portion of a paper presented at the Conference on Innovative Practices in Teacher Education sponsored by the Association of Teacher Educators in Atlanta in February of 1977. Two teachers from the course were featured in the Metro Schools' newsletter "Chalktalk" because of their community activities. And in the neighborhoods of the involved schools, more parents and more teachers are becoming partners in their important roles as educators of the children.

No One Calls Them "Oozoos" Any More
or
Multi-Cultural Education: Foreign Language in the Special Education Classroom
by Edward V. Johnson
and Ella Lett Gandy

As a doctoral student enrolled in a practicum in curriculum leadership development, Ed Johnson developed a

206

helping supervisory relationship with teachers. His task was to provide the leadership in the development of new classroom activities designed and/or adapted for multi-cultural understandings. Ella Gandy, Teacher Corps teacher at Ford Greene Elementary, was enrolled in a curriculum development field experience. Her role was to provide leadership in new curriculum developments in her classroom as well as to facilitate Johnson's new learnings about working in inner-city elementary classrooms with special education children. This selection clearly supports the idea that we are all teachers and learners. To our knowledge this multi-cultural experience in the special education classroom is a first—and without question, a success.

MC . . . (Multi-Cultural) . . . Have you ever heard the term "oozoos" applied to students in special education classes? It's shorthand slang for, "Oo, look at the zoo!" Well, we know of some students who aren't called "oozoos" anymore.

CP . . . (Curious Person) . . . Wait a minute now! What are you talking about?

MC . . . It begins with the growing concern for *true* multi-cultural education in America.

CP . . . What do you mean when you say "true?"

MC . . . We're talking about education that values diversity as well as sameness, education that doesn't ask a student to suppress or denounce the cultural values that he has grown up with.

CP . . . Where does foreign language fit in?

MC . . . Because foreign languages come from different cultures, it's natural to use them as a way to stimulate interest in other cultures—and appreciation, too.

CP . . . You mean I would teach my pupils to *speak* a foreign language?

MC . . . Well, that could be part of it, because it's fun and would really help keep the kids interested.

CP . . . What if I don't know a foreign language?

MC . . . You won't be alone there. Seriously, though, it would be good to know a little Spanish or French or something, but it isn't essential. The speaking part could be handled through tapes or records. Or maybe you could do some team teaching with a colleague who *does* speak a foreign language.

CP . . . You said speaking was just part of the idea, didn't you?

MC . . . Ah, you *were* paying attention. That's right, and it isn't even the main part.

CP . . . So what things are you shooting for?

MC . . . Let us answer that with a list of desired outcomes for students:

1. Appreciation of cultural diversity.
2. Understanding of cultural differences.
3. Awareness of elements of other cultures in American society.
4. Positive attitudes toward people from other cultures.
5. Feeling of accomplishment in using another language and knowing about other cultures.
6. Enhanced feeling of personal worth.
7. Increased understanding of the English language.

CP . . . Are those given in order of importance?

MC . . . No, not necessarily. And they probably aren't the only ones that should be considered. You might want to add some others.

CP . . . All right, they look good on paper. But what kinds of things can we *do* to reach those "desired outcomes?"

MC . . . We thought you'd never ask. We happen to have a list of suggestions for that, too. Again, you can probably think of many others to add, but here they are:

1. Talking about the people of other countries—what they look like, what they value, how they view Americans, and so on.
2. Learning about contributions of other cultures to world civilization—science, art, music, and all the rest.
3. Discussing personal feelings about people from other cultures.
4. Viewing slides and films about foreign people and places.
5. Listening to stories about famous people from other cultures, and maybe doing some role playing.
6. Learning about foreign customs and daily living.
7. Preparing and eating food that is popular in other countries.
8. Listening to familiar stories in another language.
9. Using maps of the world and selected countries.
10. Creating things—drawings, menus, skits, etc.—that relate to a foreign culture.

11. Listening to tape recordings and records in a foreign language.
12. Conversing with the teacher and each other using common foreign expressions.
13. Singing songs in a foreign language.
14. Playing guessing games using foreign words. How many? What's the missing number? Who am I? What color is it? etc.

CP . . . It still *sounds* good, but can you give me a specific example?

MC . . . Okay. Suppose we start with the story of Napoleon. That can lead to all sorts of activities, like these:

1. Learning about the man himself and why he is an important figure in world history.
2. Using a map to locate where he was born, where he fought certain battles, and where he was exiled.
3. Viewing slides of the Arc de Triomphe and other monuments erected in honor of Napoleon.
4. Discussing living conditions in France during the Napoleonic era.
5. Looking at and talking about Jacques-Louis David's painting of Napoleon's coronation.
6. Listening to Beethoven's "Emperor Concerto" and his Third Symphony.
7. Discussing the problem of judging people by their appearance, using Napoleon's slight stature as a lead-in.
8. Studying the weapons used by Napoleon's soldiers.

CP . . . Say, that covers a lot of subject areas, doesn't it?

MC . . . That's another big advantage of this approach. It has great potential for interdisciplinary study at all grade and ability levels.

CP . . . Now comes the big question. How do you know it will work?

MC . . . First of all, we don't claim to be the only teachers who have ever used this idea. But we can tell you what happened when *we* tried it. One class was a group of mildly-handicapped children, 11 and 12 years old, with both physical and learning disabilities. However, we felt that they could benefit from activities based upon a foreign language and a foreign culture. So we leaped right into the project with full enthusiasm.

209

ED: Leaving the dialogue for a minute and speaking as one of the authors, I would like to describe the process that Ella and I used in conducting this project. Ella is the regular teacher in the special education classroom, and I entered the picture as a facilitator from outside the school system. First, we recognized each other's area of expertise . . . Ella's in special education and mine in foreign language education. We set our goals, as described earlier, and made a tentative list of the kinds of activities that would likely interest the students. One of the first things we did was to let the students choose French names so that they could identify quickly with the foreign culture. From that point on, they were involved in selecting and planning many of the activities. In fact, it was their idea to produce a French "play," which was video-taped and turned out to be the big payoff activity that made them the "stars" of a TV production.

When I could be present, we concentrated mainly on oral practice and discussions about the French culture. At other times, Ella worked with the students in social studies activities. Gradually, this divided approach diminished and everything seemed to blend into a single effort.

CP . . . Right. Now, where was I? Oh yes, were the kids really interested in this business?

MC . . . They certainly were, even more than we expected. We used slides and magazine pictures to bring out questions and were really intrigued by some of them.

CP . . . Like what, for example?

MC . . . Like "Do they pray to our God?" and "Are their holidays the same as ours?" and "Do Black people speak French?" Actually, our question-answer sessions were among the most meaningful activities and led quite naturally into others.

CP . . . Okay, get specific again. Can you describe some of those "meaningful" activities?

MC . . . We'd be glad to. Try a couple on for size.

I. Greetings and Polite Sayings

Purposes: (1) to familiarize students with French language patterns and (2) to promote the importance of politeness in social relations.

Procedure: Present expressions orally at first, in written form later. After students learn to pronounce them,

210

form pairs of small groups for practice, using a role-playing approach. The teacher should also use these expressions daily in place of the similar English expressions.

Suggestions: Teacher-made flash cards are a good aid after the students have learned the expressions orally. Probably the best supplement, though, is a tape recording of the expressions with pauses where students can repeat the sayings or respond to the voice.

II. French-Speaking People

Purposes: (1) to show the sameness of people everywhere and (2) to show differences as being good.

Procedure: Use slides, films, and/or pictures that demonstrate the customs and life-styles of people from other cultures. Rather than having a highly-structured discussion, let the students ask questions and make comments about what they see. Some standard prompting questions for the teacher might be "What do you like in this picture?" or "How is that different from what you do?" or "What would you do if you were in that scene?"

Suggestions: Be alert for ideas that might develop into individual or group projects in which students can explore areas of interest.

MC . . . I could go on with these activities, but . . .

CP . . . No, that's fine. I think I have the idea. What good things came of all this effort?

MC . . . To put it directly, a whole bunch of good things happened. Let's allow Ella to speak to that from her vantage point as the classroom teacher.

ELLA: First of all, the parents liked the fact that their children are studying French. They believe it demonstrates that the children can learn. The students seem to feel the same way about it, and it obviously has increased their feelings of self-worth. They can say things that most of the other students can't say and they know facts about the world that others don't know. Certainly, their knowledge is limited, as is their speaking ability, but it makes them unique in a good way. Moreover, we have stopped hearing children talking about "oozoos" as they pass by our classroom door.

CP . . . Well, we finally got back to to your opening remark. So where do we go from here?

MC . . . Hopefully, we have stimulated some thinking on multi-cultural education, foreign language teaching, special education, and education in general. That's quite a bundle to tie together, but we see it as a beautiful challenge. We may be slightly biased on the subject, but we can see unlimited possibilities for any classroom situation. We hope you will want to gather all your creative urges and give it a try.

Multi-Cultural Education and Helping Children to Read
by Carol Stice

Carol Stice is an expert in the teaching of reading. Over the past year she has presented inservice opportunities to teachers in the Nashville Teacher Corps project. The teachers have been extremely impressed with her ability to help them improve their teaching skills. Multi-cultural education as it relates to reading is also one of Stice's priorities. In the following letter, she briefly describes how she has related multi-cultural concepts to working with reading and teaching. A number of multi-cultural activities have been generated as a result of her involvement. Dr. Stice is an Assistant Professor in the Department of Administration, Curriculum, and Instruction at Tennessee State University in Nashville.

Dear Michael,

I've thought about what I do in my courses . . . that relate to multi-cultural education . . . but I don't know how well they'd translate into activities. First, we talk about print and dialects of our language. The objectives I have for such discussions are to help teachers understand that:

1. The written language has no "dialect" in the same sense as oral language. The reader brings his/her own oral language to the printed page. This is normal and to be encouraged, especially during beginning reading.

2. Written language does have "dialect" in a sense: an author's syntax at sentence, paragraph, and story levels does operate and the good reader develops a sense of the author's language as he reads. In addition, there is a kind of dialect or syntax by story or article type. For instance, a myth or fable is different from a mystery, is different

212

from a biography, is different from a science article, etc. Readers need to have experience in reading and writing several kinds of common written materials.

3. Varieties of a language are the rule rather than the exception. There is really no such thing as "Standard English" in speech and even in print the varieties are numerous aside from spelling. "Good and bad" English is related to high status vs. low status language in terms of socio-economic and political power and not to any absolutes of right or wrong.

4. The elements of language that make one dialect different from another are phonological, syntactic, and semantic. We examine our own dialects and the dialect variations of some children as well.

5. *Ultimately* what is important is effective and creative communication and quality of content, rather than the mechanics and surface of the utterance.

6. In order for a teacher to help develop effective communication, children must feel free to express themselves, they must feel good about their own language, and the teacher must be involved with the children's ideas and the concepts they wish to express.

7. Eventually, the communication should be examined jointly by the teacher and learner for ways of improving the surface structure. Unfortunately, it is almost always the other way around; mechanics are the most important and first aspects of communication dealt with rather than the ideas themselves.

The aspects of actual reading that readily relate to multi-cultural learning involve how I want my students (a) to define the reading process and (b) to view the "errors" made by developing readers. We examine reading, our own reading and the reading of children, to demonstrate that reading is a psycholinguistic process which involves the experiential background, language (dialect), and thinking of the reader interacting with the experiential background, language, and thinking of the writer. For instance, the child who reads: "Grandfather told him the story," *Grandmother*
substituting grandmother for grandfather, may do so because she/he has more experience with her/his grandmother and so that's the word she/he thinks of first. Such a child certainly

213

doesn't have a phonic or structural analysis problem with this word. In fact, she/he may not have a problem at all. Such a child is probably interacting with the material and putting himself into what she/he is reading. On the other hand, the child

brung

who reads: "He broke my airplane," has used phonics to help with the beginning of the word but has produced a word that changes the intended meaning even though retaining the past tense. Of the two, the first child's "error" is less serious than the second child's. The second reader may be trying to process a word without thinking about how it "sounds" or whether it makes sense. In other words, reading is a complex and highly personal matter and understanding it enough to teach it requires knowing each child as an individual.

As far as individual children relating to written language is concerned, I demonstrate to teachers how difficult it is to read something in which the concepts and vocabulary are unfamiliar, or which deals with the language styles that are culturally different from our own experiences. The purposes of this and other such demonstrations are: a) to encourage the teacher to find or write revelant materials for the reader who is having trouble, materials whose subject is close to the heart and the background experiences of the reader, and b) to have the student dictate and/or write his own stories. The goals are to use all language modes to expand and reinforce each other and eventually to get the child into books. We also practice writing relevant stories, stories with eye dialect, etc., for specific children. Unfortunately, we don't have time to do enough of this sort of thing.

Then there are some other somewhat more general areas I touch upon in dealing with the teacher's attitude and the classroom atmosphere which affect learning to read. For instance:

1. Children have the right to be wrong.
2. Children have a right to exercise some self-selection over what they spend their time working on, reading, or thinking about.
3. Children have a right to know their own progress.
4. Children have a right to express themselves in writing and have their ideas dealt with rather than their grammar and spelling.
5. Children have a right to set their own purposes and goals for any given activity.

6. Children have the right to be friends with their teachers.
7. Children have the right to be listened to and have their ideas dealt with as more important than their articulation and sentence structure, etc.
8. Children have the right not to be underestimated.
9. Children have the right to be appreciated, not merely accepted or tolerated.
10. Children have the right to feel safe and pleasant in school.

I talk with teachers about these and I demonstrate how adults feel when they are treated as many children get treated in school. I wish I could be more specific in terms of how teachers are to implement these attitudes and perspectives. There are many kinds of multi-cultural activities that improve cultural literacy, develop healthy relationships with others, and improve concepts of self. These do have an impact on creating a multi-cultural school and do help children to read more successfully.

The Living/Learning Relationship in Multi-Cultural Curriculum Leadership
by Robert Eaker
and Algund Hermann

Robert Eaker, Assistant Professor of Education at Middle Tennessee State University, has worked with the Nashville Teacher Corps project almost from the beginning. Algund Hermann is an Instructor at George Peabody College. They have been actively involved in developing successful new ways to help teachers learn, teach, and grow. This brief selection relates some of the processes they utilized to help teachers improve their curriculum leadership skills and understandings as well as to implement those related to multi-cultural program purposes.

As a member of the curriculum leadership team, my primary role was to work with teachers who were engaged in individual or group curriculum development experiences. Since the teachers were developing curricula for boys and girls who were each uniquely different, it was important that we help teachers realize and capitalize on this uniqueness as they developed plans and activities for their classrooms. What follows is a brief description of a few of our ideas as we worked with this group.

The first, and we think most important point, is that as college teachers we behaved as we wanted the teachers to behave with their students. This was simple enough. If college teachers want the school teachers to be sensitive to individual kids' needs, then they must be sensitive to teachers' needs. If the college teachers want school teachers to be compassionate and understanding, then they should be compassionate and understanding. If college teachers expect school teachers to really like kids, then they should really like kids—and teachers. So the point is this: If college professors desire to help teachers become accepting and appreciative of individual differences in boys and girls, then they should be accepting and appreciative of individual differences in teachers.

Now this sounds simple enough, but what we're really describing is a particularly difficult thing for many people, especially university professors, to do. Most of us have this idea of what a "good" teacher is and how a "good" teacher behaves. (A good teacher is usually a teacher who teaches like I do, holds the values that I hold, and has a personality that is congruent with mine. See what I mean? Really, when we get down to it, isn't that what we usually really mean when we talk about "good" and "bad" teachers?) Well, our idea was to help teachers develop new teaching ideas and work in areas of curriculum improvement that *they wanted* to work in. They were encouraged to create their own purposes, make plans for achieving their goals, and implement their action plans. Our job was to help them through that process.

As simple as this idea seems, it was really quite a difficult job. Some teachers knew exactly what they wanted to do to improve their classrooms. Others had a general idea, but needed help in focusing their goals and making action plans to achieve their goals. Some teachers were very vague and never really could identify specific things to work on or develop any real plan for working. This was often frustrating. Sometimes we had to check ourselves from praising teachers who developed their program quickly—and from showing too little enthusiasm with those who needed help the most. In other words, it's easy for college professors to fall into the trap of behaving with the teachers in ways that we would not want teachers to behave with kids. Showing classroom teachers new ways of providing acceptance and appreciation of individual differences is basic and, we think, is ultimately the key to success or failure when working with teachers.

DEVELOPING CURRICULUM

Our next point is related to the idea of congruency of teaching/learning styles. It goes something like this: in the process of developing curriculum, there is always a very subtle, yet very positive pressure to develop objectives and activities that force conformity. In other words, as teachers write unit plans or even simple learning packets the tendency is to plan for kids to behave in "expected and limited" ways rather than to develop objectives and activities that encourage kids to behave in multiple and different ways.

There are, we think, two points to be made of this. One, the college instructor helped teachers learn how to develop expectation activities that allow for—and, in fact, encourage—multiple behavior possibilities on the part of the students. Two, the instructor used whatever influence and ideas he may have had to make the curricula that the teachers were engaging in flexible and somewhat open. To make this point more clear, let me note that though we college professors urge teachers to be more flexible and open with public school curricula, our college programs, by and large, are rigid and stress conforming behavior.

WORKING WITH ADMINISTRATORS

One of the exciting opportunities we college personnel had was to enjoy a uniquely close relationship with both school principals and teachers. This was also beneficial for the school administrators and teachers.

Most, if not all, teachers have some talent. Principals sometimes see teachers in particularly narrow ways or stereotype their teachers. As college instructors working with teachers, we sometimes saw teacher talents unnoticed by the principal. As we worked with the school administrators in planning programs, we assisted them in identifying new and creative ways of capitalizing on their teachers' talents.

Again, it's really the same point. If the principal wants the teachers to have a positive relationship with all of the kids in their classroom, then the principal should be open to finding ways of developing positive relationships with all of the teachers on the staff.

217

Two last points. One, the time came while working with the teachers when they needed an idea or a solution. They were stuck on the sandbar and needed a little push. Sometimes the sharing of an idea can serve as that little push. The college teacher was just the one that gave the teacher the idea that got a lot of other ideas rolling—or maybe another teacher had "that" good idea. Which brings us to the second point. Rather than limiting ideas to college people, we spent our time organizing processes where teachers got together and shared ideas. Seminars, newsletters, and visitations were just a few of the ways we, as college facilitators, helped teachers learn what others were doing in the area of planning curricula for individual differences. How multi-cultural can you get in both theory and practice? Try it.

Strategies for Living Together
by Judy Davis

Judy Davis is a doctoral student in the Human Development Counseling program at Peabody College. For one year, as a part of her professional practicum, she worked extensively as an instructor and consultant to teachers in the Teacher Corps schools. Involving children in activities designed to help them recognize and appreciate the differences in individuals was one of her specialties. In this brief selection, Davis decribes a bit of theory and practice she used which became a part of the multi-cultural program.

It is unlikely that a child will take the risk of trying to demonstrate an emerging skill if making a mistake means the ridicule of others. Within a classroom, affective intrusions (such as fear of performing because of the reaction of others) can interfere with cognitive learning. If a child is unable to behave in a manner which demonstrates what is being learned cognitively, then there is little opportunity for that cognitive skill to be used as a building block for further learning. Therefore, how a child feels about himself within a classroom environment and the attitudes that a child has about the classroom environment influence how that child performs in school.

Learning occurs within relationships. We learn one thing in relation to another. We learn in order to live as comfortably as possible in our individual worlds. Learning is the process of surviving. The teaching-learning process is an interaction between individuals learning and refining skills needed to negotiate within their worlds more comfortably and successfully. The process of interactions between all the individuals within a classroom is transactional in nature. Each interaction is based upon the experience of previous interactions within that environment. This transactional process of interactions building upon one another creates the classroom world or classroom climate in which children learn strategies of how to live together comfortably and productively.

As a teacher, I try to help children learn skills that they will use in twenty years as productive adult members of society. Since I can only make educated predictions as to what some of the skills are that individuals will need in order to be productive in the future, it seems that developing a questioning and curious approach to the world becomes a crucial element in children's education.

As an educator, I am concerned with providing children with optimum opportunities for learning within the classroom environment. Part of my responsibility, in providing optimum learning opportunities, is to create a classroom climate that is conducive to the children's experimenting with new and developing skills. Teachers, as designated leaders of classroom groups, become the models for learners, and primary determinants of the classroom climate. This means it's the teacher's responsibility to set the tone of respecting and valuing all members of the classroom group.

A child needs to feel free to practice the skills being learned in order to integrate these skills into moment-to-moment behavior and to be able to use these skills as a foundation for subsequent learning. This freedom to practice in learning occurs when an individual feels respected by others. This respect within a classroom environment involves children learning to recognize and appreciate the differences in individuals. This suggests that the classroom climate must enhance children's developing a value for individual differences and learning how to live comfortably and successfully with these individual differences. It is within a climate of value and respect for the individual that children are able to risk asking questions and practicing skills in a classroom

219

without fear of the reactions of others. The classroom climate becomes conducive to a questioning-feedback model of teaching-learning, which can provide a greater number of opportunities for children to learn how to participate more constructively in the classroom world.

I attempt to help teachers and students understand the problems of living together in a classroom and the feelings in interactions that may interfere with optimum cognitive learning. I call this affective education. It is a structured way of becoming aware of the interactions within a classroom and then learning to act constructively upon that awareness so as to enhance the performance of cognitive learning.

There is nothing different about affective education than what teachers do all day long in the classroom. It is merely the focusing of attention on creating a classroom climate that encourages children to operate in a questioning-feedback model of teaching-learning. It is looking at cognition in children in reference to their capacity to engage with others in relations characterized by cooperation, fairness, and mutuality. It implies the growing awareness of individuality, respect for individual differences, and learning to work together. It involves a process of providing opportunities for children to learn new strategies in dealing with feelings that may interfere with their ability to demonstrate cognitive skills successfully in their performance within the classroom world.

I attempted to help teachers learn and create a variety of approaches that can be used in helping children demonstrate respect for one another, learn how to work together to complete tasks successfully, and learn from one another. One such approach involves integrating into the academic curriculum a component of developing awareness of the relationship between how a child feels and how a child performs in school. It is a task-oriented approach to dealing with affect as it relates to the successful completion of a cognitive task; it fosters a problem-solving attitude of dealing with distractions to learning while reinforcing the cognitive skills being learned. It is a process that need not involve any additional teacher preparation time or special time allotment in the daily classroom schedule. It can be incorporated into the daily teaching-learning process and provide an added dimension to the academic tasks. This classroom activity approach is one of a few which follow as examples of tasks which can be incorporated into daily lessons, can reinforce concepts being learned, and can also provide opportunities for children to learn how to work together and respect one another. As a result of my efforts in this area, the multi-cultural climate of the Teacher Corps schools has been improved.

COOPERATIVE CHAIRS

Instruct the entire class group to choose and arrange their chairs into a geometric shape (not a circle or a square) presently being studied. In order to provide the children with an opportunity to learn about decision-making and problem-solving within a group, they must come to some consensus as to the shape in which they will arrange their chairs. In addition to maintaining a memory image of the shape to be formed and remembering its name, they must cooperate and work constructively with one another to complete the task successfully. Your responsibility, as the teacher, is to be the observer of the group process and be responsible for noting conflicts which arise and the time involved in completing the task. Your primary role is to ask questions of the group which will focus attention on how the task was accomplished by the group. The questioning is a process of directing attention to the interactions, to the strategies used, and to exploration of possible alternative strategies that could be used in completing the task. Your comments and questions could include the following: "I heard several people make suggestions for different shapes. How did you finally decide which shape to form? Did any one person take charge in deciding that shape, or in helping everyone move into place? I wonder if anyone can think of any other ways that you could have decided the shape and moved your chairs into that shape?"

INTRODUCING DIFFERENCES

Direct the children to sit in a circle. Have all members in the circle count off "A, B, A, B . . ." all the way around the circle. Instruct all A and B pairs to break away from the large group and share with one another their favorite food, hobby, television program, and school subject. Tell the children that they will be responsible for introducing their partners to the group when the total class group returns to the circle. This task provides the children opportunities for exposure to several skills. The children must remember a series of questions and answers, and relate these verbally to the class group. Each child is provided an op-

221

portunity to practice speaking out in the class group. The class develops an awareness of differences and likenesses between individuals. Also, the children are exposed to the experience of sitting in a group and listening to one another share information in a systematic fashion.

You, as a member of the classroom group, should participate in the activity. You will probably need to remind the group that each member is sharing important information with the group and that when it is not an individual's turn to speak, that individual should be listening to others. It may be possible to explore how it feels to be introduced and have one's favorite things expressed by another person.

GROUP EXPECTATIONS

Instruct children to sit in a circle and generate a "what we can expect from one another in this classroom group" list. This activity provides an opportunity for children to identify and express verbally how they would like others to behave towards them, and how they would like to behave towards others. Discussion provides exposure to thinking about how behavior influences the feelings of others. Your role is to support and seek clarification of the meaning of the children's ideas. You should help the children to assume responsibilities for recording expectations as they are verbalized, for making a class chart of these expectations, and for deciding how they would like to use the chart.

Quietly ask two or three students to create a distraction while the remainder of the group are working on their spelling (or similar lesson). Instruct the group to sit at their desks and write out, in sequence, a list of spelling words which the teacher will read in series of three or four words each. Follow up with a group discussion in which you ask questions which will lead the children to explore how the distractions influenced their ability to complete the task. Explore with the children the different strategies that individuals used in attempts to screen out the distractions, and why they worked or did not work. Discussion should also focus on the different feelings that children experienced, and the influence of these feelings, in doing the task.

The children will work on demonstrating sequential memory in the face of external distractions. They will develop an awareness of possible alternative strategies that can be used to screen out distractions in order to complete tasks successfully.

Multi-Cultural Curriculum Leadership:
in Schools and on Campus
by James Huffman

James Huffman, Assistant Professor of Education at Middle Tennessee State University, has had a broad range of successes while working in the areas of curriculum and supervision with Nashville Teacher Corps projects. One manner in which he provided a support system for "teacher learning" is reflected in the following selection. Multi-cultural education and its integration into the curriculum of the school frequently occurred because of Huffman's involvement.

As a member of the curriculum leadership team, it was my intent to serve as a facilitator of human potential. Since most people (including teachers and students) have extensive potential to achieve significant learnings, it is important that a consultant work with them in growth-inducing ways. By growth-inducing ways, I mean exhibiting accepting, supportive, and freeing behavior. If we expect teachers to exhibit such behavior while working with children, it seems essential that those who work with teachers (consultants, supervisors, administrators, etc.) exhibit the same kind of behavior in their relationships with teachers. Consequently, accepting and even encouraging differences in values, beliefs, and methods among teachers becomes very important. This behavior seems to be consistent with much of the thrust of multi-cultural education. If I am unable to accept differences in teachers, I cannot help them to accept differences in their students or suggest that they encourage children to be accepting of other children or adults. I attempted to behave with teachers in ways that would demonstrate consistency with what we were encouraging for their students.

Implementing this philosophy as a way of working with teachers required that I become familiar with their teaching situations and their feelings and aspirations regarding their work. Teachers defined ways in which they desired to improve some aspect of their teaching and I attempted to provide resources, ideas, suggestions, encouragement, and support for their endeavors. I communicated with the teachers on an individual basis and at regular intervals.

In working with teachers on various improvement projects, I

was constantly alert for opportunities to make suggestions or present ideas that would help them integrate multi-cultural activities into their classes and lessons. Generally, I found teachers to be receptive and often even excited about the idea of developing multi-cultural activities for their classrooms.

When teachers began developing specific activities, I was frequently able to bring them into contact with materials of a multi-cultural nature and with available resource people. Teachers who decided to implement multi-cultural activities had this very strong support system available to them. I am sure that teachers could not have accomplished nearly as much as they did without such support.

An example of a particular teacher's efforts to integrate multi-cultural activities into his teaching units will further explain my initiating and supporting role as a consultant. I began working with one junior high school social studies teacher who was teaching his classes from a rather strict physical geography approach. Concern was with topographical features, agriculture, and natural resources of various countries of the world. As the teacher was explaining his procedures, materials, activities, and the like to me, I suggested that his students might be quite interested in the customs, beliefs, and ways of life of the people in those various countries. The teacher expressed interest in doing "something like that." I gave him some ideas that I had seen other social studies teachers use with some success. It was not long before the teacher was trying activities that focused on the people of one culture. As his interest in teaching about cultures increased, he was able to draw on the expertise of other consultants and to utilize materials available to him through the support system. By the end of the semester, the teacher was effectively teaching physical geography integrated with cultural considerations.

I wish to mention one other factor which has resulted from my work on the curriculum leadership team to promote multi-cultural considerations in the curriculum. As I work with student teachers in our regular university program, I find that I am constantly alert to opportunities for encouraging their use of multi-cultural education. As a member of the curriculum leadership team, I hope that I have had some effect in facilitating multi-cultural approaches in classrooms. I know that my experiences in working toward that end have taught me much and have had a definite effect on the way I work in other settings.

The Community and Multi-Cultural Education

Without a successful community action program, multicultural education is weakened considerably. Attempting to help students learn new ethnic and cultural understandings without community involvement would be functioning unrealistically. The continuity between home and school is essential for children to become multi-culturally oriented. Elizabeth Thompson and Joan Johnson are community coordinators with the Nashville Teacher Corps project. They are extremely able and successful. The community program was this Teacher Corps's first thrust into multi-cultural education. Many of the multi-cultural experiences and activities that have been developed have been a direct result of the efforts of Thompson and Johnson. Their guidance and leadership have been invaluable to the development of a healthier multi-cultural climate in the schools. In the following selections they report some of their experiences as community coordinators; the linkage to the multi-cultural education program is obvious.

Providing Community and Multi-Cultural Opportunities
by Joan Johnson

One of the most powerful and beneficial aspects of the Teacher Corps program has been the involvement of trainers and school personnel in the milieu of the community. A second part of the community program has been the successful involvement of parents, other adults in the neighborhood, and family oriented service agencies of the community in joint efforts with school faculty.

Opportunities in the community program for inservice and preservice personnel were geared to meet the assessed needs of the individual participants. However, the major purpose remained clear: Community-based education was a vehicle for creating responsive schools.

In my role as community coordinator, I planned with public schools and university personnel to see that Teacher Corps participants were provided educational experiences that would de-

225

velop those skills required for effective community involvement. Activities were designed to enable educational personnel to: 1) understand the home background and environment of the student, 2) communicate and work more effectively with parents, 3) identify and utilize community resources in the classroom, and 4) increase the involvement of parents in school programs.

Cooperative efforts on the part of the university, the school system, and the community afforded the opportunity for prospective teachers to have on-the-job educational practice, and for experienced teachers to have practical inservice training. Community-based education was field-based and field-referenced; therefore, each community project and activity responded to community-felt and community-expressed needs. Project participants were encouraged to teach community members how to continue projects and activities, using Teacher Corps resources in advisory capacities. My work as a community coordinator was with professional educators; but the major focus of my efforts, and the most rewarding personally, was to involve parents and community resources in the learning experiences of children.

The school population which made up "my community" was mostly Black and White Americans with some Vietnamese and Korean persons. Some students lived within several blocks of the school and others were bused from distances up to eight miles per day. Family income ranged from welfare levels to above $25,000. While the school community had differences, it had many things in common, too. Our common goal at Wharton Junior High was to open the school building in the evening. I saw this happen! Wharton became a meeting place for students and adults to spend leisure hours in activities such as arts, handwork crafts, guitar, happy homework club, karate, cake decorating, and sports for young and old. I saw an inner-city school in a high-crime rate area of Nashville opened in the evening, but I also saw much more. I observed children from different backgrounds, who attended classes together each day, have the opportunity to learn more about one another, to become *friends* in a controlled but less structured situation during the evening. Parents from the suburbs drove into a neighborhood which once was unknown and forbidding but now was the location of a familiar school building filled with people who shared a common concern, "the education of children." "Family Fun Night" at Wharton provided for extended educational and recreational opportunities in an area which was devoid of such a program previously, and it also provided for people of diverse cultures the opportunity to develop a program which respected and responded to the cultural differences in the school community.

Bringing People Together
by Elizabeth Thompson

As community coordinator for the Teacher Corps program, it has been my responsibility to provide day-by-day coordination between the home and school. I needed to be aware of the attitudes and the feelings within the community and to be empathetic, especially to the families in the low-income brackets. I explained community needs to school personnel and promoted, publicized, and interpreted the Teacher Corps concept to the residents of the community. They perceived the program as a service agency sensitive to their needs. It has been a great pleasure to serve in this capacity. The program has opened doors of success for lay community people. It has enabled participants who were qualified to further their education.

The community program of Teacher Corps has operated in this area for four years. Some decisions about the program were made at grassroots level. The most successful part of my involvement dealt with working with the community advisory council and the community school. The role of the advisory council has been to make all the decisions about community affairs such as the community school organization, the responsibilities of staff, and the response to concerns from community residents. The council is made up of parents, teachers, community personnel, and agency representatives. It has enlightened this group of people to know that parents can be decision makers. The chairperson of the council is Rev. Dr. Amos Jones, Sr., a minister within the community. Rev. Jones has been an asset to the overall community programs, bringing in expertise in the workings of the people and the community. He has also inspired other ministers to lend support to the programs. I have seen this community develop into a place of peace and successful communication between its residents, young and old. I have also seen crime decrease, the pride of persons being able to acquire a job, and, most of all, respect for each other.

The community school has closed the gap of hostility. It offers a gathering place for people, an alternative to living in the streets day and night. The program has operated four years, two nights a week in the fall, five nights a week during the summer. Some of the classes offered are: arts-crafts, slimnastics, dramatics, karate, sports, sewing, consumer education, early childhood, music, and Red Cross nursing. In talking with parents who have experienced the community school, one recurring response has been that "It's the best thing that ever happened!" for their children.

Working in an inner-city Black community, of which I am a part, is a long, hard struggle. First you have to work at being accepted and trusted, even if you are Black. Let me assure you, it's not an easy task. The Teacher Corps program ended as of June 1977. In this community area, residents are very saddened over this termination, but happy about the community school being left at Washington Jr. High School. The program will be financed by the Inter-Denominational Ministers Forum, an organization of two hundred ministers in the Davidson County area. If I had my job to do over, it would be a pleasure. The last four years have been a great experience for everyone involved.

Helping Teachers Develop Healthy Human Relationships in Their Classrooms
by Robert Dellanoce

As a facilitator in the multi-cultural training program, Robert Dellanoce developed a helping supervisory relationship with teachers. His task was to provide the leadership in the development and implementation of new classroom activities designed and/or adapted to enhance healthier self-concepts and human relationships as a means of increasing multi-cultural understandings between children and teachers. The following is Dellanoce's description of some of the basic assumptions, implementation processes, new learnings, and activities which occurred in the training process.

Many of the teachers I worked with became involved in this particular learning process by signing up for practicum and field experience opportunities offered by the Curriculum Leadership Program at Peabody College through TEAM/Teacher Corps. Within this context the teachers and this "facilitator" outlined some appropriate and common goals we held as educators. Those goals were:

To implement new curriculum which would enhance student-student and student-teacher relationships,

To implement new curriculum which would enhance self-concept, and

To implement new curriculum which would introduce and develop a feeling of multi-cultural awareness and appreciation.

These became the beginning for our multi-cultural learning process. It was a process that would allow the multi-cultural approach to ensue via the day-by-day school experiences of students. From these goals and the related feelings of the individuals involved, one constant developed in our many interactions. We realized that all individuals are important and unique and that our classroom experiences should be adjusted to capitalize on and draw from these important likenesses and uniquenesses.

SOME BASIC ASSUMPTIONS

The following statements briefly describe the basic assumptions and frame of reference of our multi-cultural curriculum development and implementation.

1. The process of multi-cultural education is unfolding, dynamic, and totally individual. It is a process that depends upon a school, its personnel, and their interpretations of multi-cultural awareness and appreciation. It becomes a process of self-analysis in terms of a school system, its needs, and its views and concerns toward growth.

2. Multi-cultural education cannot follow a predetermined format. The direction it takes as a learning force relies heavily on the goals and objectives of its implementors. Fostering new viewpoints and ideas, multi-cultural education encounters a school curriculum and provides it with a fresh emphasis, a new purpose.

3. One way to help develop a new multi-cultural emphasis or purpose is to deal with a multi-cultural dimension concerned with human relationships and self-concept. Basic to most changes—especially multi-cultural enlightenment—are people. In order to teach those concerned—to reach and expose them to others—it is necessary to encounter their own feelings, their own values, and their own opinions as people. We strived to do just that. It attempts to engage people in the process of being themselves.

229

It attempts to stimulate them both intellectually and affectively so that each and every person "surfaces" and is shared with others.

This doing and giving together becomes a foundation on which greater multi-cultural awareness and appreciation are built. We learn about ourselves—what we are and what we feel inside. We also learn about others and what they feel inside. We recognize differences and likenesses which may have been previously unnoticed. Hopefully, we learn to realize or cope with our new learnings and to grow as a result of our learning.

A basic theme within this context is acceptance—acceptance of ourselves and of others. Acceptance may reduce our anxieties and allow us to incorporate the positions of others into our thinking so as to stimulate a multi-cultural approach to life. Our reactions, decisions, and dealings may not reflect the *I* in our self-concepts nor the importance and appreciation of the *You.* Our interactions may become synthetic growing experiences utilizing the growth within our own culture and within cultures of others.

4. The overall attempt is to increase or expand and deepen multi-cultural awareness through the development of healthy human relationships and self-concepts.

MAJOR PHASES IN IMPLEMENTATION

The implementation steps which followed from our basic assumptions are outlined in the subsequent discussion.

Step 1. Teachers began to identify their needs specifically through the exploration and evaluation of classroom social interactions. Both teachers and this facilitator were alert to small group formations, cliques, or other intra-class boundaries in social interaction. The question of *who* was interacting in the classroom became of prime importance. Were children free to interact with others? Were there blocks to interpersonal relationships, and if so, could these blocks be identified? Teachers also recorded their own experiences in interacting with their class members. Their own self-awareness in regard to teaching and caring for students became another significant consideration. Informal discussions, conversations, verbal as well as non-verbal cues (withdrawal, shyness, non-cooperation) were noted and served as input for our total awareness of the quality of relationships in the classrooms.

Step 2. Since the improvement process was based on the interactions and feelings of the people involved, communication

230

became paramount. It seemed to us that a successful communication system would serve our project well in its endeavor to create activities for a more multi-cultural curriculum. The following became our avenues for increased project communication and participation.

Scheduled meetings between teachers and the multi-cultural facilitator.

Advertisement of the multi-cultural project through faculty meetings (to encounter newly interested teachers and to gather new school awareness, feedback, etc.).

The creation of a multi-cultural project newsletter. The letter communicated our ideas, understandings, and project goals to others within the school system.

Informal communication between the general faculty, project teachers, and the facilitator, and the sharing of ideas and information, was always encouraged.

Step 3. Basic to any multi-cultural awareness project is the idea of the cultural potential inherent in any classroom of children. Before finding, sharing, and implementing activities for a refreshed curriculum, the teacher's personal observations in his/her classroom were stressed.

In many instances, the teachers and facilitator encountered groups of children representing a variety of ethnic origins, value systems, differences, likenesses, and cultural experiences. The children were of all races; some had lived their life within the geographic school district, while others came from various countries and states within the country; some familial structures were matriarchal, some patriarchal, while others were balanced between the two. Children came from nuclear, extended, and one-parent families. Other factors such as role formation and social, physical, and emotional development were at play within the classroom settings. Thus, students who were more socially, physically, and emotionally mature were grouped with less mature individuals. Numerous factors such as these were totally dynamic. Also occurring at times were differences which served as social barriers; sex, maturity, socio-economic status, and race being some examples. It was also noted that a type of tenseness and insecurity existed within certain classrooms. Basically, the quality of trust among and between many individuals needed strengthening and reinforcement. Acceptance of differences as

231

well as appreciation of likenesses would help address needs and initiate improvement.

Step 4. The process led to the mutual development of new directions. The major components influencing the process of implementing our purposes were the *needs* that grew from the various classroom situations. New directions formed from various problems, ideas, recommendations, and comments which generated within specific classrooms and project meetings. Concerns were focused in on improved interpersonal relationships which hopefully would enhance multi-cultural understandings, and thus, better human learning and growing conditions. Comments reflecting the need for appropriate activities were:

"My kids need to trust me and each other more."

"I'd like to see certain students feel more comfortable interacting with each other in class."

"I'm sure he has the ability and probably the desire to be more involved, but. . . ."

"I'm having a hard time with my kids—I'd like to develop a better rapport with them."

"I want to develop a more accepting climate in my room. There are a lot of problems on their minds."

"There's a subtle tension between groups in my class and I'd like to deal with it."

Step 5. Both the teachers and this facilitator became interested in finding, adapting, or developing activities to resolve classroom concerns. We were led to sources which were used for starting discussion, theater games, group awareness, and sensitivity and encounter training. The activities selected or developed were usually designed to bring people together, to provide common ground from which to begin interaction, and hopefully, to develop trust and mutual cooperation. Some activities were simple and direct; for example, "getting to know one another" type games. Others, dealing with personal values and feelings, were somewhat more sophisticated and elicited deeper response. The overall process became one of "doing." The following are examples of the activities which were implemented.

Group Fantasy—Groups of children were assembled for the purposes of providing a fantasy experience. The participants— sixth graders and their teachers—were led through an open-ended verbal fantasy trip. They were urged to develop the fantasy trip according to their own preferences; all details were de-

232

veloped by the participants. All individuals were then urged to share their individual and unique fantasies. The focus became the feeling that all contributions reflected personal feelings and, in a broader sense, individuals' cultures. All contributions were equally important and equally valuable to all who listened.

Lend a Hand—Touching or the idea of physical closeness became incorporated into the activity called "Lend a Hand." Simply, a person with eyes closed examines someone's hands. The examined then becomes a member of a surrounding group. The examiner tries (with eyes opened) to locate the person's hands originally explored. The activity brought forth feelings of personal space and reactions to touching. Conversational feedback allowed participants to hear how differently individuals reacted to the exercise. Values, mores, and acculturation seemed to differentiate the responses. The acceptability and "rightness" of all reactions was the lesson of importance.

Blind Walk—Participants were grouped into dyads, one person being a sighted leader and the other a blind follower. The leader attempted to provide his/her partner with an interesting short journey, focusing on the stimulation of senses other than sight. The "blind" partner concentrated on different textures, temperatures, etc., encountered during the journey. The exercise focused on trust and interpersonal cooperation. The children demonstrated and verbalized their individual reactions during and after the blind walk. Reactions ranged from "comfortable, trusting feelings" to feelings of uneasiness and mistrust. As in "Lend a Hand," the significant learning was the fact that reactions were different for different reasons and that all reactions were important, valid, and equally valuable.

The "Art Lesson"—Placed in small groups, participants were requested to depict the concepts of love and peace in a drawing. It was required also that the drawing be a group product. As in the other activities, the process and not the product became the learning. Participants discussed their cooperation as a group engaged in a purposeful activity. Group differences in drawing art items as well as intra-group differences reflected value, feeling, and cultural influences.

Four Corners—Perhaps the most verbal exercise explored was one entitled "Four Corners." Four corners of a discussion room are labeled as follows: S.A.—strongly agree; S.D.—strongly disagree; A.—agree; and D.—disagree. The class, as a group,

233

is read statements to which each student must respond with one of the four choices. Usually, statements are controversial or deal with relevant, timely issues. Participants listen to statements and then stand by the signs according to their responses. Again, all differences are valued and every rationale is accepted. The exercise again allowed participants to be "themselves" and support their individual differences via a non-threatening, non-judgmental group exploration.

Points of View—Various prepared stories were selected and read to classes. The stories chosen reflect the points of view of different story characters. Participants were urged to project their own values, feelings, or opinions when evaluating each story, character, or situation. All reactions were encouraged. No right answer, but rather the realization of many alternatives, was encouraged.

Cultural Compliments—Group members were requested to choose a positive quality or attribute of a classroom friend. Then, reactions to these compliments were requested and discussed. Feelings were shared among group members, who were both originators and receivers of the compliments. The value of the experience was that unique backgrounds gave rise to differences in the admired qualities which were complimented.

Reviewing—Certain of the aforementioned activities were either photographed, filmed, or videotaped. In viewing and recapitulating these activities, all participants were able to "see, hear, and evaluate" their behaviors. After a number of the exercises, and an improvement in group cohesiveness, acceptance, and cooperation, an "It's OK to be OK" or "differences and likenesses are good" feeling became evident.

SUMMARY

For project teachers, children, and the facilitator, the multicultural process became an unfolding one since its inception. It began with concerns and ideas which identified needs. Needs were met by the development of appropriate activities which were incorporated into daily routines. But, as with most educational processes, growth was not always tangible, but rather was evidenced in indirect and subtle ways. Evaluation of multicultural growth was similar to the cues and behaviors that helped shape its direction earlier. Teachers had identified behaviors in students and classroom conditions which lead to activities. Now, the same teachers and students were encountered in order to see whether positive changes and differences in their behaviors and feelings had occurred.

Tensions were subtly decreased. Inhibitions which controlled student involvement were replaced by the nuances of creative behavior. Shy, reticent individuals were seen to raise hands and answer questions; more important, they were able to communicate who and what they were and how they felt about issues and ideas. Groups of kids gathered when necessary to implement ideas or to attempt tasks. Their commonality became their support or enthusiasm for learning and not societal norms which would dictate or influence their behaviors. In essence, children and teachers alike were operating and learning on a different level. Individuals were individuals in a secure atmosphere and not individuals in an unsure place. Note, for instance, the following statements:

—A teacher commented: "I'm hearing from students that never spoke up before."
—Another stated: "I decided to combine my teaching efforts with some other teachers who were interested in multicultural approaches. It's more human and accepting."
—Several students commented: "I like being here. Mrs. _____ makes it easy to talk and work with everybody in the class." "I like everybody in my class. People can work things out. Everybody has the same feelings, sometimes."
—A teaching intern replied after finishing the project: "You know, my kids and I like each other more. I didn't realize how we had threatened each other before."

Multi-cultural education is a process of growing. It is a shift in emphasis, a new approach and purpose for kids going to school in order to learn about themselves and their society. It provides a curriculum that addresses the importance of multiple talents and teaches people how to support societal differences. Its impact, albeit difficult to measure, lies in climate and feelings one experiences when spending time in a school building filled with teachers, administrators, and students. Multi-cultural education is pride and acceptance. It is security in knowing one is different from another. It is being shown—taught, as it may be— that likenesses and differences are important and right. Multi-cultural education is seeing and hearing diverse children work, cooperate, and enjoy one another. It is experiencing the decline

235

of social barriers that prevent the sharing of knowledge and experience. It is watching individuals in a more secure learning environment that reflects a loss of fear and separatism. Multi-cultural education is pluralism in education. More specifically, it is children liking one another as people. It becomes their feeling OK to *be* OK. Multi-cultural education is a way of knowing why we have become the people we are.

Toward Working with Teachers in a Multi-Cultural Helping Process
by Martis M. Okpalobi

Martis Okpalobi has been an instructor in the Nashville Teacher Corps multi-cultural program almost from its inception, and recently completed her doctoral studies at Peabody College in Curriculum Leadership. She was successful in working with teachers to develop new approaches designed to help children learn multi-cultural concepts. Some of her experiences in working in a leadership role with teachers were linked to her graduate program. In the following article Okpalobi identifies some of the helping processes she used to help teachers learn and grow.

I worked as a facilitator/instructor in a supervisory/helping relationship with classroom teachers who were enrolled in a program focused on curriculum improvement. It happened on-site, in their own classrooms, and was designed to improve *their* educational environments.

The purposes and goals which each teacher set for his/her self-improvement experience were different. Therefore, I had a different helping relationship with each. For example, one teacher wanted to identify and examine social studies textbooks and other related materials available for use at the middle school level. She evaluated the quality of the textbooks and curriculum materials used in the teaching/learning process as to their treatment along various multi-cultural dimensions—multi-ethnicity, cultural differences, sexism, values, lifestyles, and so on. Her purpose was to assume a leadership position in her school in order to recommend alternative curriculum materials which other teachers in her school could use. She tried to locate materials that reflected the cultural pluralism of American society.

Another teacher decided to use both innovative and exemplary teaching/learning materials which would help children have more positive concepts of themselves and build healthy human relationships in the classroom. Still another teacher proposed to plan a teaching/learning unit which would help students become aware of and appreciative of the nature of cultural pluralism. By exploring and investigating the historical and cultural roots of various ethnic groups, students came to appreciate the varied lifestyles, cultural differences, dialects and other linguistic differences, values, beliefs, and social behaviors of the multi-ethnic groups in American society—especially those groups represented in the culture of the school.

As facilitator, my role involved being a resource person, i.e., one to recommend specific books and other materials, their locations, and means of acquiring them. I also worked in a supervisory/helping relationship with teachers to help them recognize alternative ways of planning and implementing teaching/learning experiences with children—ways by which students could participate in planning the learning experiences which would affect them. For example, one teacher had identified various cultures to be included in his multi-cultural, multi-ethnic unit, "America's Megapolis—Culturally Different Roots and Emerging Lifestyles." This teacher asked me to help him identify some activities, a process for achieving group decision-making, some resource materials to supplement text and other school-supplied references, and appropriate learning experiences to help him move from a teacher-centered classroom to a teacher-facilitated resource center in which students participate in curriculum decision-making.

As I worked with the teacher, my approach to helping resolve his curriculum concerns was to meet with him in his classroom bi-weekly during the regular school hours. I employed a question technique: What are you trying to accomplish? Have you tried . . .? Did it work? Why is this important? Who are the benefactors? The same line of questioning was carried over by the teacher in his unit planning with kids in the classroom. At the end of our "formal" helping relationship, this particular teacher expressed his belief that by "providing a viable process for himself and his students to work together in planning, organizing, implementing, and evaluating the learning unit, he and his students now experience happier, more positive feelings in the classroom."

237

This particular teacher learned that he could become a "facilitator-helper" to students. This positive transition did not develop overnight. It occurred only after many weeks of working with him. It happened by gradually trying student-centered activities such as encouraging kids to evaluate their own work and assist with peer evaluations, teaching kids to work through small group decision-making processes to reach group consensus, and asking students to share various cultural characteristics of their homes that were unique to their own culture. Both teacher and kids began to feel more comfortable with their role changes.

While helping the teacher in this transition, I suggested related activities. The teacher would try them over the next two to three days. He would then give me immediate feedback on whether or not the suggested activities worked and to what extent. We sometimes planned by telephone after the school day. We questioned a lot of what we suggested and tried. He preferred that I question rather than tell him what to do or how to do it.

In my work with still another teacher, I felt that our best role-relationship was one in which I could advise her on the potential effectiveness of her curriculum materials (both teacher-made and commercial) and could help her evaluate the worth of activities after they were implemented. This teacher had a specific goal of helping students build positive concepts of self and healthy human relationships in the classroom. She felt secure in trying multi-cultural activities, but wanted me to explore with her whether or not the activities she was trying were actually working. As we met in her classroom during her regular Tuesday planning periods, she would tell me what she had tried, explain her implementation processes, and relate her student feedback strategies. She would ask me for suggestions to improve the activities and for new activity ideas.

When we first began working together, this teacher seemed a bit tense. She conveyed an attitude that she was the expert and I had nothing constructive to offer her. She had much to teach me. My follow-up approach was to withdraw and allow her many opportunities to try, test, evaluate, and communicate the multi-cultural activities she had developed. My role was that of a listener. As the teacher-teller, supervisor-listener relationship continued, she gradually began to ask me for suggestions. I felt I was helping her and she felt she was learning. We were pleased with our working relationship.

With each teacher, I attempted to establish a relationship designed to help her/him become more conscious of her/his own education belief system, values, and culture and of how those related to classroom teaching, learning, and living. I also attempted to help each teacher identify, use, and recommend to others the available multi-cultural resource materials and the sources for obtaining such materials. The materials used and recommended were especially helpful in the process of understanding, emphasizing, and supporting diversities which existed in their classrooms. I wanted to develop a sense of "we're all okay" in the classroom.

In order to succeed with my purposes, I met with teachers weekly, and sometimes more frequently, depending on the nature of the needs felt and expressed by teachers and myself. These sessions took place on the teachers' turf. My approach was to initiate conversations with teachers about the learning experiences they had with students, look at any materials they used, and explore possible new directions. Instead of "telling" teachers what to do, I used a questioning approach. I would ask questions to explore how, what, when, why, and who the teacher teaches. Teachers seemed open and unthreatened in their responses. In addition to this face-to-face contact, the teachers sent me a weekly summary of the activities they initiated in their classes, how they felt about the processes, and some new directions for future learning experiences.

At varying intervals each teacher was asked to indicate how our inservice experiences helped them alleviate some of their classroom problems and achieve their purposes. One teacher now feels more comfortable in assuming a leadership role among professional peers in her school. She said that next semester she will chair the textbook selection committee. In addition, when she first approached teachers with her concerns about the mono-cultural emphases conveyed in the middle schools' social studies books, her peer teachers virtually ignored her and were physically rude to her. They now come to her for suggestions and recommendations on where and how to find multi-cultural materials. Another teacher is planning to continue classroom learning/living experiences to help children develop positive

239

self-concepts. She has acquired a sense of confidence and wants to continue her efforts.

The new directions initiated by teachers have required a long-term commitment to deal with cultural pluralism. They have found success . . . hopefully, they will continue.

The Role of the Team Leader in Multi-Cultural Education
by John Lifsey

John Lifsey served as Team Leader during the development of the multi-cultural program by the Nashville Teacher Corps. Lifsey has been identified by many of his team leader colleagues nationally for leadership roles within their ranks. His ability to function successfully in helping teachers experience personal and professional growth is well recognized. In the following article, Lifsey briefly describes some of the ways he has worked toward improving the multi-cultural climate of his school, and these provide useful ideas for any role groups within a school that may be moving toward multi-cultural goals.

As Team Leader, I worked with the intern team and inservice teachers to facilitate their acquisition of knowledge, changes in their attitudes, changes in their individual behavior, and changes in their group behavior. All of these were to occur along multi-cultural dimensions. Even though I attempted to use similar methods with the intern team and other teachers, a more intensive involvement with the intern team developed. This was due, in part, to the commitment of time I designated for intern development and/or in response to the expressed desires of the interns in having such involvement.

The intern team, which included the teachers of record, the interns, and myself, became active in the early stages of the multi-cultural program's development. This involvement began with the needs assessment process—finding out what new multi-cultural understandings the interns and teachers perceived as needed. This was necessary if the training they received was to be relevant. Information from the needs assessment process indicated the desirability of establishing a multi-cultural foundations seminar. This seemed a desirable first step, and I encouraged all with whom I worked to participate. All four interns, teachers of record, and myself participated in this seminar, and it produced a number of results which were beneficial.

Seminar involvement helped the team gain a common basis of understandings related to multi-cultural concepts. These concepts developed from sharing the same experiences and from having learned some of the same terminology.

The team members initiated discussions about multi-cultural topics. As individuals, they began to clarify the attitudes and understandings of other team members as well as their own. As team leader, I was involved in these same processes.

The seminars served as a vehicle for helping team members begin informal contacts with each other. This helped us learn more about each other's cultural frame of reference and value system. The foundation seminars helped team members better understand their own uniqueness and unique aspects of others.

As important as understanding uniqueness was, that alone was not enough. It was the next step, the acceptance and eventual valuing of individual differences, that was truly important. As team leader, it is difficult for me to determine what role, if any, I played in helping this to happen. It did occur, as reflected by the successful operation of the team as both a planning and instructional team.

The only factor in my own behavior which I can identify as possibly being instrumental in this change process was my behavior toward team members. I attempted to demonstrate by my actions that I valued the unique contributions of each team member. I encouraged team members to respond with their own ideas and feelings during team planning. I supported diverse teaching styles and activities. I was interested in hearing and knowing the team members' perspectives on any topic. I attempted to help point out the way in which the diversity of the group added to its strength. These actions, I feel, had a positive influence on team interactions.

Thus, the style of team interactions became supportive of differences among adults. This made the transfer of such behaviors by teachers toward children likely, but did not assure that this would happen, or that the curriculum would reflect such a change.

Team planning meetings were a time when opportunities for incorporating multi-cultural activities into the curriculum were developed. I utilized team planning time to support or elicit suggestions concerning appropriate multi-cultural activities along multi-cultural dimensions, and to support the unique styles and ideas of team members. These actions seemed to help the classroom instruction begin to reflect a belief in and a valuing of individual uniqueness.

As activities were planned and implemented by the intern team, I began to look for opportunities to share successful activities. Activities were disseminated to several groups and individuals. Parents were kept informed as to the purposes and goals of the team. This was done in several ways. A newsletter published by the children and distributed to parents was an effective method. Open house or parent nights, where multi-media presentations were given, were also effective. Other personal contacts, reports sent home by teachers including samples of instruction, and home visitations were also employed to keep parents informed.

Other teachers in the building became aware of activities through informal conversations, through department chairpersons or lead teachers, or at faculty meetings. Other interested people were also kept informed as to the activities which occurred. These included project staff, building principals, and university trainers.

As team leader I also attempted to serve as a resource link. I identified opportunities for instructional improvement within the school building. I was also aware of the human and non-human resources available within and outside of the building. I attempted to link these two—opportunities and resources—whenever possible.

In summary, I believe my three most important functions as a team leader in this multi-cultural program were:

Demonstrating by my personal interactions with people a support for individual uniqueness.

Eliciting curriculum opportunities during team planning meetings.

Serving as a resource link for the intern team and in-service teachers.

Classroom Strategies for Teaching Thinking and Valuing

by Charles B. Myers

Charles B. Myers is an Associate Professor of History and Social Science Education at George Peabody College for Teachers. He is also Director of Programs for Educators of Youth. Dr. Myers has been involved in the development and implementation of inservice and preservice experiences with Metro Nashville Public Schools and the Teacher Education Alliance for Metro over a seven-year period. This past year, he successfully helped Teacher Corps teacher-community participants learn new classroom strategies for teaching thinking and valuing. In the following, Myers briefly describes the instructional processes he used. The linkage and significance for creating multi-cultural schools is obvious.

The two field-based and field-referenced courses, Classroom Strategies for Teaching Thinking and Classroom Strategies for Teaching Valuing, were offered to participants in the Nashville Teacher Corps Program during the 1976-77 school year. The first focused on thinking in the cognitive domain and was offered in the fall; the second focused on more affective situations. Forty-two participants were involved in the first course and sixteen in the second.

The course on thinking involved the use in the classroom of three discussion-type classroom strategies that teachers could use to stimulate higher levels of thought on the part of their students. The three strategies were:

1. Developing Concepts
2. Developing Generalizations
3. Applying Generalizations

These strategies were originally developed by the Taba Curriculum Development Project at San Francisco State University and have been revised by a variety of people, including Jack Fraenkel, Mary Durkin, and myself. The basic steps in each of these three strategies are given in the charts on the next two pages.

DEVELOPING CONCEPTS

Teacher	Student	Teacher Follow-through

What do you see (notice. find) here?	Gives items.	Makes sure items are accessible to all students. For example:
		  Chalkboard lists
		  Transparency lists
		  Individual lists
		  Pictures
		  Item cards

Do any of these items seem to belong together?	Finds some similarity as a basis for grouping items.	Communicate grouping. For example:
		  Underlines in colored chalk
		  Marks with symbols
		  Arranges pictures or cards

Why would you group them together?*	Identifies and verbalizes the common characteristics of items in a group.	Seeks clarification of responses when necessary.
What would you call these groups you have formed?	Verbalizes a label (perhaps more than one word) that appropriately encompasses all items.	Records.
Could some of these belong in more than one group?	States different relationships.	Records.
Can we put these same items in different groups?** Why would you group them that way?	States additional different relationships.	Communicates grouping.

 * Sometimes you may ask the same child "why" when he offers the grouping, and other times you may wish to get many groups before considering "why" things are grouped together.

** Although this step is important because it encourages flexibility, it will not be appropriate on all occasions.

DEVELOPING GENERALIZATIONS

Teacher	Student	Teacher Follow-through
What did you notice? See? Find? What differences did you notice (with reference to a particular question)?	Gives items.	Makes sure items are accessible. For example: Chalkboard list Transparency list Individual lists Pictures Item cards Choose the items to pursue.
Why do you think this happened? or How do you account for these differences?	Gives explanation which may be based on factual information and/or inferences.	Accepts explanation. Seeks clarification if necessary.
What does this tell you about . . . (e.g., the way people behave)?	Gives generalization.	Encourages variety of generalization, and seeks clarification where necessary.

Note: This pattern of inviting reasons to account for observed phenomena and generalizing beyond the data is repeated and expanded to include more and more aspects of the data and to reach more abstract generalizations.

APPLYING GENERALIZATIONS

Teacher	Student	Teacher Follow-through
Suppose that . . . (a particular event occurred given certain conditions), what would happen?	Makes inferences.	Encourages additional inference. Selects inference(s) to develop.
What makes you think that would happen?	States explanation, identifies relationships.	Accepts explanation and seeks clarification if necessary.
What would be needed for that to happen?	Identifies facts necessary to a particular inference.	Decides whether these facts are sufficient and could be assumed to be present in the given situation.
Can someone give a different idea about what would happen?	States new inferences that differ in some respects from preceding ones.	Encourages alternative inferences, requests explanations and necessary conditions. Seeks clarification where necessary.
If, as one of you predicted, such-and-such happened, what do you think would happen after that?	Makes inferences related to the given inference.	Encourages additional inferences and selects those to pursue further.

Note: This pattern of inviting inferences, requiring explanations, identifying necessary conditions, and encouraging divergent views is continued until the teacher decides to terminate the activity.

245

The format of the course instruction followed a three-cycle approach in which (1) I used the strategy in a demonstration situation and the demonstration was analyzed by the participants; (2) the participants in a large group situation planned a similar discussion lesson on a different topic, the participants in a number of teams planned a second lesson which was taught by the teams to other participants in the groups; (3) individual participants planned lessons for their classrooms, these classroom lessons were taught and tape recorded, and the classroom lessons were analyzed by the participants, myself, and my assistants, Elizabeth Bivens and Philip George.

EXPLORING FEELINGS

Teacher	Student	Teacher Follow-through
What happened?	Restates facts.	Sees that all facts are given and agreed upon. If students make inferences, ask that they be set aside temporarily.
How do you think...feel?*	Makes inference as to feelings.	Accepts inference.
Why do you think he would feel that way?	Explains.	Seeks clarification, if necessary.
Who has a different idea about how he felt?	Makes alternative inferences and explanations.	Seeks variety, if necessary. Asks for reasons, if necessary.
How did . . . (other persons in the situation) feel?	States inference about the feelings of additional persons.	Seeks clarification, if necessary. Encourages students to consider how other people in the situation felt.
Have you ever had something like this happen to you?**	Describes similar event in his own life.	Ensures description of event.
How did you feel?*	Describes his feelings, may re-experience emotions.	Seeks clarification, if necessary. Provides support, if necessary.
Why do you think you felt that way?	Offers explanation. Attempts to relate his feelings to events he has recalled.	Asks additional questions, if necessary, to get beyond stereotyped or superficial explanation.

* These questions are repeated in sequence several times in order to obtain a variety of inferences and personal experiences.

** If students have difficulty responding, you may wish to ask, "If this should happen to you, how do you think you would feel?" or "Has something like this happened to someone you know?" Another useful device may be for the teacher to describe such an event in his own life.

During the spring, the strategies that were more affective than those in the fall were pursued in the same pattern as during the fall course. The strategies were:

1. Exploring Feelings
2. Resolution of Conflict
3. Analyzing Values

Charts which indicate the basic steps in each of these three strategies appear on pages 246-248.

RESOLUTION OF CONFLICTS

Teacher	Student	Teacher Follow-through
What happened? or What did . . . do?	Describes events.	Sees that all events are given. Tries to get agreement, or, if not possible, a clear statement of differences in perception of what occurred.
What do you think . . . (a protagonist) should do? Why?	Gives response.	Accepts response; seeks clarification, if necessary.
How do you think . . . (others) would react if he did that? Why?	Makes inference and explains.	Accepts. Seeks clarification, if necessary.
Has something like that ever happened to you?*	Relates similar event in his life.	Provides support, if necessary.
What did you do?**	Relates recalled behavior.	Seeks clarification, if necessary.
As you think back now, do you think that was a good or bad thing to do?	Judges past actions.	Encourages student to judge his own past actions. The teacher may need to prevent others from entering the discussion at this point.
Why do you think so?	States reasons.	Accepts reasons. If necessary, asks additional questions to make clear the criteria or values which the student is using in judging his actions.
Is there anything you could have done differently?	Offers alternative behavior.	Accepts. Asks additional questions to point up inconsistencies where they occur, e.g., "How does that agree with reasons you gave earlier?"

* If students have difficulty responding, you may wish to ask, "If this should happen to you, how do you think you would feel?" or "Has something like this happened to someone you know?" Another useful device is for the teacher to describe an event in his own life.

** These questions are repeated in sequence several times in order to obtain a variety of responses.

Teacher	Student	Teacher Follow-through
What did they do . . . (with reference to some matter)?	Describes behavior.	Sees that description is complete and accurate.
What do you think were their reasons for doing / saying what they did?	States inferences.	Accepts. Seeks clarification, if necessary.
What do these reasons tell you about what is important to them?*	States inferences regarding values.	Restates or asks additional questions to ensure focus on values.
If you . . . (teacher specifies similar situations directly related to student, e.g., "if you accidentally tore a page in someone else's book") what would you do? Why?**	States behavior and gives explanation.	Accepts. May seek clarification.
What does this show about what *you* think is important?	States inferences about his own values.	Accepts. Seeks clarification, if necessary.
What differences do you see in what all these people think is important?	Makes comparisons.	Ensures that all values identified are compared.

* This sequence is repeated for each group or person whose values are to be analyzed. Each group is specified by the teacher and has been previously studied.

** This sequence is repeated in order to get reactions from several students.

In both courses, specific efforts were made to relate the classroom strategies to situations in which people develop and apply generalizations about people and groups of people. The affective strategies lend themselves readily to this application. However, the cognitive strategies, since they involved the developing of generalizations, the categorizing of ideas, and the applying of generalizations in new situations, are, in fact, the major components in all generalization processes. It is these thinking processes which all people use as they confront new cultural groups, different cultural settings, and individuals who are different from themselves.

Teachers who know these discussion techniques can apply them to multi-cultural lessons in all content fields. They can also use specific components of the discussion techniques to deal with classroom lessons that relate directly to intercultural understanding among students and teachers. The affective strategies are effective in these ways in classrooms that do not necessarily include heavy humanistic, cultural, and social studies content.

Some selected sample topics teachers initially chose to develop and use with students as they learned the teaching thinking and valuing strategies are presented in the following list. (The limit is only your own imagination.)

—The amount and kind of experiences people have with different kinds of people.

—How people treat people different from themselves.

—Learning about actions and values of people in given value-involved situations and generalizing about the values people hold.

—Feelings (and reasons for them) of people in a specific situation . . . to describe and explain one's personal feelings in a similar situation.

—Solutions to a conflict situation in which a person must decide if he should do something wrong because a friend wants him to.

—Developing solutions to a conflict situation in which two people want to use the same thing at the same time . . . the feelings of people involved, possible solutions, consequences, and ways people handle conflict.

—Students' concepts of school (concept development).

—When deprived of one form of entertainment, people will search for another (application of generalizations).

—When a rule is not enforced fairly, much unhappiness can result (generalizations).

—Values involved in a situation where two people will profit if they lie.